THE
REIGN OF GRACE
FROM ITS
RISE TO ITS CONSUMMATION

BY

ABRAHAM BOOTH

WITH

AN INTRODUCTORY ESSAY
BY THOMAS CHALMERS

WIPF & STOCK · Eugene, Oregon

Wipf and Stock Publishers
199 W 8th Ave, Suite 3
Eugene, OR 97401

The Reign of Grace
From Its Rise to its Consummation
By Booth, Abraham
ISBN 13: 978-1-55635-713-8
ISBN 10: 1-55635-713-3
Publication date 11/8/2007
Previously published by Reiner Publications, 1809

CONTENTS.

	Page
MEMOIR OF THE AUTHOR..	5
THE AUTHOR'S PREFACE..	37
INTRODUCTION...	39
CHAP. I.—Concerning the Signification of the term Grace.....	46
II.—Of Grace, as it reigns in our Salvation in general....	48
III.—Of Grace, as it reigns in our Election..............	53
IV.—Of Grace, as it reigns in our effectual Calling......	98
V.—Of Grace, as it reigns in a full, free, and everlasting Pardon......................................	113
VI.—Of Grace as it reigns in our Justification...........	143
VII.—Of Grace, as it reigns in our Adoption..............	189
VIII.—Of Grace, as it reigns in our Sanctification.........	198
IX.—Concerning the Necessity and Usefulness of Holiness, and of Good Works............................	218
X.—Of Grace, as it reigns in the Perseverance of the Saints to eternal Glory........................	229
XI.—Concerning the Person of Christ, by whom Grace reigns..	244
XII.—Concerning the Work of Christ, through which Grace reigns...................................	261
XIII.—Concerning the Consummation of the Glorious Reign of Grace.....................................	268

INTRODUCTION

TO

THE REIGN OF GRACE.

BY

THOMAS CHALMERS, D. D.

There is no one term which is more frequently employed in the Bible, to denote our relationship to God, than the term *covenant*. But though the import of this term is sufficiently understood when it relates to the intercourse between man and man, we fear it is very indistinctly apprehended when it expresses our relation to God. A covenant is an agreement between at least two parties, and it is generally at first proposed by one of them, and then acceded to by the other. If the former be very distinct, and absolute, and peremptory in the terms that he lays down, the latter, in the act of giving his acquiescence, feels that he is coming under very distinct and certain obligations. The engagement is just felt to be as formal upon the one side, as it is upon the other —and when it is a contract between man and man, there is a strict and definite understanding, both with him who originated the articles, and him who complies with them.

It is thus, in any social or earthly covenant. We there see how anxiously the utmost explicitness is secured, by one clause and one stipulation after another, that each may know the distinct place he has to occupy, and the distinct part he has to perform. There is a certain relative position in which the one party stands to the other, so that when the one enters upon his place in the covenant, and then acts the part that is assigned to him, the other conforms to the covenant by entering upon his place, and acting the part that is assigned to him. Were there a loose or obscure understanding on the one side, then, on the other side, there might be freedom for a loose and obscure understanding also. But a well-framed covenant does away all looseness, and admits of nothing but what is strict and determinate; so that all who are concerned may have a clear and well-defined path to walk in. The formal and peremptory attitude of one party in the covenant, calls for a corresponding attitude from the other, and summons him to an observation just as pointed and as rigorous as the terms that are imposed. And the line of performance for each is so marked out, that each is fully aware when he keeps by it, and as fully aware when he steps aside into any track of deviation.

Now, if such be the real force and import of a covenant, what a lesson does it hold forth, when this is the very term that the Bible so often employs in expressing that transaction by which a man enters into a right relationship with God. What a power of rebuke is conveyed by this single term, on the loose, and indefinite, and floating imaginations of almost every man, as to the right position which he himself should occupy, and as to the question, whether he has actually and personally entered upon it. What a fell denunciation does this one vocable carry with it, not merely on the unsettledness of his accounts with God, but on the unsettledness even of his conceptions, as to the footing upon which, if we may use the expression, the account is opened with Him. How vague the apprehensions of the vast majority are, as to the terms in which an agreement is struck with God, and as to the way and method in which that agreement is kept up and maintained with Him. And this charge extends a great deal farther than to those who profess no care and no concern about the matter.

How many may be specified of those who are versant in the whole orthodoxy of the New Covenant, and yet with whom the question is altogether undetermined, whether it be a covenant that they have individually laid hold of. They love the evangelical language, and they like to breathe in the atmosphere of an evangelical society, and they feel that the decided preference of their taste is towards the tone and habit of evangelical professorship, and yet, with all this, they have not set themselves to the question, "What shall I do to be saved?" with that pointedness, and formality, and mature deliberation upon articles, which the very term of a covenant appears to demand of them. They breathe, perhaps, many good desires, and are in the way of many good impulses, and give their most cordial assent to the truth and importance of all the scriptural doctrine that is proposed to them ; nay, can speak soundly and well about the new covenant, and yet have never distinctly, and solemnly, and individually, charged the obligation of its articles upon themselves—living very much adrift and at random after all—with no distinct place of relationship to God, personally and actually in occupation—with no urgent or practical sense of any clearly articled engagement between Him and them, viewed in the light of two parties linked together by the tie of mutual promises, and respectively bound to certain mutual performances, and habitually unconscious, all the day long, of having taken up any position in which they have certain appropriate duties to discharge, and every occupier of which has the right to look from the other party in the contract, for the fulfillment of certain stipulations.

Meanwhile there is no want either of clearness or of precision with God. All is pointed and peremptory in the manifesto that He has given of Himself to the world. He wills us to enter into covenant with him, but lays down the terms of it in a way so distinct and so authoritative, as to preclude and lay an interdict upon all others. In framing the articles of this covenant, all the high and unchanging principles of heaven's jurisprudence were concerned—and we behold upon the face of it, the sure impress of that moral character which obtains in the sanctuary above. It is a document which announces the truth, and the justice, and the uncompromising dignity of the government by which it has been issued; and there is indeed a striking contrast between the disregard in which it is held by men on earth, and the intense earnestness of that gaze which it drew from the choirs and the companies of the celestial. "Which things the angels desire to look into." So that there is no lightness, and no looseness, in the terms of that proposal which came down to us from heaven. The question, of how an alliance between God and sinners could be struck, and how a right ceremonial of approach and meeting between the parties could be adjusted, and what sort of compact ought to be devised, so as to satisfy the claims, and suit itself to the character of each—these are questions which, however slighted in a world, where all that is above, is looked to through the dull medium of its gross and incumbent carnality—they are questions which have exercised the purest and mightiest intelligences in nature, and which belong to the very essence of the rectitude that is everlasting. They are questions, for the right determination of which, we see all heaven, as it were, in a busy movement of concern—and the public mind of God's unfallen universe, at least, directed in solemn contemplation towards them, and an overture made out with all the form and circumstance of a covenant that was to be unalterable; and this delivered into the hands of a Mediator, who, both by the dignity of His person, and the power of His high, though mysterious achievements, has added to the weight and sacredness of the whole transaction;—and thus has it been ushered in with a style of authority to the notice of our species; who are called to listen, that they may hear of the only way in which God will be approached, and of the only terms in which He will treat with them. And is not this a call upon us to look more strictly into the matter of our relationship with God, and a reproach to us for the vague indifference of our minds upon the subject, and an urgent application to our conscience, whether we have taken up our part in the account, and whether there has been such an event in our history, as a great federal transaction between us and the Lawgiver in heaven; whether we have struck with Him, or closed with Him, upon His own terms; whether the fulfillment of our part of the covenant in time, is our habitual business, and the fulfillment of His part of it, both in time and in eternity, is our habitual expectation—in a word, whether we are living as we list, or living by the terms of a treaty actually concluded and entered upon between us and God.

These are questions that need to be addressed, not merely to those on whom the terms and the obligations of religion have no hold, but to those who are longing after it, though in hitherto fruitless aspirations; to those who, yet wrapt in a kind of general mistiness, have never seen the certainty of that track which they have to pursue, and never felt the solidity of that ground which they have to walk upon—who sigh, and expatiate, and spend their earnestness among fruitless generalities—who still feel themselves bewildered in the haze of undefined speculation—and have neither the confident look, nor yet the confirmed footstep of him who knows his calling, and who has actually taken hold of a sure and a well-ordered covenant.

We apprehend that there is an actual, and a highly interesting class, who exemplify the very condition of mind which we now attempt to characterize. The truth is, it marks a sort of transitive state in the progress from nature to grace, which the great generality of inquirers have to undergo. There is such a thing as a longing desirousness to be right, but without any clear or steady perception of the avenue that leads to it—an honest, but yet an undirected inclination of the mind towards God—a heart under the visitation of strong concern, that its possessor should be what he ought, and do what he ought, but still laboring in the midst of many fears and many fluctuations; and that, just because he looks with a still clouded eye, on the field of spiritual contemplation that lies before him. This is a state, which reminds us somewhat of the exercise of the Psalmist, when he says, "My soul breaketh for the longing that it hath unto thy judgments at all times," and that, shortly after he had said, in the perplexity of his felt darkness, "Open thou mine eyes, that I may behold wondrous things out of thy law." Now we would pronounce of him who is in this state, that his face is towards Zion. He is seeking the Lord, if haply he may feel after Him and find Him; and laboring to enter upon a rest which he hath not yet attained to—familiar with all the sounds and all the doctrines of orthodoxy, but without being conscious, as yet, of having taken up that position which orthodoxy would assign individually to him—rather trying to put himself into the attitude of readiness for the Lord, than actually waiting in that attitude for the coming of the Lord—thoroughly aware that there is a posture of preparation, but utterly in the dark, whether it is a posture that he has personally assumed—and in the face of a covenant offered from heaven for his acceptance, with all its articles penned under the dictates of clear and unerring wisdom, still "running as uncertainly, still fighting even as one that beateth the air."

This a matter which ought not to be left in a state of unsettledness. If ever there was a business which it were desirable should be brought to a point, it is surely that which involves in it the state of a creature towards God. Of all the questions that lie within the compass of human speculation, this ought not to be abandoned to the caprices of a loose and floating imagination. "What shall I do to be saved?" and "wherewithal shall I come before God?" these are interrogatories precise in the object of them, nor should we rest satisfied with anything short of a precise and clearly intelligible solution. It is woful to think of the frivolity wherewith the mind can shift itself away from the urgency of these questions, and by an act of indefinite postponement, can commit them to a futurity that, in all likelihood, will ever be receding till that hour which separates its misspent time from its unprovided eternity. Were there anything slack or indeterminate in the articles of God's message to the world, this might well apologise for a corresponding remissness on the part of man. But when this message has come in pointed application to us, and armed with all the rigor and imperative force of an *ultimatum*, and has taken the shape of a covenant, in which God offers His terms, and both demands and entreats our compliance with them—there is no room left for parrying or evasion; nor do we meet aright this advancing movement on the part of God, but by our distinct response to His distinct and peremptory overtures.

It were well, if, under the impulse of such considerations, we were to take up the language of the Prophet, and say, "Come then, and let us join ourselves to the Lord." There is one way of setting forth upon this movement, to which nature feels a very strong and general inclination. Nothing can be more natural than the conclusion —that hitherto we have done wrong, and are therefore out of terms and out of friendship with God. Let us henceforth do right, and thus we shall recover the ground from which our own sins have disposted us. There is a universal propensity among men to feel in this manner—It is by our own doings that we have forfeited our claim upon God; and it is by our own doings that the claim is to be re-established. The truth is, that though the old covenant of—" Do this and live," is now an utter wreck, in virtue of man's disobedience, yet the feelings and tendencies of man's unrenewed nature still retain, as it were, the very mould and impress of such a covenant; and we are not aware of a more prevailing imagination, or of one that lurks more insidiously, and operates more powerfully in the human bosom, than that acceptance with God can somehow be carried by a certain character of meritoriousness, in the desire of our own hearts, and in the doing of our own hands. And this, our first attempt, is so to manage as that heaven shall be rightfully ours, in virtue of our rendered services, and that it shall come to us on the footing of a legal payment, by which value is given for the value that has been received. The secret, but certain aim, in the first instance, of every man who goes out in quest of immortality, is so to qualify himself, as that he may demand it as a right at the bar of justice, instead of suing for it as a boon at the bar of mercy. And this is what the Bible calls "going about to establish a righteousness of our own"—founding a plea on which we may challenge heaven as our well-earned remuneration, or as the fulfillment of a bargain between two parties —standing on the even ground of "work and win," upon the one side, and "accept of that work, and bestow an adequate reward for it," upon the other. The man who works with this for his object, is said to work in the spirit of legality; and this we hold to be the aspiring and universal spirit of nature, in its first attempts to reunite with the God from whom sin has so widely dissevered it.

This fond and clinging tendency on the part of man, to get into terms with God on the footing of the Old Covenant, after that covenant has been broken into shreds, or, if he persist in his tendency, will gather itself up against him into a body of overwhelming condemnation, has come down to us from our first parents, and is deeply incorporated with that nature which they have transmitted over the whole family of their descendants. It is not peculiar to Jews, who wanted to make a righteousness out of their Mosaic law. It extends to the men of all countries, and of all colors, who, out of the law of conscience, or the law of conventional propriety in their neighborhood, or the law to which tradition, and revelation, and custom, have made their respective contributions, still want to rear a righteousness of their own, which God, on the principles of justice, shall be bound to accept, and, on the same principles, shall be bound to reward. This spirit of legality, whatever may be its disguises, has a prompting and a presiding influence at the outset of all our returning movements unto God. And it is a spirit to which He has most broadly adverted in the New Covenant, that he has framed for the purpose of bringing sinners again into fellowship with Himself, and there He peremptorily refuses to give it any countenance. He utterly refuses to enter into any degrading compromise with human sinfulness—and, setting up the authority of His law, as a thing that was unchangeable and irreducible, He holds that, by one act of disobedience, the foundation of merit, on the part of the creature, is utterly cut away. It is said of God, that He cannot lie, and therefore may it be of Him, that He cannot accept the unfinished conformities of man to a rule that is inflexible—He cannot accept of these as the claims to which are to be adjudged the high rewards of heaven's jurisprudence. We are outcasts from the Old Covenant, if, in a single instance, we have made free with the authority of God, or trampled on any of

His requirements. And on the face of the New Covenant, there is nothing that stands out more strongly, than the decisive check which it has laid on the spirit of legality, than the wide and welcome way in which it throws open the gate of heaven to all, if willing to enter there on the footing of a divine grant; and the firm interdict which, at the same time, it throws across the path of all who offer to approach on the footing of their own merits. There is not one more obvious or prominent characteristic of the Gospel, than just the way in which it meets and encounters the spirit of legality at the very outset, and must either conquer it into entire submission, or decline to treat with it altogether. It holds forth an alternative, on the one side of which the access between God and man is hopelessly and everlastingly barred, and on the other side of which there is a patent way of approach, even to the place "where His honor dwelleth," and where his favor is as free as the elements of air and light, to all who will. All who propose to join themselves to the Lord in that covenant, to which He has actually put His consenting hand, ought to be aware of this—nor are they prepared for such a movement, till brought to acquiesce in the saying, "that not by works of righteousness which we have done, but according to His mercy He hath saved us."

But it is altogether worthy of remark, that the mercy by which we are saved, is mercy in conjunction with righteousness. On the work of our redemption, the sacredness of the Godhead stands as prominently out as does the tenderness of the Godhead. God did not so love the world, as, under the simple instigation of a compassionate feeling towards it, to send a message of forgiveness, and thus make known to sinners the mere clemency of His nature. He so loved the world, as to send His only begotten Son into it, who took upon Him the punishment of our guilt, and the whole burden of that obedience which we should have rendered; and thus made known the righteousness of His nature, as well as its clemency, in that He thereby approved Himself just, while the Justifier of those who believe in Jesus. This is the leading characteristic of the Gospel dispensation. It is a dispensation of mercy, but of mercy in alliance with truth; a mercy illustrative of all those high and unchangeable perfections which belong to the great moral Sovereign of the universe. He makes us all welcome to pardon, but it is to pardon sealed by the blood of a divine atonement. He beckons the guiltiest of men to draw nigh, but it is only by the path of an appointed and consecrated mediatorship. He holds out the remission of sins to one and to every; yet it is not a simple sentence of remission that He passes upon any, but a sentence of justification; or, in other words, a sentence given in consideration of a righteousness. To every sinner there is declared the offer of his remission, that in laying hold of it, he may do homage to the gentle and compassionate attributes of the Deity. But to every sinner there is declared at the same time, the righteousness on which this deed of remission is founded, that he may also do homage to the august and holy attributes of the Deity.

He who confides in the general mercy of God, would break up this association, which God will never consent to dissolve. His hatred of sin, and the high moral regard He bears to the worth and the rectitude of virtue, are stamped on every feature of that economy which He has instituted for the acceptance and recovery of the sinful. It is thus that the priesthood of Christ stands forward to observation, in characters of sanctity, as bright and legible as it does in the characters of benignity. And therefore it is not a proffer of bare mercy, but of propitiated mercy, that is held out for our acceptance. God does not set forth Himself with a general declaration of pardon to the sins of mankind; but He sets forth His Son a propitiation for the sins of mankind. And what we have to look to, is not the mercy of God unguarded and unqualified; but the mercy of God in Christ, and through Christ, reconciling the world.

There is no question that appears to have been more solemnly entertained, and more deliberately weighed in the counsels of the upper sanctuary, than how to determine the footing on which the guilty shall be taken back again, into acceptance with the God whom they had offended. And to provide a solid footing, Christ had both to serve and to suffer in our stead. Lest our sins should pass unreckoned, and so escape the punishment that was due to them, they were reckoned unto Christ; and lest the righteousness that He as Mediator has brought in, should pass unreckoned, and so miss of a reward, it is reckoned unto us. And thus, in the highest exhibition of generosity that ever was given to the world, we behold, at the same time, all the precision of a justice that could not deviate, and all the unchangeableness of a truth that could not fail. Had we fulfilled the law of God, heaven would have been ours, and it would have been given to us because of our righteousness. We have broken that law, and yet heaven may be ours, not because of our righteousness, but still because of a righteousness; and the honor of God is deeply involved in the question, What and whose righteousness this is? It is not the righteousness of man, but the righteousness of Christ reckoned unto man. The whole distinction between a covenant that is now exploded, and the covenant that is now in force, hinges upon this alternative. If we make a confidence of the former plea, we shall perish; and if of the latter, we shall have life everlasting.

God is merciful; and in virtue of this, it was His longing desire to frame a deed of reconciliation, and to convey it to our world. But God is also righteous; and in virtue of this, the very peculiar economy of a mediatorship, and an incarnation, and a sacrifice, had to be instituted, through which this deed of mercy was to pass; and in its way, it became tinged as it were, with the full expression of the entire and unbroken character of the Godhead. So that, when it reaches the sinner, it bears upon it the impress of the divine justice, as well as of the divine benignity. It is only by the acceptance of this deed on the part of the sinner, that God will consent on His part to take the sinner into acceptance. He will not enter into fellowship with the guilty, but in such a way as shall secure their complete recognition of all the attributes of His nature. Forgiveness by a mere demonstration of mercy is not that way. Reward from Him as a generous master, to man for his own righteousness, though an unworthy service, is not that way. The way must be such as to manifest not a degraded, but a vindicated Sovereign; and so, that the mercy which He awards shall be that, not of fallen, but of exalted majesty. And hence the peremptory announcement, that no man cometh unto the Father but by the Son; and the no less peremptory rejection of every man who offers by any other approach, to draw nigh unto the sanctuary. The whole character of heaven's jurisprudence hangs upon the question, Whether man shall stand before God, upon his own righteousness, or the righteousness of Christ? nor is there a more direct and pointed article in that covenant by which a sinner joins himself to God, than, that on the one ground he will never meet with acceptance, and on the other ground, he will never miss it.

It is painful to be told of the insecurity of all those refuges to which nature most fondly clings, and in which she most rejoices as her favorite hiding-place. Man is never more in his element, than when building a security before God, on some plea or palliation of his own; and it is not without a sigh, or without a struggle, that he can behold the foundation of all merit in himself utterly swept away. The only redress we can offer, is to assure him of the stability of that other, and that only foundation on which we invite him to build. It is to announce to him, in the language of Scripture, that as he has failed in making out a righteousness by his own obedience to the law, "Christ is the end of the law for this righteousness, to every one that believeth." It is to make him perceive, that if he will only consent to stand on the righteousness of Christ, as the alone ground of his dependence, God will stand by the articles of His own covenant, for the fulfillment of which we have both His affirmation and His oath, as our immutable guaranties. He will never mock the confidence which His own word has inspired, and therefore one and all should encourage themselves on the strength of this assurance, and cast the cause of their acceptance on that unfailing plea, that is never lifted up by man without ascending in welcome to the throne of God. The merit of His will-beloved Son is to Him the incense of a sweet-smelling savor, so that the guiltiest creature who takes shelter there, has posted himself on the very avenue, along which there ever rolls the tide of divine complacency. We should invest ourselves then with this merit, and wrap ourselves firmly in it, as in a covering. We should put on Christ, who is offered to us without money and without price. We should present ourselves before God, with His invitation as our alone warrant, and the truth of His promises, which are yea and amen in Christ Jesus, as our alone confidence. His place in the new covenant is to declare our forgiveness, through the blood of a satisfying atonement. Our place in the covenant, is to give credit to that declaration. If each of the parties take his own place, all the promises that have passed from the one to the other will have their fulfillment. If we have faith in God, according to our faith, so will be His faithfulness.

The act of laying hold of this covenant, is primarily and essentially an act of the mind. It is a business, at the doing of which, there may have been no visible or external movement at all; a transaction entered upon, and completed in no other character of agency, than the character of thought, and the fruit of a silent interview between the Spirit of God and the spirit of man, the former showing unto the latter the things of Christ, and the latter rendering the consent of his understanding and belief to this demonstration. These are the unseen but substantial steps, by which an act of reconciliation is struck between the two parties, and both the overtures on the one side, and the responses on the other, may be altogether mental. When God makes it known to the sinner, by His word and Spirit, that Christ hath wrought out a perfect righteousness, to the whole use and validity of which he is just as welcome as if the righteousness were personally his own; and when the sinner, persuaded of the truth of this, is simply translated into the same confidence before God that he would have had, had his own personal righteousness been perfect like that of Christ; then the covenant of grace is in very deed entered upon, and without any other forth-putting on the part of God, than the exhibition of His word to man, and any other forth-putting on the part of man, than the acquiescence that he has rendered thereto. God's declaration of a righteousness unto all, and upon all who believe, constitutes His offer. The credit we give to this declaration constitutes our acceptance. To receive Christ, we have only to believe in His name. It is altogether a mental process. Our renunciation of the plea of our own righteousness, is a mental act. Our reliance on the plea of the righteousness of Christ, is a mental act. Our drawing upon God for forgiveness and justification in the name of this righteousness, is a mental act. And God hath graciously bound Himself to accept and to honor this method of drawing. He has so ordered the covenant between us and Him, that on our simply counting Him faithful who hath promised, He counts Himself pledged to the fulfillment on us of what is so promised.—Could we state the thing more freely we would do it, for sure we are that the more freely it is stated, the more truly it is stated. We have failed in making out a title-deed to God's favor by our own obedience. Christ hath made one out for us by His obedience. If we believe it to be a good title-deed, it is ours, if we will. Should we be satisfied with it, God is. We are putting honor upon Christ, when we trust in the plea of His righteousness; and God is putting honor upon Christ, when He sustains the validity of this plea. Thus, there is a common place of meeting between God and the sinner, when the belief of the one, and the blessing of the other, come into close and rejoicing fellowship. Should any one who reads his Bible, and relying on God's testimony, conceive this belief, then, on the strength of this mental inclination alone, he has laid hold of the covenant. He has become invested with a complete righteousness, the whole reward of which will be conferred on him, simply because of his reliance upon it. It is his by faith. A negotiation has been going on between God and his soul, and such is the force and obligation of the contract which has resulted from it, between the two parties—that while the one is bound to depend, the other is bound not to disappoint him.

We never shall obtain any secure or legitimate rest to our minds, till we have thus found it in Jesus Christ, as the Lord our righteousness—till we have come to trust wholly in His merit, and not at all in our own, as our alone plea of meritorious acceptance with the righteous Lawgiver—till the free offer of a title to eternal life, through the obedience of another, be met by our faithful acceptance of it; and on cleaving to it as our single but sufficient claim to reconciliation, have learned in this attitude to walk in quietness, and with confidence before God.

It is not in our power to reason any one into this confidence. It springs in the heart of man, on the simple statement of the truth, and by the manifestation of that truth, by the Spirit, unto the conscience. Argument and eloquence are alike unavailing towards the production of it. It is by the doctrine being presented to the mind, and the mind perceiving in the doctrine a counterpart to its own wants; it is thus that the faith comes which is unto salvation. We have endeavored to offer a faithful exhibition of the truth as it is in Jesus; and it is the part of the inquirer to ponder it attentively; and the Spirit may so convince of sin, and may so manifest the suitableness of the proffered Saviour, as to assure him, that this is indeed the wished-for remedy to the grievous and deep felt disease. And therefore would we state the averments of Scripture, on this most essential and interesting of all subjects, with the view of putting it to those who have sought for rest, and have not yet found it, whether these words bear not the evidence of a testimony from heaven, seeing it is only by a sure and simple reliance upon them, that they can reach the object they have so long and so vainly been in quest of.

"Christ was delivered for our offences." "Christ hath made an end of transgressions, and brought in an everlasting righteousness." "God hath set Him forth a propitiation for the sins of the world." "He died, the just for the unjust, to bring us to God." "He has been made sin for us, though He knew no sin, that we might become the righteousness of God in Him." "Justified by faith, we have peace with God, through Jesus Christ our Lord." "And all who believe in Him, are justified from all things, from which they could not be justified by the law." Inasmuch that one shall say, "In the Lord have I righteousness;" and "this is the name whereby He shall be called, The Lord our righteousness." The labor of a whole life directed to the object of establishing a merit of our own, will only widen our distance from peace; and, we know of nothing that will send this visitant to our agitated bosoms, but a firm and simple reliance on these declarations. The unbelief of man is the only obstacle which the mercy of God in Christ has to struggle with; nor do we know of one other step that is necessary, but an act of faith on the part of the sinner, that this mercy may take its ample effect and fulfillment upon his person. It is simply by an act of believing, by a pure act of the mind, that he enters into reconciliation, and a covenant is established, as steadfast and immutable as it is in the power of solemn guaranties to make it—a covenant with only one tie, but that a most sufficient one, to bind it, even the tie which subsists between the faith of the creature, and the faithfulness of the Creator.

And it is for the purpose of presenting to our readers a full and very able exposition of the truths on which we have been insisting, that we have introduced into our series of Christian Authors the following Treatise, on "*The Reign of Grace, from its rise to its consummation,*" by ABRAHAM BOOTH; which we earnestly recommend to their attentive perusal, as one of the most powerful and luminous, and comprehensive expositions of the dispensations of grace with which we are acquainted. In this Treatise, they will find the Gospel of the Grace of God exhibited in all the fullness and freeness of its unrestricted offers of mercy, through the Saviour, to guilty man—in all the extent of its exuberant blessings—in its rich provisions for deliverance from condemnation and guilt, and restoration to the favor and friendship of God—in all the efficacy of its renovating and sanctifying influences in forming us to holiness, and in assimilating us to the spirit and character of God—and in all the benign and diversified operations, which a God of infinite wisdom and love has fitted it to produce, by causing it to reign unto eternal life through Jesus Christ, as made of God unto us wisdom, and righteousness, and sanctification, and complete redemption.

Originating, as those blessings and privileges do, in this grace, it is of mighty importance for us to ascertain, whether we have closed with God on the terms of His own covenant, and thus have been made partakers of this grace, and whether its reign has been established in our hearts. And we cannot refer the reader, who is in earnest about his salvation, to any treatise better fitted than that of Abraham Booth, to give him sure and satisfying evidences for ascertaining the soundness and security of his hopes for eternity. He presents grace, as reigning through Jesus Christ unto eternal life, to sinners; and he invites the chief of sinners, by putting faith in the testimony of God, to lay hold of the offered grace, and thus appropriate to themselves the blessings of pardon, and peace, and justification, which God has provided through the atonement and righteousness of Christ; and which, in the proclamations of the Gospel, are freely and unreservedly offered to all who will. On this, the alone warrant of faith, he invites all to enter into peace and reconciliation with God, and by judging Him faithful who hath promised, to enjoy the blessedness of the man whose sins are covered, and to whom the Lord does not impute transgression.

But while faith in the free grace and offered pardon of the Gospel puts peace and joy into the heart of the believer, it is no less fitted to produce purity and holiness. This, indeed is the tendency, as well as the main and ultimate design of the Gospel, and it is on this account that we estimate so highly the Treatise we are now recommending, that it so nobly vindicates the doctrines of grace as doctrines according to godliness. And if there is any portion of this work to which, more than another, we would particularly direct the attention of our readers, it is to those chapters " On Grace as it reigns in our Sanctification," and " On the Necessity of Holiness and good Works." There is, in the minds of many, a fancied alliance between free grace and an immunity to sin; that, since pardon is the free gift of God, through the blood of the atonement, there is no restraint laid on men's inclination to sin— that since we are justified wholly by the righteousness of another, the necessity of personal righteousness is as wholly superseded—and that since we cannot earn heaven by our own obedience, all the motives and securities for obedience are removed. We have not room to attempt an exposure of this oft-repeated, but unfounded, assertion—an assertion, to which the clearest averments of Scripture, and the experience of every true believer, give the most triumphant refutation. And we count it unnecessary to enter into any defence of the doctrines of grace from the charge of licentiousness, after the able and unanswerable vindication which the present volume furnishes. We do not indeed deny, that many professors of the Gospel give some color for such an impeachment, by profaning that holy name by which they are called, and by failing to adorn the doctrines of grace by lives and conversations becoming the Gospel; but such men have never felt the *reign of grace* in their hearts, otherwise it would not have failed to teach them " to deny ungodliness and worldly lusts, and to live soberly, righteously, and godly in the world;" and, while such men repose a fancied confidence in the death of Christ as their deliverance from condemnation, and as their passport to heaven, they have utterly mistaken one of the main designs of Christ's death, which was "to deliver us from all iniquity, and to purify us unto Himself a peculiar people zealous of good works." If heaven consists in God's manifesting the spiritual glories of His holy and perfect character, then must our spirit and character be kindred to His own, before we can delight in the love and contemplation of such glory. To love and enjoy God, we must be like God. And they utterly mistake the design of the Gospel, who conceive of it as a mere act of indemnity; and the Gospel has not been believed by them at all, if it has not come to them in the power and beneficence of holiness and grace, to change their hearts and their affections into the love of what is holy, and righteous, and excellent; nor can they entertain any well-founded hopes of heaven hereafter, in whom there is no process of restoration going at present to the lost image of the Godhead, and in whose hearts grace is not exerting its reigning power, to assimilate them to the spirit and character of God.

Whatever there may be now, in the days of Paul, at least, there were men who turned the grace of God into licentiousness, and who ranked among the privileges of the Gospel an immunity for sin. And it is striking to observe the effect of this corruption on the mind of the apostle;—that he who braved all the terrors of persecuting violence, that he who stood undismayed before kings and governors, and could lift his intrepid testimony in the hearing of an enraged multitude—that he who, when bound by a chain between two soldiers, still sustained an invincible constancy of spirit, and could live in fearlessness, and triumph, with the dark imagery of an approaching execution in his eye—that he who counted not his life dear unto him, and whose manly breast bore him up amidst all the threats of human tyranny, and the grim apparatus of martyrdom—that this man so firm and so undaunted, wept like a child when he heard of those disciples that turned the pardon of the cross into an encouragement for doing evil. The fiercest hostilities of the Gospel's open enemies he could brave, but when he heard of the foul dishonor done to the name of his Master, by the moral worthlessness of those who were the Gospel's professing friends, this he could not bear—all that firmness, which so upheld him unfaltering and unappalled in the battles of the faith, forsook him then; and this noblest of champions on the field of conflict and of controversy, when he heard of the profligacy of his own converts, was fairly overcome by the tidings, and gave way to all the softness of womanhood. When every other argument fails, for keeping us on the path of integrity and holiness, we should think of the argument of Paul in tears. It may be truly termed a picturesque argument, nor are we aware of a more impressive testimony in the whole compass of Scripture, to the indispensable need of virtue and moral goodness in a believer, than is to be found in that passage where Paul says of these unworthy professors of the faith, "For many walk, of whom I have told you often, and now tell you even weeping, that they are the enemies of the cross of Christ; whose end is destruction, whose god is their belly, and whose glory is in their shame, who mind earthly things."

This page intentionally left blank

This page intentionally left blank

This page intentionally left blank

This page intentionally left blank

MEMOIR.

Abraham Booth was born at Blackwell, in Derbyshire, on the 20th of May, 1734, old style. In the first year of his life, his parents removed from Blackwell to Annesley Woodhouse, a small hamlet in the parish of Annesley, Nottinghamshire, where they occupied a farm belonging to the Duke of Portland. Of a numerous family of children, Abraham was the oldest, and there the first fifteen or sixteen years of his life were passed, assisting his father as soon as he was able in his agricultural concerns.

The advantages of education, which are of such unspeakable importance to the cultivation of our mental powers, are generally of difficult attainment in villages and the retired districts of the country; and a century ago they were probably more so than at present. This may help to account for a circumstance which Mr. Booth has often been heard to mention amongst his friends—that until he quitted the farming business, he never spent six months at school. His father taught him to read, making it a general practice to hear his lesson every day after dinner.

It is certainly a very just remark, that there are no characters, however eminent among our species, whose biography is more instructive, or in which we feel more interested, than those which exhibit to our view persevering efforts surmounting formidable obstacles, and dis tinguished eminence gradually arising out of obscurity and depression. Such is the discipline through which many of the greatest names in the republic of letters have passed ; nor have any of the original favourites of nature or the children of affluence attained a superiority so solid and durable as that which has been acquired by such a course of cultivation.

The energy of young Booth's mind, which appeared so conspicuously throughout the subsequent period of his life, began very early to develope itself. He was indebted almost entirely to his own industry and application for his proficiency in the art of writing, and in the science of arithmetic. And as he grew up, so devoted did he become to his studies, that he cheerfully sacrificed the hours usually allotted to repose and recreation, for the pleasure he found in prosecuting them. When the other members of the family retired to rest, Abraham withdrew to cultivate his mind. The parents of our author were members of the church of England; and of course trained up their son in a customary reverence for the national establishment of religion. The first direction of his mind towards the dissenters took place when he was about ten years of age ; and was occasioned by the preaching of some plain and illiterate teachers belonging to the denomination of General (or Arminian) Baptists who occasionally visited his neighbourhood. They drew the attention of the family ; and under their discourses our author was first awakened to a concern about the salvation of his soul. His convictions were permanent and increased with his years ; but it is plain from the history of his own mind, that it was long after this ere he attained any just and clear views of the true grace of God, or was enlightened into the important doctrine of accept ance with God as revealed in the New Testament. He, however, applied to the society of General Baptists to be admitted into their communion, and was accordingly baptized on a profession of his faith, by Mr. Francis Smith, at Barton, in 1755, at which time he was about the age of twenty-one.

Some years previous to this, young Booth had relinquished the farming business; and, induced probably by the hope of being able to pursue his studies with less interruption, he had applied himself to learn the business of a stocking maker, but was never articled as an apprentice to the trade. He, however, managed to support himself by that means, from the age of sixteen to that of four-and-twenty, at which period he married Miss Elizabeth Bowmar, the daughter of a neighbouring farmer, with whom he enjoyed much domestic felicity during more than forty years.

But possessing so vigorous a mind, it was not likely that Mr. Booth should long continue a mechanic. He had now been diligently occupied for several years in the acquisition of useful knowledge; his capacity had attained to a considerable degree of maturity; he had entered into an important domestic relation; and he had before him the prospect of a numerous family for whom he was bound to provide; and he therefore adopted the resolution of opening a school at Sutton Ashfield, about two miles from Kirby, for the instruction of youth. Mrs. Booth assisted the undertaking by instructing the female pupils in the useful branches of needle-work, for which she had been eminently qualified by her education.

The society of General Baptists, with which Mr. Booth now stood connected, had sufficient discernment to perceive that he possessed abilities which only required cultivation to mature and raise to excellence. They accordingly invited him to assist occasionally in the public preaching of the word; and so rapid was his improvement, that in a little time he was considered as a leading person among them. Their profession increased considerably throughout the neighbouring districts; and our author was frequently at Melbourne, Barton, Loughborough, Diseworth, and other places, at the distance of twenty, thirty, and even forty miles from home, preaching the glad tidings of salvation to his fellow-sinners, according to the views which he then had of divine truth. In the year 1760, it was thought advisable to collect into churches those who had professed the faith and been baptized, and to appoint over them pastors and teachers, after the example of the first churches. The society of Kirby-Woodhouse was accordingly submitted to the superintendence of Mr. Booth, who continued for several years to labour among them in the ministry of the word; though, for reasons which do not appear, he declined to take upon himself the pastoral office. His preaching is, nevertheless, said to have been with considerable acceptance and success; and in the regulation of these newly-formed societies he proved highly instrumental. We find him in the same year assisting at the ordination of Mr. F. Smith and Mr. T. Parkins over the General Baptist church at Melbourne, and delivering a solemn charge to them from Acts xx. 28. *Take heed unto yourselves and to all the flock*, &c.

In this stage of their proceedings, however, a memorable and important change took place in the religious sentiments of Mr. Booth. He had hitherto held the Arminian doctrine, and been a strenuous advocate for the universality of divine grace. He had written and printed a poem on "Absolute Predestination," in which the fervour of his zeal for what he then esteemed truth, had vented itself in reviling the doctrine of election and particular redemption, in language as replete with contumely and reproach as is to be found in the writings of Wesley or Fletcher. It may indeed be pleaded as some apology for its author, that he wrote it when only twenty years of age; and it is important, as serving to demonstrate the greatness of the change which afterwards took place in his mind relative to the character of the Supreme Being.

Mr. Booth was fully aware that the change which his sentiments had undergone was of such a nature as to render it utterly impossible for himself and his friends to walk any longer together in a way that would be productive of mutual comfort; and he had too much integrity to conceal the difference. The change itself was the fruit of deep conviction, and thus at a future period of his life we find his own pen recording it. "The doctrine of sovereign, distinguishing grace, as commonly and justly stated by Calvinists, it must be acknowledged, is too generally exploded. This the writer knows by experience, to his grief and shame. Through the ignorance of his mind, the pride of his heart, and the prejudice of his education, he, in his younger years, often opposed it with much warmth, though with no small weakness; but after an impartial inquiry, and many prayers, he found reason to alter his judgment; he found it to be the doctrine of the Bible, and a dictate of the unerring Spirit. Thus patronized, he received the once obnoxious sentiment, under a full conviction of its being a divine truth."

The revolution that had now taken place in his sentiments was soon observed by his friends, and it occasioned considerable uneasiness in their minds. They respected his character and approved his ministry. Meetings were held for the purpose of investigating the differences which subsisted between them, when each party produced the best arguments they could in behalf of their respective tenets; but neither party succeeding in convincing the other, they mutually agreed to part. In vindication of the principles of Christian integrity, which on this occasion governed his conduct, Mr. Booth chose as the foundation of his farewell discourse, the parable of the unjust steward, which naturally led him to remark, that fraud and concealment of various kinds may obtain the friendship of men; that when friendship is obtained by such means, he who gains it, and they who grant it, are chargeable with injustice peculiarly execrable; and that Scripture, reason, and conscience, unite their authority in recommending universal fidelity to accountable creatures, and especially to the ministers and professors of religion, in the view of the great day of account, when they must all give up their stewardship!

Mr. Booth's separation from the General Baptists suspended for a while his public ministrations; but in a short time a place was procured at Sutton Ashfield, called Bore's Hall, which was licensed for the purpose, and in which he recommenced his labours as a preacher of the gospel of peace. Here he gathered in process of time a small society of the Calvinistic or Particular Baptist denomination; and it was at this time that he composed his invaluable treatise, "The Reign of Grace." The substance of that excellent work was originally delivered in a series of discourses at Sutton Ashfield, and afterwards at Nottingham and Chesterfield; at both of which towns he for several years was in the practice of preaching on alternate Sabbaths.

The exertions of Mr. Booth during this period will, to many, appear to have been truly astonishing. He had to labour throughout the week for the support of a family every year increasing, and even then become numerous. He had frequently to travel the distance of twelve or fifteen miles on the Lord's-day morning, and afterwards to preach twice or thrice during the day, for which the only remuneration he accepted was barely the expense of horse hire, which at no time exceeded ten pounds a year; and it was under these unfavourable circumstances that he wrote *The Reign of Grace*. But to such as have " tasted that the Lord is gracious," the solution of the problem will not be difficult. When we examine his publication, and remark what the subjects are which then occupied his public ministrations, viz. : the nature and properties of divine grace—when we think of him as tracing that grace in all its rich aboundings; as reigning in our election—effectual calling—the pardon of sin—justification—adoption—sanctification—perseverance—and at length crowning the sinner with eternal glory, we may safely conclude that " the word of Christ dwelt richly in him," and that he " spake of these things out of the abundance of his heart," bringing forth that which was good to the use of edifying and which ministered grace to the hearers." When the mind is filled with the doctrines of divine grace, it delights to dwell upon so transporting a theme, and the tongue speaks of it with inexpressible pleasure.

When the manuscript of the Reign of Grace was completed, it was shown by the author to some of his friends, though probably without any view to immediate publication. He was yet an obscure and unfriended individual, little known even in the circle of his own denomination; and he might possibly recollect the maxim of the poet, that

"Slow rises worth by poverty depressed!"—

At any rate we are said to owe its first publication to the following train of circumstances. A friend of Mr. Booth's who had perused the work in manuscript, happening to be at Huddersfield, in Yorkshire, called upon Mr. Henry Venn, a clergyman professing evangelical sentiments, and well known as the author of a popular work, entitled "The Complete Duty of Man," to whom he mentioned Mr. Booth's intended publication, and gave such an account of it as excited in Mr. Venn an eager desire to see it. The manuscript was accordingly transmitted to him, and so strongly prepossessed was he by a perusal of it, that he took a journey from Huddersfield to Sutton Ashfield, that he might enjoy the pleasure of a personal interview with the author. The result was an acquaintance which ripened into intimacy; and notwithstanding the dissimilarity of their views respecting the nature, constitution, and order of a Christian church, that intimacy was cemented by the bonds of reciprocal esteem and friendship which continued with unabated ardour through life. Mr. Venn strongly urged upon his friend the publication of his manuscript, and with a view of making it more generally known, wrote a recommendatory preface to the work.

The "Reign of Grace" was first published in April, 1768, and soon attracted pretty general regard. The Particular Baptist Church in Little Prescot Street, Goodman's Fields, London, had recently lost their pastor, Mr. Samuel Burford, and were then looking out for a successor. Some of the members of the church happening to meet with Mr. Booth's book, and approving the per formance, they came to the resolution of taking a journey into Nottinghamshire, to see the author. The result of this visit was an invitation to our author to supply the church in Goodman's Fields, for a few Sabbaths, to which he consented; and in the month of June following, he arrived in London and preached to them three Lord's days in succession. This led to a second invitation for further assistance, with which also, after visiting his own family, he complied, and preached four Sabbaths more: and in the issue the church unanimously agreed to invite him to become their pastor. By a letter bearing date October 1st, 1768, he signified his acquiescence with their call; and on the sixteenth day of February, 1769, was ordained by prayer and the imposition of hands. On this solemn occasion, he delivered before the church a public and explicit confession of his faith which was afterwards printed.

Mr. Booth's settlement in London forms a new era in the history of his life. He was now called to move in a new circle, and the change which he underwent in being translated from an obscure country village to the metropolis of the kingdom, must have been striking even to his own mind. Instead of preaching to a few plain unlettered people in a barn or humble school-room, he was now to discharge the duties of the pastoral office over one of the most respectable churches amongst the English dissenters. He was doubtless fully impressed with the importance of the trust, and the high responsibility which attached to it: a consideration of which could not fail to stimulate a vigorous mind like his to a sedulous improvement of its powers. Hitherto his acquirements had scarcely carried him beyond the rudiments of English grammar. But he rejoiced that Providence had now favoured him with auspicious opportunities of increasing his knowledge; and, conscious of his deficiencies, he became insatiable in his thirst after learning. The first object to which he devoted his attention was an acquaintance with the Latin and Greek languages; and in the pursuit of that, his progress was considerably facilitated by the assistance which he derived from an eminent classical scholar, who had formerly been a Roman Catholic priest. Of this gentleman's erudition, Mr. Booth always spoke in terms of high commendation; and thus aided, it is natural to suppose that his improvement would be rapid. The tutor usually came in the morning, and after breakfasting with his pupil, they retired together into the study for business. This was the only assistance worth mentioning with which he was ever favoured; and with that exception, he might be fairly denominated—a self-taught scholar.

In prosecuting his studies, however, Mr. Booth never lost sight of the important ends of his office as a minister of the gospel of Christ. It was no object of his ambition to become a profound metaphysician, or an adept in the higher branches of the mathematics. He made no pretensions to the character of an accomplished Hebrician, nor to any intimate acquaintance with the oriental languages. But a familiar knowledge of the Latin gave him an easy access to the exhaustless stores of theology published upon the continent of Europe, and which are to be met with in the writings of the many eminent professors that have filled the chairs of Foreign Universities among the reformed churches, such as Witsius, Turretine, Stapferus, Vitringa, and Venema. Not many of his cotemporaries were so deeply read in the Popish controversy; and the fruits of his reading may be found in the adroitness with which he has employed the best arguments by which the reformation was defended, in vindication of his own sentiments as an Antipædobaptist. Ecclesiastical history was a favourite subject with him and the writers of that class, viz.: Dupin, Cave, Bingham, Venema, Spanheim, and the Magdeburg Centuriators were familiar to him; as were also Lewis, Jennings, Reland, Spencer, Ikenius, Carpzovius, Fabricius of Hamburgh, and others on the article of Jewish Antiquities. Among the writers of his own country, there was none that engaged so much of his regard, as Dr. John Owen, to whose evangelical and learned works he has in various ways frequently acknowledged his obligations; and from whom there will be found more quotations in his writings, than from any other author, ancient or modern, if we except the sacred volume.

It is a true though hackneyed observation, that the history of an author must be found in his works; and the justice of its application to Mr. Booth will be apparent from the present narrative. We may trace him in his studies and in his labours by means of the press, during almost every successive year, from the time of his removal to London, to the period of his death. In 1770, which was only the first year after his ordination, he published *The Death of Legal Hope, the Life of Evangelical Obedience*, in an Essay on Gal. ii. 19.

The main design of this Essay is to prove that the grace which brings salvation to guilty men, and which "reigns through righteousness unto eternal life by Jesus Christ our Lord," has no tendency to relax their obligations to holiness, but that, on the contrary, it is a doctrine according to godliness.

One of the most pernicious sentiments arising from an abuse of the doctrines of grace, is a denial that the moral law is the rule of life to believers. This unscriptural and absurd principle was probably never more prevalent in England than at that period; and Mr. Booth had to sustain a testimony against it both in his writings and in his personal conduct as the pastor of a Christian church.

About the time Mr. Booth came to settle in London, the question concerning the divinity of Christ was the subject of much controversy in this country. Several respectable clergymen of the established church resigned their benefices, and took their lot among the Socinian dissenters, because they could not conscientiously conform to Trinitarian worship. The dispute was kept in agitation during several years; and certainly a formidable phalanx of talent appeared against this leading article of the Christian faith. It was upon this occasion that Mr. Booth was induced in the year 1777, to present the public with a new edition of a work, entitled, *The Deity of Jesus Christ, essential to the Christian Religion*, written originally in French, by *Dr. James Abaddie*, dean of Killaloe in Ireland. An English translation of it had appeared many years before, but it was greatly improved by our author, who revised, corrected, and by judiciously retrenching it in some parts, concentrated the author's reasoning, and much enhanced its value and usefulness.

In the following year (1778) he published "*An Apology for the Baptists, in which they are vindicated from the imputation of laying an unwarrantable stress on the ordinance of Baptism.*" The object of the publication is to oppose the principle of mixed communion, which had been introduced among some of the Baptist churches in England, about the middle of the seventeenth century, and which has more or less prevailed among them to the present time. A consideration of the subject was partly forced upon our author, by one of his brethren in the ministry, who had been invited to take the pastoral care of a society of this mixed kind; but having scruples in his own mind upon the propriety of this practice, he submitted the thing to the judgment of Mr. Booth, and requested to be favoured with his sentiments upon it. The substance of "The Apology" was consequently transmitted to his friend in a series of letters; and, in the hope that what was originally intended for the information of an individual, might prove useful to the denomination at large, he was afterwards induced to publish it in its present form.

Mr. Booth was, shortly after this, called to take up his pen in defence of the ordinance of Baptism itself. In the year 1784, he was induced to lay before the public his "*Pædobaptism examined, on the Principles, Concessions, and Reasonings of the most learned Pædobaptists.*" In the preface to that work, he informs us that having observed for a course of years, that many of the most learned and eminent Pædobaptists, when theological subjects are under discussion, frequently argue on such principles, admit such facts, interpret various texts of Scripture in such a manner, and make such concessions, as are greatly in favour of the Baptists; he extracted a number of passages from their publications, and made many references to others, which he thought might be fairly pleaded against infant sprinkling. On reviewing these quotations and memoranda, he had concluded merely for his own private use, to employ some leisure hours in transcribing and arranging them under different heads of the Pædobaptist controversy.

He has taken up the subject upon much more general grounds, than that which is occupied by any individual writer that has hitherto appeared on either side of this long litigated question; and his method of discussing the subject is entitled to the full praise of originality. Of the ability displayed by the author in the execution of this work, it is unnecessary in this place to enlarge. The public voice, which is perhaps after all the surest test of criticism, has long ago stamped upon it the sanction of its applause. It may be safely made a question, if the subject was ever handled in a more masterly manner, by any writer in any age or language. He meets his opponents on their own ground, avails himself of their own weapons, and with singular dexterity turns them against themselves. The Monthly Review for September, 1784, smartly remarked, that "He sets his opponents together by the ears, and leaves them to overthrow the very cause, in defence of which they professed to take the field." The book was so well received that the whole impression was soon disposed of; and in the year 1787, our author gave to the public the second edition of Pædobaptism Examined, now enlarged by additional quotations, illustrations, and remarks, from one to two thick volumes. The performance, in its present state, may, almost without a hyperbole, be said to have exhausted the controversy on the Baptist side of the question; and the simple inquirer after truth who is not convinced by Mr. Booth's volumes can hardly be expected to yield his judgment to any thing that man can say upon this long contested point.

The "*Essay on the Kingdom of Christ*" was first

published in 1788. It relates to a subject of great importance; for it is evident that just views of it lie at the foundation of all rational principles of dissent from the national religious establishment. Yet it is remarkable that before the publication of this essay, the subject had been very little discussed among the English Nonconformists, though it had been fiercely litigated among the Episcopalians. Mr. Booth's Essay is a scriptural illustration of the subject, designed to show that as the kingdom of Christ is not of this world, it must in its nature be different from that of the kingdom of David, and the entire constitution of things under the Jewish theocracy. Hence he justly infers that it is quite absurd to reason from what took place under the Mosaic economy, to the nature of the Christian church, and the rights, privileges, and duties of the subjects of the Messiah's kingdom, since these are as different as flesh and spirit, temporal and spiritual. Keeping this distinction in view, he proceeds to elucidate his subject by showing that the gospel church is not of this world in regard to its origin—its subjects—the means of its establishment and support—the laws by which it is governed—that it does not resemble the kingdoms of this world in regard to its splendour—nor in respect of its immunities, riches, and honours. The discussion of these several particulars leads him not only to vindicate his own principles of dissent from the national establishment, but to animadvert with considerable severity on various things among its members which appear to him in the light of political artifices calculated to impeach the dominion of Christ in his own kingdom, or to degrade and corrupt that worship which he requires.

His next publication is entitled " *Glad Tidings to Pe-*

rishing Sinners; or, The Genuine Gospel, a complete Warrant for the Ungodly to believe in Jesus Christ;" the first edition of which appeared in 1796, and was followed by a second in 1800, with such considerable additions and improvements as almost to constitute a new work. Even among those who admit the truth of the gospel in the most unqualified terms, it has nevertheless been a subject of much debate, " to what description of persons it should be preached;" though surely, when we consider that it is the command of the Divine Author that it be preached " to every creature," it may justly excite surprise that such a question should ever have been started.

" The Amen to Social Prayer, illustrated and improved;" first published in the year 1800, is a sermon which had previously been delivered at one of the monthly meetings of ministers belonging to the Particular baptist denomination. It having been agreed to preach a series of Discourses on the different branches of the Lord's prayer, Dr. Jenkins commenced with a sermon on the words " Our Father, who art in heaven;" and it fell to the lot of Mr. Booth to close the whole with a discourse on the word " Amen." As no man was ever more averse than our author to the practice of selecting detached words and phrases, or of choosing any part of Scripture for the base purpose of making it the subject of a trial of skill, with the view of exciting popularity, or of affording amusement to the giddy multitude, it may be readily supposed that the task allotted him on this occasion, of preaching from a single word, would excite no small share of pleasantry among his friends. They could not forbear calling to mind the strong terms in which, in his " Essay on the Kingdom of Christ," he had entered his solemn protest against this practice, condemning it with the most

marked reprobation, as a disgrace to the pulpit, and a profanation of the sacred ministry ; and a general interest was excited to know how the preacher would extricate himself from what was considered a species of dilemma. He even appears to have personally felt the delicacy of his situation : but his good sense and solid judgment extricated him without much difficulty from the embarrassment. In fact, the result was such as to make it rather a matter of regret that he was not oftener placed in circumstances which, like the present, called forth the superior powers of his mind, than that it happened to him on this occasion. It produced a discourse on the subject of prayer, in which the duty and the privileges of it are illustrated in so masterly a manner, and such important instructions are given, both to ministers and people respecting that branch of public worship, that the pastor or private Christian who can peruse it without being both humbled and edified must either have very little experimental acquaintance with these interesting things, or have made an advance in the divine life, far beyond what falls to the generality of professors.

We now arrive at that period of our author's life, when, according to the ordinary course of nature, it might reasonably be expected, that his powers both of body and of mind would be rapidly declining. He had nearly attained the limit commonly allotted to the life of man; for he was fast advancing upon seventy years of age. But whatever ravages those infirmities of nature which are the usual concomitants of old age had made upon his earthly tabernacle, he gave the most indubitable proof that the powers of his mind had not sustained the smallest diminution. The productions of his pen, which it yet remains for us to notice, under whatever point of view they may be examined, will be allowed by every competent and impartial judge, not to yield the palm of excellence to the ablest of his former publications.

In the year 1803, at one of the monthly meetings of his Baptist brethren, he delivered a discourse which was soon afterwards published under the title of "*Divine Justice essential to the Divine Character* ;" a discourse which, had he left to the world no other fruits of his pen, would alone have been sufficient to stamp his character as one of the closest thinkers, and ablest reasoners, and most judicious divines of the century in which he lived.

In 1805, the last year of his life, he published his "*Pastoral Cautions*," the substance of which he had twenty years before delivered from the pulpit as a charge, at the ordination of Mr. Thomas Hopkins, over the Baptist Church in Eagle Street, Red Lion Square, London. He had now been fifty years engaged in the work of the ministry, and of that period more than thirty-five pastor of the church in Prescot Street. Independent of his native good sense and superior talents, it is natural to conclude that his age and long experience must have eminently qualified him for instructing his younger brethren on a subject of such vital importance to the welfare of the churches, and the honour of the Christian profession. It formed no part of his plan in this publication, to point out the topics which should constitute the subject matter of their ministrations; but to caution them how they should behave themselves in the house of God, in their families, and in the world, so as to exemplify the character of the Christian pastor, and, by a corresponding deportment, adorn the high and honourable office in which they are placed. The discourse is replete with maxims of prudence, and abounds in that wise and salutary counsel which is the result of mature years and valuable experience in union with disinterested and fervent affection; which combine in this instance, to administer profitable instruction to the inexperienced. The lessons are such as it became one to deliver, who had grown gray in his Master's service, and who obviously considered himself standing on the brink of the grave: and they are such as it well becomes those who survive him to make familiar, and by them to regulate their conversation in the church and in the world.

Several "*Funeral Sermons*" and "*Addresses*" delivered at the interment of his friends, were also published at different periods of his ministry; and they are what such compositions ought to be,—simple, chaste, solemn, and pathetic appeals to the living on the uncertainty of human life—the certainty of death—the necessity of being prepared for that event—the folly of trifling with the interests of the immortal soul, and neglecting the things that concern our everlasting peace—the importance of the gospel of Jesus Christ as the one thing needful, as that which alone can give effectual relief to the mind of a sinner under the dread of death and the judgment. They exhibit no high-wrought eulogies on the character of the deceased—no detail of compliments to surviving relatives—no flights of fancy, nothing trifling, nothing extraneous. All is solemn and affecting as the scene before us; and they may be safely held up as models of address which young ministers would do well in spirit and manner to imitate, when called to officiate on such mournfu occasions.

Mr. Booth was indebted to the goodness of God for a sound constitution of body; and he enjoyed as great a portion of good health as commonly falls to the lot ot man. His frame was muscular, though never inclined to corpulency; and during the far greater part of his life, he was seldom interrupted by ill-health in the discharge of his pastoral duties. But after he was sixty years old the effects of his intense application to study were very perceptible. He was increasingly afflicted with the asthma, particularly during the winter seasons; and the last three which he passed were severe and threatening, insomuch that he became impressed with the conviction that the time of his departure was at hand. About four years previous to his own dissolution, he sustained a severe shock in the loss of his dear partner in life; though his resignation to the will of God under that trying dispensation, appeared truly remarkable.

Some months before his death, having been attending a meeting of his ministering brethren in the city, he was taken suddenly ill on his way home, and from that time was mostly laid aside from his public labours. He was now called, in his own personal experience, to prove the validity of those principles which he had spent his life in recommending to others. His friends had now the satisfaction of seeing that in the immediate prospect of death his mind retained all its wonted calmness and serenity. To their anxious inquiries, his answer uniformly was, "I have no fears about my state"—

> "The gospel bears my spirit up;
> A faithful and unchanging God
> Lays the foundation of my hope
> In oaths, and promises, and blood."

Although in a great measure precluded from the discharge of his public official duties for several months before his death, he employed himself in revising and finishing for the press, "*An Essay on the Love of God* to his chosen *People*," and another on " *A Conduct and Character formed under the Influence of Evangelical Truth*," which he delivered into the hands of a particular friend just before his death, and by whom they were subsequently published. Nor are those excellent essays the only fruit that remains to us of his departing hours. Only a day or two before he left the world, he gave into the hands of the same friend a manuscript entitled, " *Thoughts on Dr. Edward Williams's Hypothesis relative to the Origin of Moral Evil*." This subject, in itself metaphysical and curious, has always been regarded as one of the most abstruse and difficult that can possibly employ the human intellect; and in the examination of Dr. Williams's " Hypothesis" Mr. Booth has evinced that he was still as competent as ever he had been to exert the powers of a sound and discriminating judgment—to grapple with the unwieldly or to chase the subtle. His manuscript bears internal evidence of having been composed during the last year of his life. Having carefully examined Dr. Williams's theory, and exposed its fallaciousness, Mr. Booth thus terminates the last of his literary labours: " Were my opinion asked respecting the origin of moral evil, the answer would be, I have no opinion upon the subject; nor dare I form conjectures about it. Having long been fully persuaded that a satisfactory solution of the question lies far beyond the reach of human intellect, I consider it as more becoming my feeble reason, and much more respectful to Divine Providence, to exclaim with Paul, ' O the depth !' than to indulge speculation on a subject so mysterious; lest I should fall under the righteous reproof of Jehovah's interrogatory to Job, ' Who is this that darkeneth counsel by words without knowledge ?' Of this, however, I have no doubt, that the existence and prevalence of moral evil in the rational creation, are completely consistent with all the perfections of God, and with all his eternal decrees; and that under the management of Supreme Wisdom, when the great system of Providence respecting both angels and men is finished, the conduct of God in reference to evil, both moral and natural, will be to the praise of his glory, in the eyes of all holy creatures." What a picture do these few lines exhibit of an humble, ingenuous, and pious mind. What a contrast to that rash and presumptuous spirit of speculation which, vainly puffed up by a fleshly mind, scorns to bound its investigations by the limits of revelation, and daringly intrudes into things which God has thought fit to veil from human ken. How expressive also of his reverence for the Supreme Being, his unshaken confidence in his wisdom, his power, his justice, holiness, and truth: how descriptive of the consciousness which possessed him of the very limited extent of his own faculties. The paragraph is worthy to be printed in letters of gold; it is worthy of the pen of Abraham Booth; and in no part of all his valuable writings does his Christian character appear more truly great, than in this concluding sentence of his works.

From the time that he was compelled to give up preaching, to the period of his death, he had many opportunities of evincing to his friends the steadfastness of his faith and hope, as well as the importance which he now attached to those precious doctrines which he had spent his life in publishing among them. "I now live," said he, "upon what I have been teaching others' His experience corresponded to the solid and judicious views of Divine truth, which formed the basis of his public discourses, and that characterize all his writings. He expressed no enthusiastic raptures; nor is there any reason to suppose that he was anxious about them. His mind was serene and peaceful; and with eternity in his immediate view, and considering the time of his departure at hand, he blessed God for a good hope through grace, breathed after heaven and perfect conformity to the image of Christ, and, in patient submission to the will of God, waited for the coming of his Lord and Saviour, to receive him to his kingdom.

On the Saturday preceding his death he requested to see a much esteemed friend, that he might communicate to him his last instructions, to whom, among other things, he said, "I am peaceful but not elevated." The following day, the same gentleman desired his son to inquire after his health. He replied to the inquiry, and then added, "Young man, think of your soul; if you lose that, you lose all. Be not half a Christian. Some people have just religion enough to make them miserable; not enough to make them happy. The ways of religion are good ways. I have found them such these sixty years." This was on the Lord's-day, during some part of which he was able to sit up in his study. His friends, however, were apprehensive that his dissolution was near, and several of them went to see him, as they rightly supposed for the last time. Though rendered almost incapable of conversation, he affectionately dropped a word to one and then to another, particularly to his young friends who were anxious to take leave of him. "But a little while" said he to one of them, "and I shall be with your dear father and mother." To another, "I have often borne you on my heart before the Lord; now you need to pray for me, and you must pray for yourself." To a third, in reference to a well-known Socinian minister, he said with much solemnity, "Beware of ———'s sentiments." Thus he studied to redeem the few hours yet allotted him, in counselling the young, and establishing them in the ways of the Lord. The evening was spent in the bosom of his endeared family. Two of his daughters and their husbands continued with him, and before their departure one of the latter engaged in family worship, with which he joined. About nine o'clock, he was put to bed, and lay down to rise no more until the resurrection morn! He expired the next day, without a struggle or a sigh; aged seventy-one.

The following extracts from the records of the church in Little Prescot Street, over which Mr. Booth had so long exercised the pastoral office, may here be appropriately inserted:

"By this dispensation of Providence, the church are bereaved of an under shepherd whom they highly valued, in whom there was an union of piety and talent rarely to be met with.

"In the pulpit he was always solemn and devotional; his prayers were the fervent effusions of the heart, and often brought his fellow-worshippers—where he appeared to be—near to the divine footstool. His discourses were solid, judicious, and interesting; nothing fell from his lips but what tended to edification. He aimed to alarm the conscience, and to awaken the heart, with an energy that plainly evinced how deeply he was convinced of the importance of those truths which he preached to others. His doctrinal views of religion were formed upon the closest investigations of Scripture, accompanied with earnest prayer. Doctrinal truth he considered as the only foundation of evangelical obedience; while *notions* of religious truth, however correct, would prove of no avail, any farther than their sanctifying influence was felt upon the heart, and evidenced by a holy walk and conversation. His own exemplary conduct was a striking comment on the doctrines he believed and preached.

"Integrity and uprightness were prominent traits in his character, acknowledged by all who knew him; and the pages of this church record-book show with what diligence, fervour, and affection he watched over the spiritual interests of his beloved people.

"To the poor of his flock he was kind and attentive; they were never neglected by him whilst able to go abroad, and to the lowest among his brethren and sisters, his humility and condescension were manifest. To the chambers of sickness and distress he was ever ready to direct his steps, to pray with, to console, and to advise the afflicted inmate. In every time of need he was a valuable friend, and in his pastoral visits many of us can say that he was frequently instrumental, by his cheerful demeanour and pious conversation, in mitigating our sorrows, and increasing our joys.

"He possessed a noble disinterestedness of spirit; he sought not ours but us. He was truly the servant of this church for Jesus' sake. A pastor, in the language of Jeremiah, according to God's heart, who fed his people with knowledge and understanding. There are, perhaps, but few instances in the church of Christ, of one who has better exemplified the character of a Christian bishop, as drawn by the pen of the apostle Paul. Titus i. 7—9."

As a testimony of esteem for this eminent servant of Christ, the church has erected a neat marble tablet, in the chapel in Little Prescot Street, Goodman's Fields, where he had so long officiated as their pastor; with the following inscription:

THIS TABLET

was erected by the Church in grateful Remembrance
of their beloved and venerable Pastor,

ABRAHAM BOOTH:

who, with unremitted Fidelity, discharged his ministerial Labours
in this place, thirty-seven Years.
As a Man, and as a Christian, he was highly and deservedly esteemed;
As a Minister, he was solemn and devout:
His addresses were perspicuous, energetic, and impressive;
they were directed to the Understanding, the Conscience, and the Heart
Profound Knowledge, sound Wisdom, and unaffected Piety
were strikingly exemplified
in the Conduct of this excellent Man.
In him the poor have lost a humane and generous Benefactor;
the Afflicted and the Distressed a wise and sympathetic Counsellor;
and this Church
a disinterested, affectionate, and faithful Pastor:
nor will his name or writings be forgotten,
while Evangelical truth shall be revered; Genius admired, or Integrity respected.
He departed this Life on the 27th January, 1806,
In the 72d year of his Age.

The following condensed and elaborate view of his character, is from the pen of one of his contemporary ministering brethren, the Rev. Dr. Newman.

As a Christian, he was pre-eminent. Called by divine grace when about twelve years of age, he experienced, in the long course of threescore years, many alternations of hope and fear, of joy and sorrow, with many changes of trials and temptations. Yet with respect to his personal interest in the divine favour, he seems to have been carried on in an even tenor, without any remarkable elevations or depressions. His common conversation breathed much of a devotional spirit, and discovered the strong sense he had of his own sinfulness before God and the simplicity of his dependence on the Holy Spirit. Firm in his attachment to his religious principles, he despised the popular cant about charity, and cultivated that genuine candour, which is alike remote from the laxity of latitudinarians, and the censoriousness of bigots. He was conspicuous for self-denial, and contempt of the world, walking humbly with God. His moral character was pure and unblemished. Perhaps there never was a man of more stern, unbending integrity, he would have been admired and revered by *Aristides the Just*. Sincerity clear as crystal, consistency with himself, and unbroken uniformity of conduct were always to be seen by the ten thousand eyes that were continually fixed upon him. He was temperate, even to abstemiousness : in fortitude " bold as a lion." Caution was interwoven with the texture of his mind, yet he would sometimes say, " We have need of caution against caution itself, lest we be over cautious." He once observed that " in morals, integrity holds the first place, benevolence the second, and prudence the third. Where the first is not, the second cannot be ; and where the third is not, the other two will be often brought into suspicion." In his attendance on public worship, he was remarkable for an exemplary punctuality, which also extended to all appointments in meetings for business. His manners were simple, grave, and unaffected; frequently enlivened with an agreeable pleasantry. It was edifying and delightful to observe how he perpetually breathed after more conformity to Christ—more heavenly-mindedness. That man must have been extremely wise or extremely foolish, who could spend an hour in his company without being made wiser and better.

As a Divine, he was a star of the first magnitude. A

Protestant, and a Protestant Dissenter, on principle, are one of the brightest ornaments of the Baptist denomination to which he belonged. A Calvinist, and in some particulars approaching what is called High-Calvinism; but he has sometimes declared, as many other great men nave done, that he never saw any human system which he could fully and entirely adopt. From the pulpit, his sermons were plain and textual, highly instructive, always savoury and acceptable to persons of evangelical taste; for the glory, the government, and the grace of Christ were his favourite themes. He aimed to counteract, with equal care, self-righteous legality on the one hand, and, on the other, Antinomian licentiousness. Such was the excellence of his personal character, that he needed not the arts of the orator and the graces of elocution to gain attention. His audience listened with profound veneration, and hung upon his lips. He had the gift of prayer in a very high degree; and whoever heard him was powerfully impressed with the idea that he was a man who prayed much in secret. From the press, he appeared to the greatest advantage. Nor will it be denied by any, that his writings are very elaborate and exquisitely polished. No bagatelles, no airy speculations —all solid and useful. His *"Reign of Grace,"* and indeed all his works, will continue to instruct and delight the Christian world to the end of time.

As a Christian Pastor, he shone with distinguished lustre. Every member of the church in which he presided, had a share in his affection. The poor were as welcome to his advice and assistance as the rich: and his faithful reproofs were given, without partiality to either, as occasion required. It was justly remarked at his grave, that he has unintentionally drawn his own picture.

in his sermon entitled " Pastoral Cautions." He was not a lord over God's heritage. It has been said he appeared always willing to give up almost every thing to the decision of the church; and the consequence was, the church gave up almost every thing to *his* decision. His attention to the poor and the afflicted of his congregation was highly exemplary. Nor did he content himself with saying, " Be ye warmed, and be ye filled," but liberally contributed to the supply of their wants, according to his ability. The economical system he established at home, furnished him with a considerable fund for charitable uses abroad. His charity was never ostentatious; none but the Omniscient eye knew the extent of it, and therefore it is impossible to say how many of the sons and daughters of affliction have lost, by his death, a most generous benefactor.

As a literary man, he was generally acknowledged to belong to the first class among Protestant Dissenters. Without the advantages of a liberal education, he had cut his own way, by the force of a strong, keen mind, through rocks and deserts. His memory was amazingly tenacious; his reasoning powers acute; his apprehension quick; his deliberation cool and patient; his determination slow and decided. His application must have been very intense, to which his vigorous and robust constitution of body was happily subservient. Though he perused a prodigious multitude of books, and respected the opinions of wise and learned men, he ever maintained a sublime independence of mind, and thought for himself. His knowledge of languages was very considerable. Not many of the *literati* of this country have had so intimate an acquaintance with the grace and force of words, or have written with such correctness and energy united

Yet he has been heard to say, that he had a wife and family before he knew any thing of the theory of English grammar. He was not unacquainted with the Greek and Roman classics; they were, however, by no means his favourite authors. It would surprise the public to know what loads of ponderous Latin quartos he read, of French, Dutch, and German divines! The Greek Testament he went through nearly fifty times, by the simple expedient of reading one chapter every morning, the first thing, not so much for the purpose of criticism as of devotion. General science and literature claimed a share of his attention; and every one was astonished to observe the fund of information he possessed on all subjects. In history civil and ecclesiastical; in antiquities, Jewish and Christian; in theological controversy and the creeds of all denominations, he was equalled by few, and excelled by none It is pleasing to recollect, that all his learning was solemnly consecrated to the cross of Christ; and that, while he was disgusted, as he often was, with the illiteracy and ignorance of books which he perceived even among educated preachers in many instances, he was very far from supposing human literature to be essential to the gospel ministry.

As a universal friend and counsellor, he was exceedingly beloved. His extensive and diversified knowledge, his well-tried integrity, his penetration, prudence, and benevolence, occasioned numberless applications for his counsel, not merely from the Baptists, but from Christians of almost all parties. Difficult texts of Scripture, knotty points of controversy, disputes in churches, and private cases of conscience were laid before him in abundance. Seldom was there an appeal made to the judgment of any other man. It was like "taking counsel at Abel, and so they ended the matter," Yet he was no dictator. When he had patiently heard the case, and candidly given his opinion, he would usually say, " Consult other friends, and then judge for yourself." Such a degree of majesty attended him, plain as he was in exterior, that if he sat down with you but a few minutes, you could not help feeling that you had a prince or a great man in the house. It would sometimes appear to strangers that he was deficient in that winning grace which accompanies softness and sweetness of manner; but those who were most intimately acquainted with him, are fully prepared to say, there was in general the greatest delicacy of genuine politeness in his conduct. Many young ministers will long deplore their loss. Never surely can they forget how readily he granted them access to him at all times; how kindly he counselled them in their difficulties; how faithfully he warned them of their dangers! With a mournful pleasure they must often recollect his gentleness in correcting their mistakes; his tenderness in imploring the Divine benediction upon them; his cordial congratulations when he witnessed their prosperity!

PREFACE

TO THE

LAST CORRECTED EDITION

I SHALL not offer any apology to the public, on behalf of the ensuing treatise. For if the leading sentiments adopted and defended in it correspond with the unerring oracles, I have no apprehensions from the frowns of men; and if not, it would be impossible, by the most laboured apology, to justify my conduct.

The doctrine of sovereign grace is here maintained and handled in a practical manner. It has been my endeavour, in the following pages, not only to state and defend the capital truths of the gospel, in a doctrinal way; but also to point out their peculiar importance, as happily adapted to awaken the conscience, and comfort the heart; to elevate the affections, and influence the whole conduct in the way of holiness.

To this edition of *The Reign of Grace*, I have made large additions. The principal of which is, an entire chapter upon *Election;* which renders the scheme of doctrines more complete, and the contents of the book more answerable to the title. I also thought it my duty, in a particular manner, to bear a public testimony to that important part of revealed truth; having in my younger years greatly opposed it, in a poem *On absolute Predestination.* Which poem, if considered in a critical light, is despicable; if in a theological view, detestable: as it is an impotent attack on the honour of Divine grace, in regard to its glorious freeness; and a bold opposition to the sovereignty of God. So I now consider it, and as such I here renounce it.

However the doctrine of Reigning Grace may be decried as licentious, it is that very truth which God in all ages has delighted to honour; which the Divine Spirit has owned for the information and comfort, for the holiness and happiness of sinful men. Were I not fully persuaded of this, rather than appear as an advocate for it, I would condemn my tongue to everlasting silence, and my pen to perpetual rest.

I have nothing further to add, by way of preface, except my ardent prayers, that a divine blessing may attend every perusal of the following chapters; so as to make the performance really useful, and cause it to answer some valuable purposes for the great Redeemer's glory.

A. BOOTH

THE

REIGN OF GRACE

INTRODUCTION

The gospel of Reigning Grace, being a doctrine truly divine, has ever been the object of the world's contempt. It was of old a stumbling-block to the self-righteous Jew, and foolishness to the philosophic Greek. Paul, who was a resolute asserter of the honours of grace, and indefatigable in preaching Christ, found it so by repeated experience; and that not only among the illiterate and profane, but also among the learned and the devout. Nay, he had frequent occasion to observe, that the religious devotees of his age were the first in opposing the doctrine he preached, and the most hardened enemies against the truth of God. The polite, the learned, the religious, were all agreed to load both his character and his doctrine with the foulest reproaches. Nor was this treatment peculiar to Paul, but common to all his contemporaries, who espoused the same glorious cause, and laboured in the same beneficent work. The doctrine they preached was charged with licentiousness. Their enemies boldly affirmed that they said; *Let us do evil that good may come.* Thus were their character and their labours impeached: that, as hateful to God; these, as destructive to man.

But what was the ground of this impious charge? Were they loose in their morals, or scandalous in their lives. No such thing. Had they not as much regard for practical religion and true morality as any of their objectors? More, far more than they all. Did they never mention good works as necessary to answer any valuable end in the Christian life? They often pressed the performance of them, as absolutely necessary to answer various important purposes, both in the sight of God and man. What then could be the reason of so hateful a charge? Because their doctrine was not in the least adapted to gratify the pride of man. They taught, that without the atonement made on the cross, and the grace revealed in redeeming blood, the state of the best men would have been absolutely desperate—desperate as that of the devils, and of those already damned. And as the apostles were free to declare, that the state of the most respectable part of mankind was evil—dreadfully evil—evil as to those things, for the sake of which they most highly esteemed themselves; so they boldly preached a perfect Saviour, and a finished salvation, to the most worthless and vile.

These primitive teachers and infallible guides were not in the least acquainted with those terms and conditions, prerequisites and qualifications, the performing and attaining of which are, by many, accounted so necessary to acceptance with God. They knew but of one way in which a sinner might be accepted of God, and justified before him; and that was entirely of grace, through the perfect work of Christ alone. The way of justification which they taught is absolutely pure and unmixed. In their doctrine, on this important subject, grace does not only appear; it shines, reigns, triumphs: it is the *only* thing. There is not discernible in it the least tincture of those notions which foster pride, or cherish self-esteem. All those fine distinctions, invented by the proud philosopher, or the self-righteous moralist, which tend in any degree to support the opinion of human worthiness, and to obscure our views of divine grace, are by them entirely set aside, and totally annihilated. The most shining deeds and valuable qualities that can be found among men, though highly useful and truly excellent, when set in their proper places, and referred to suitable ends, are, as to the grand article of justification treated as nonentities. In this respect, the most zealous professor, with all his laboured performances, stands on a level with the most profane. The apostolic truth addressing all to whom it comes, as guilty, condemned, perishing wretches, leaves no room for preference or boasting in any; that so the whole glory of our salvation m ıy be secured to that grace which is infinitely rich and absolutely free.

At this, the devout Pharisee and the decent moralist are highly offended. Such doctrines being advanced, they think it incumbent upon them to stand up in defence of what they call an holy life: and to support the sinking credit of good works, as having a considerable efficacy in procuring our acceptance with God. This many persons frequently do, much more by talking about their necessity, than by performing them. Now they think it their duty to rail at the preacher as an avowed enemy to holiness; nor will they spare to give him the honourable title of, *A friend of publicans and sinners.* Now innumerable slanders are cast on the doctrine of grace, as being licentious; and on the ministers of it, as opening the floodgates of all iniquity. For they suppose that every thing bad may be justly expected from those who openly disavow all dependence on their own duties; and whose hope of eternal happiness arises, not from services which they perform, but from grace which the gospel reveals— not from the worth which they possess, but from the work which Christ has wrought. Thus they despise the gospel under the fair pretence of a more than common concern for the interests of holiness.

Nor is this the only offence which the gospel gives. For as it is entirely inconsistent with the natural notions of men concerning acceptance with God, and contrary to every scheme of salvation which human reason suggests; as it will admit of no copartner in relieving a distressed conscience, or in bringing deliverance to a guilty soul, but leaves every one that slights it and seeks for assistance from any other quarter, to perish under an everlasting curse; so the pride of the self-sufficient kindles into resentment against it, as a most uncharitable doctrine and quite unsociable. Nor can the faithful dispensers of sacred truth fail to share in the honour of these reproaches.

For while they dare to affirm that this gospel, so hateful to the sons of pride, exhibits the only way of a sinner's access to his offended Sovereign; and that all who oppose it, and all who embrace its counterfeit, are left in the hands of divine justice without a Mediator; they are sure to be accounted persons of contracted minds, and very far from a liberal way of thinking. They are considered as the dupes of bigotry, and little better than the enemies of mankind. He, indeed, who pretends to be a friend to revealed truth, but is cool and indifferent to its honour and interest; whose extensive charity is such, that he can allow those who widely differ from him in the capital articles of the Christian faith, to be safe in their own way; may enjoy his peculiar sentiments without much fear of disturbance. But though such conduct may be applauded, under a false notion of Christian candour, and of a catholic spirit; though it may be the way to maintain a friendly intercourse among multitudes whose leading sentiments are widely different; yet it will be deemed, by the God of truth, as deserving no better name, than a *joint opposition* to the spirit and design of his gospel. For such a timid and lukewarm profession of truth is little better than a denial of it—than open hostility against it. To seek for peace at the expense of truth, will be found in the end, no other than a wicked conspiracy against both God and man. Such, however, as love the truth, will boldly declare against all its counterfeits, and every deviation from it: and, whatever may be the consequence, they will say with him of old; *Though we, or an angel from heaven, preach any other gospel, let him be accursed.*

Thus the genuine gospel will always appear like an insult on the taste of the public. Wherever it comes, if it be not received, it awakens disgust and provokes abhorrence. Nor can it be otherwise. For its principal design is to mortify the pride of man, and to display the glory of grace; to throw all human excellence down to the dust, and to elevate, even to thrones of glory, the needy and the wretched; to show that every thing which exalteth itself against the knowledge of Christ, is an abomination in the sight of God; and that He who is despised of men and abhorred by the nations, is Jehovah's eternal delight.* The ancient gospel is an unceremonious thing. It pays no respect to the academic because of his profound learning; nor to the moralist on account of his upright conduct. It has not the least regard to the courtier, because of his pompous honours; nor to the devotee, for the sake of his zeal or his righteousness. No, the potent prince and the abject slave, the wise philosopher and the ignorant rustic, the virtuous lady and the infamous prostitute, stand on the same level in its comprehensive sight. Its business is with the worthless and the miserable, whomsoever they be. If these be relieved, its end is gained. If these be made happy, its Author is glorified, whatever may become of the rest. Towards these it constantly wears the most friendly aspect, and rejoices to do them good. But the self-sufficient of every rank are treated by it with the utmost reserve, and beheld with a steady contempt. *The hungry it filleth with good things, but the rich it sendeth empty away.*

These considerations may serve to show us the true state of the case, as it stood between Paul and his opponents. The situation of things was much the same between Protestants and Papists, at, and for some time after the Reformation. Nor will the apostolic doctrine ever fail to be attended with strenuous opposition and foul reproaches, while ignorance of its real nature, and legal pride, prevail in the hearts of men. Many, indeed, are the methods that have been devised, to render the unpalatable truth more generally acceptable, and to obviate *the offence of the cross.* But what have been the consequences? The gospel has been corrupted; the consciences of awakened sinners have been left to grope in the dark, for that consolation which nothing but the unadulterated truth could give; and, instead of promoting holiness, the reverse has been awfully manifest. It therefore behooves every lover of sacred truth, to let it stand on

---

* Isa. xlix. 7. Matt. iii. 17.

its own basis, and not to tamper with it. To leave all its credit and all its success in the world, to its own intrinsic worth—to that authority with which it is closed, and to the management of that sovereign Being who ordained it for his own glory.

But however the doctrine of reigning grace may be despised by the self-sufficient, it will ever be revered by *the poor in spirit.* For by it they are informed of an honourable way of escape from the wrath to come, which they know they have justly deserved. To the sensible sinner, therefore, it must always be a *joyful sound.* And though such persons as are ignorant of its nature, tendency, and design, are always ready to imagine that it has an unfriendly aspect upon morality and good works, when preached in its glorious freeness; yet we may boldly affirm, that it is the grand instrument ordained by a holy God, for informing the ignorant, comforting the disconsolate, and rescuing the profligate from that worst of vassalage, the servitude of sin, and subjection to Satan. Such is the benign tendency of the glorious gospel! Such is its friendly and sanctifying influence on the hearts of men!

It will indeed be acknowledged that this doctrine may be held in licentiousness by those that profess it. But then it will be as confidently maintained, that whoever holds it in unrighteousness never received the love of that sacred truth, or experienced the power of it. For, to have a bare conviction of divine truth in the mind, and to experience its power on the heart, are very different things. The former may produce an outward profession: the latter will elevate the affections, turn the corrupt bias of the will, and influence the whole conduct. With the steadiest persuasion, therefore, of the holy nature and tendency of the doctrine of divine grace, as it is in itself, and as it operates on the minds and manners of all those who know it in truth; I proceed to give, not a full display, (that is infinitely too high for mortals,) but some brief hints concerning that grace which reigns; and of the way in which it is manifested, so as to demonstrate its power, glory, and majesty, in the salvation of sinners.

This I shall do by endeavouring to illustrate that important and charming passage, recorded in Romans the fifth and twenty-first; EVEN SO MIGHT GRACE REIGN, THROUGH RIGHTEOUSNESS, UNTO ETERNAL LIFE, BY JESUS CHRIST OUR LORD. And while the author, conscious of his own insufficiency, looks up to the Spirit of wisdom for divine illumination, that he may write with all the precision and sanctity of truth, in opening the noble subject of the ensuing treatise; he would entreat the reader to peruse, with candour and impartiality, the contents of the following pages.

CHAPTER I.

CONCERNING THE SIGNIFICATION OF THE TERM GRACE.

THAT we may proceed with greater clearness and certainty in our following inquiries, it is necessary to consider what is implied in the term *grace*. The primary and principal sense of the word, is *free favour; unmerited kindness*. In this acceptation it is most frequently used in the inspired volume; and thus it is to be understood in the words of the Holy Ghost under consideration. *Grace*, in the writings of Paul, stands in direct opposition to works and worthiness—all works and worthiness of every kind, and of every degree. This appears from the following passages. *Now to him that worketh the reward is not reckoned of grace, but of debt   Therefore it is of faith, that it might be by grace.   For by grace are ye saved—not of works, lest any man should boast.   Who hath saved us—not according to our works, but according to his own purpose and grace.**

As the word *mercy*, in its primary signification, has relation to some creature, either actually in a *suffering* state, or obnoxious to it; so *grace*, in its proper and strict sense, always presupposes *unworthiness* in its object. Hence, whenever any thing valuable is communicated by the blessed God to any of Adam's apostate offspring, the communication of it cannot be of *grace*, any further than the person on whom it is conferred is considered as *unworthy*. For, so far as any degree of worth appears, the province of grace ceases, and that of equity takes place. Grace and worthiness, therefore, cannot be connected in the same act, and for the same end. The one must necessarily give place to the other, according to that remarkable text: *If by grace, then it is no more of works; otherwise grace is no more grace. But if it be of works, then it is no more grace; other-*

---
* Rom. iv. 4, 16.   Eph. ii. 8, 9.   2 Tim. i. 9.

wise work is no more work.* From the apostle's reasoning it is evident, that whatever is of works, is not of grace at all; and, that whatever is of grace, is not of works in any degree. In the apostle's view of things, works and grace are essentially opposite, and equally irreconcilable as light and darkness. Besides, when Paul represents the capital blessings of salvation as flowing from divine grace, we are led to consider the persons on whom they are bestowed not only as having no claim to those benefits, but as deserving quite the reverse—as having incurred a tremendous curse, and as justly exposed to eternal ruin.

That grace, therefore, about which we treat, may be thus defined: *It is the eternal and absolutely free favour of God, manifested in the vouchsafement of spiritual and eternal blessings to the guilty and the unworthy.* What those blessings are, we shall endeavour to show in the subsequent pages. Meanwhile be it observed, that, according to this definition, the grace of God is *eternal.* Agreeable to the import of those reviving words; *Yea, I have loved thee with an everlasting love.*† It is divinely free, and infinitely rich. Entirely detached from every supposition of human worth, and operating independently of all conditions performed by man; it rises superior to human guilt, and superabounds over human unworthiness. Such is the eternal origin, such the glorious basis, of our salvation! Hence it proceeds and is carried on to perfection. Grace shines through the whole. For, as an elegant writer observes, it is "not like a fringe of gold, bordering the garment; not like an embroidery of gold, decorating the robe; but like the mercy-seat of the ancient tabernacle, which was gold—pure gold—all gold throughout."

Yes, reader, this is the inexhaustible source of all those inestimable blessings which the Lord bestows on his unworthy creatures, in this or in a future world. It is this which, in all that he does, or ever will do for sinners, he intends to render everlastingly glorious in their eyes, and in the eyes of all holy intelligence. The indelible

* Rom. xi. 6 † Jer. xxxi. 3.

motto inscribed by the hand of Jehovah on all the blessings of the unchangeable covenant, is, TO THE PRAISE OF THE GLORY OF HIS GRACE.

Hence we may learn, that if grace in its own nature, and as it is exercised in our salvation, be directly opposite to all works and worthiness; then those persons are awfully deceived, who seek to join them together in the same work and for the same end. However high their pretences may be to holiness, it is plain from the word of God, and may in some degree appear from the nature of the thing, that they take an effectual way to ruin their souls forever, except that very grace prevent, of which they have such false and corrupt ideas. For divine grace disdains to be assisted in the performance of that work which peculiarly belongs to itself, by the poor, imperfect performances of men. Attempts to complete what grace begins, betray our pride and offend the Lord; but cannot promote our spiritual interest. Let the reader, therefore, carefully remember, that grace is either absolutely free, or it is not at all: and, that he who professes to look for salvation by grace, either believes in his heart to be saved entirely by it, or he acts inconsistently in affairs of the greatest importance.

CHAPTER II.

OF GRACE, AS IT REIGNS IN OUR SALVATION IN GENERAL.

GRACE, in our text, is compared to a sovereign. Now a sovereign, considered as such, is invested with regal power, and the highest authority. Grace, therefore, in her beneficent government, must exert and manifest sovereign power—must supersede the reign, and counteract the mighty and destructive operations of sin; or she cannot bring the sinner to eternal life. For the Holy Spirit has compared sin to a sovereign, whose reign terminates in death.

As *sin* appears, clothed in horrid deformity, and armed

with destructive power, inflicting temporal death, and menacing eternal flames; so *Grace* appears on the throne, arrayed in the beauties of holiness, and smiling with divine benevolence; touched with feelings of the tenderest compassion, and armed with all the magnificence of invincible power. Fully determined to exert her authority and gratify her compassion, under the conduct of infinite wisdom; to the everlasting honour of inflexible justice, inviolable veracity, and every divine perfection—by rescuing the condemned offender from the jaws of destruction; by speaking peace to the alarmed consciences of damnable delinquents; by restoring to apostate creatures and vile miscreants a supreme love to God and delight in the ways of holiness; and, finally, by bringing them safe to everlasting honour and joy. In a word, the heart of this mighty sovereign is compassion itself: her looks are love; her language is balm to the bleeding soul, and her arm salvation. Such a sovereign is GRACE. Those who are delivered by her must enjoy a complete salvation. Those who live under her most benign government must be happy indeed.

Divine grace, as reigning in our salvation, not only appears, but appears with majesty: not only shines, but triumphs: providing all things, freely bestowing all things necessary to our eternal happiness. Grace does not set our salvation on foot, by accommodating its terms and conditions to the enfeebled capacities of lapsed creatures; but begins, carries on, and completes the arduous work. Grace, as a sovereign, does not rescue the sinner from deserved ruin, furnish him with new abilities, and then leave him, by their proper use, to resist the tempter, to mortify his lusts, to attain those holy qualities, and perform those righteous acts, which render him fit for eternal happiness, and give him a title to it. No; for if the province and work of grace were circumscribed in this manner, things of the last importance to the glory of God and the felicity of man, would be left in the most uncertain and perilous situation. And, admitting the possibility of any sinner being saved in such a way, there would be ample scope for the exertions of spiritual pride, and much room for boasting; which would be diametrically contrary to the honour of the Most High, and frustrate the noble designs of grace. This matchless favour, far from being satisfied with laying the foundation, rears the superstructure also: it not only settles the preliminaries, but executes the very business itself. The Pharisee in the parable made his acknowledgments to preventing and assisting grace: for, *God, I thank thee*, was his language. It is evident, however, that his views of grace were very contracted; and his hopes arising from it very deceitful. Would we then view grace as reigning, we must consider it as the alpha and omega, the beginning and the end of our salvation; that the unrivalled honour of that greatest of all works may be given to *the God of all grace*.

Having taken this general view of reigning grace, I would now ask, What think you, reader, of this wonderful favour? Is it worthy of God? Is it suitable to your case? Or know you not, that you are by nature under the guilt and dominion of sin? Of sin, that dreadful sovereign; of sin, that worst of tyrants. *Sin reigns*, says the apostle; and the end of its reign, where the sovereignty of grace does not interpose, is eternal death. Can you sleep away your time, and dream of being finally happy, while under the power of so malignant a sovereign. Shall the toys and trifles of a transitory world amuse, when your *soul*, your immortal ALL, is at stake? If so, how lamentable your condition! how dreadful your state! Awake!—arise!—Bow the knee to divine grace, O stubborn rebel! while she holds out the golden sceptre of pardon and of peace. Acknowledge her supremacy, submit to her government, before justice ascend the throne and vengeance launch her bolts. For then an eternal bar will lie against every application for mercy, though arising from the most pressing want.

Or, if awake in your conscience, do you think it possible to effect your own deliverance? Alas! you are entirely without strength to perform any such thing; and grace was never intended as an auxiliary to help the weak, but well-disposed, to save themselves. The mercy of God and the gospel of Christ, were never designed to assist and reward the righteous; but to relieve the miserable and save the desperate—to deliver those who have no other assistance, nor any other hope. Were you acquainted with your abject vassalage, were you convinced by the Spirit of truth, that there is no possible way of escape, but by reigning grace; then would you cry for help, and then the relief that grace affords would be *all your salvation, and all your desire.*

If, on the other hand, you are burdened with sin and harassed by clamorous fears of being cast into hell; if, sensible of your native depravity, the multiplied iniquities of your life, the many shameful defects attending your best services, and your present absolute unworthiness, you are ready to sink in despondency; O remember, that *grace* has erected her throne! This forbids despair. For her wonderful throne is erected, not on the ruins of justice, not on the dishonour of the law; but, on the BLOOD OF THE LAMB. The inconceivably perfect obedience, and the infinitely meritorious death of the Son of God, form its mighty basis. Here grace is highly exalted: here grace appears in state, dispensing her favours and showing her glory. To such a benevolent and condescending sovereign, the basest may have free access. By such a powerful sovereign the most various, multiplied, and pressing wants may be relieved with the utmost ease and greatest alacrity. Remember, disconsolate soul, that the name, the nature, the office of GRACE ENTHRONED, loudly attest, that the greatest unworthiness and the most profligate crimes are no bar to the sinner in coming to Christ for salvation; in looking to sovereign favour for all that he wants. Nay, they demonstrate, that the unworthy and sinful are the *only* persons with whom grace is at all concerned: This is amazing! this is delightful!

Ho! all ye children of want and sons of wretchedness! hither ye may come with the utmost freedom. Be it know to you, be it never forgotten by you, that JEHOVAH considered your indigent case, and designed your complete relief, when he erected this wonderful

throne. Your names are not omitted in the heavenly
grant: nay, ye are the *only* persons that are blessed with
a right of access to this mercy-seat. Did sinners more
generally know their state, and the glorious nature of
grace as *exalted in majesty;* how would the throne of
this mighty sovereign be crowded!—crowded, not by persons adorned with fine accomplishments—but, with *the
poor, the maimed, the halt, and the blind.* With longing
hearts and uplifted hands, big with expectation and sure
of success, they would throng her courts. Thither they
would flee, as a *cloud* for number, and as *doves* for speed:
for there is provision made to supply all their wants.
As persons of all ranks and of every character are equally
destitute of any righteous or valid plea for admission
into the eternal kingdom ; so, feeling their want of spiritual blessings, they have equally free access to this mu
nificent sovereign, and the same ground to expect complete relief. Here, and in this respect, there is no difference between the devout professor, and the abandoned
profligate ; the chaste virgin, and the infamous prostitute.
For, being all criminals, and under the same condemnation, they have not the smallest gleam of hope, except
what shines upon them in that compassionate proclamation which is issued from the throne of grace by the eternal Sovereign.* But, as that proclamation is expressive
of the freest favour and the richest grace ; including offenders of the worst characters, publishing pardon for
sins of the deepest dye, and all ratified by veracity itself;
it affords sufficient encouragement to the vilest wretch
that lives, who is willing to owe his all to divine bounty,
without hesitation to receive the heavenly blessing, and
with gratitude to rejoice in the royal donation.—" Yes,
thine it is, O SOVEREIGN GRACE! to raise the poor from
the dunghill, and the needy out of the dust. Thine
it is, to set them on thrones of glory, and to number
them among the princes of heaven." Remember this,
my soul, and be this thy comfort: and may the Lord

---

* Isa. lv. 1—3. Matt. xi. 28. John vi. 37, and vii. 37. Rev.
xxii. 17.

enable both the author and the reader to see eye to eye the riches of *reigning grace!*

Having endeavoured to show how grace reigns in our salvation in general; I shall now proceed, in the following chapters, to make it appear that grace reigns more particularly, in our *election—calling—pardon—justification—adoption—sanctification—*and *perseverance* in the faith to eternal life. These are so many essential branches of our salvation; and in the vouchsafement of these capital blessings, grace reigns; manifesting an authority and exerting a power truly divine and infinitely glorious.

CHAPTER III.

OF GRACE, AS IT REIGNS IN OUR ELECTION.

AMONG the various blessings which flow from sovereign goodness, and are dispensed by reigning grace, that of *election* deservedly claims our first regard. It was in the decree of election that the grace of our infinite Sovereign did first appear, in choosing Christ as the head, and in him, as his members, all that should ever be saved. Election, therefore, is the first link in the golden chain of our salvation: and the corner-stone in the amazing fabric of human happiness.

As JEHOVAH is the former of universal nature, the supporter and governor of all worlds; and as it is not consistent with the perfection of an infinite Agent, to act without the highest and noblest design; so the adored Creator, before he imparted existence, or time commenced, proposed and appointed an end worthy of himself, in all he determined to do. This was his own glory. This was his grand design in all the various ranks of existence to which his almighty *fiat* gave birth. Not a single creature in the vast scale of dependent being, but is connected with this as its ultimate end. The loftiest seraph that surrounds the throne, and the meanest insect that crawls in the dust, have the same origina

Parent, and are designed, in different ways, to answer the same exalted end. To deny this, or to suppose that the most perfect Agent did not act for the most worthy purpose, is highly derogatory to the dignity of the First Cause.

Nobly conspicuous, among the various orders of animate and inanimate existence in this lower creation, was man, when first formed and recent from the hands of his Maker. Man, therefore, as bearing the lively impress of his great Creator's image; possessing such elevated faculties and large capacities for operation and enjoyment; was designed, in a peculiar manner, to answer this highest of all purposes. Nor was the entrance of sin subversive of the grand design, but made subservient to it in various ways. It was impossible such an event should bring confusion into that stupendous plan of divine operation which consummate wisdom had formed. For, *known to* the omniscient *God, are all his works,* and all events, *from the beginning of the world.* All that is comprehended in what men call *contingent,* is absolute certainty with Him who is perfect in knowledge. The entrance of sin, therefore, among moral agents, whether angels or men, could not possibly frustrate JEHOVAH's purpose, or render his original designs abortive. *The counsel of the Lord shall stand, and he will do all his pleasure.*—Though the entrance of moral evil among mankind was an awful event; though Adam, and every individual of his numerous offspring were contaminated, injured, and ruined by it; yet it appears from divine revelation, that He *who declares the end from the beginning,* not only foresaw it, but from eternity determined to display his perfections and promote his glory by it. His determination was, to glorify himself in the complete salvation and endless felicity of some of the apostate race, and in the righteous condemnation of others: so that a revenue of glory shall arise to the great Supreme from all mankind. This glory shall arise, as well from that haughty Egyptian monarch, who renounced God's dominion and said: *Who is* JEHOVAH *that I should obey him?* as from the king of Israel, whose exalted character is, *A man after God's own heart*. As well from a traitorous Judas, who sold his Master's blood ; as from a faithful Paul, who counted not his very life dear, so that he might finish his course with joy, and promote the Saviour's honour. These shall be the monuments of sovereign grace ; those, of righteous vengeance, and both for the glory of God to all eternity. Nor is any thing more agreeable to right reason, or the sacred Scripture, than to conclude, That as JEHOVAH is the first Cause, so he should be the last End ; and that he should be at the most perfect liberty to dispose of his offending creatures in what way he pleases, for his own glory. To dispute this, is to deny his divine supremacy, and, with Pharaoh, to renounce his eternal dominion.

Such being the final cause of the creation in general, and of mankind in particular, that Sovereign Being who has an absolute right to do what he will with his own, having determined to create man and to leave him to the freedom of his own will, foreseeing he would certainly fall; of his *free distinguishing love, chose a certain number out of the apostate race of Adam, and ordained them to a participation of grace here, and to the enjoyment of glory hereafter.* In the execution of which purpose, by means every way becoming himself, he determined to glorify all his infinite excellencies. Such is that immanent act of God which is commonly called *election*, and is the subject of this chapter.

The doctrine of election, or, which is the same thing, the doctrine of distinguishing grace, is now very much exploded. It is generally deemed unworthy of serious notice, by the learned and philosophic gentlemen of the present age. Though it cannot be denied to have made a considerable figure in those systems of divinity, that were adopted by men of eminence for piety and learning in former ages; and particularly by our first reformers from Popery ; yet now it is ranked, by many, among the rash opinions of a credulous antiquity. It is cashiered, as a doctrine abhorrent from reason, and as at eternal war with the moral perfections of God. It is consigned over to oblivion, as worthy of no more regard than the bold inquiries and wild conclusions; the laborious trifling and learned lumber, of the ancient, doting, Popish schoolmen. It is also traduced as a declared enemy to practical piety, and as highly injurious to the comfort and hope of mankind. This being the case, we need not wonder that it is now become quite unfashionable.

But what is the reason of this tragical outcry against it? If I be not greatly deceived, it is as follows. This doctrine lays the axe at the root of all our boasted moral excellence. This doctrine, in its native consequences, demolishes every subterfuge of human pride; as it leaves not the shadow of a difference between one man and another, why the Deity should regard and save this person rather than that; but teaches all who know and all who embrace it, to rest in that memorable maxim; EVEN SO, FATHER, FOR SO IT SEEMED GOOD IN THY SIGHT; resolving the whole into divine grace and divine sovereignty. Without paying the least compliment to the learning, sagacity, or character of any who dare to arraign the divine conduct, it repels their insolence in the following blunt manner; *Nay, but, O man! who art thou that repliest against God?*—It further teaches, that as unmerited kindness and sovereign favour began the work of salvation: so the same grace must carry it on and complete the vast design: while the Most High, ever jealous of his honour, is determined to have all the glory. Other reasons might be mentioned; but these may suffice to show, that the spirit of independence which is natural to man, and reigns in the unregenerate, must be fired with resentment by such an attack upon it. Hence the few votaries of this unpopular doctrine must expect reproach and ridicule, if not something more severe, to attend the profession of a tenet so unpolite.

It is not, however, my present design to enter upon a laboured defence of this offensive doctrine. I shall leave that to the friends of truth, who have more leisure and greater abilities. This, indeed, has been already often performed with great advantage to the church of God. I shall, therefore, content myself with taking a short view of the principal branches of this article of the Christian faith ; with proposing a few arguments, which appear to me plain and pertinent in vindication of it; and with pointing out its proper improvement.

That those who in the volume of inspiration are called the *elect*, are a people distinguished from others, and that all mankind are not included under this denomination ; are so apparent as hardly to need any proof. These things are so obvious, from the allowed signification of the term, and the tenor of divine revelation, as to leave no room for dispute. From the *signification of the term* —Because where all, whether persons or things, are equally accepted, there is no preference given ; there is no choice made ; there are none left. For to *elect* and to *choose*, are the same thing. Where any are chosen, others must be refused. From the *tenor of divine revelation*—As it is written ; *I speak not of you all ; I know whom I have chosen—I have chosen you out of the world—The election hath obtained it, and the rest were blinded.*

That those who are so denominated are not collective bodies, appears with superior evidence from what is asserted concerning them, in the same infallible rule of our faith and practice. They are described as having their *names written in heaven*, and *in the book of life*. They are said to be *ordained to eternal life*, and *chosen to salvation*. And, in the boldest manner imaginable, it is asked by one, who was thoroughly acquainted with their state and privileges ; *Who shall lay any thing to the charge of God's elect ?*

Now a small degree of discernment will enable us to conclude, that these things cannot with truth be affirmed concerning nations, churches, or communities of any sort, considered as such. But, on the contrary, they strongly imply, that the elect, as distinguished from others, are particular persons, whose names are in a peculiar manner known to God; that election relates to spiritual blessings and eternal enjoyments ; and that the objects of it are dear to God, and forever precious in his sight.

That the objects of election are particular persons, may further appear from hence. From the beginning Jehovah designed to manifest his love in the salvation of sinners. The damnation inflicted on many puts it beyond a doubt, that this design extended only to some; for all are not saved, and the divine purpose cannot be rendered void. That salvation was to be wrought by his own Son, as invested with the character, and as performing the work of a Mediator and Surety. As a Mediator and Substitute, he was to obey, and bleed, and die; die, under a charge of the blackest guilt, and feeling the weight of the heaviest curse.* It was necessary, therefore, to be determined, how many, and who in particular, should be interested in this wonderful work, and saved by it. Their persons, as well as their situation and wants, must be known to him and distinguished from others. For it is absurd to suppose, that he should engage as a substitute, to perform obedience and pour his blood; to lay down his life as a ransom to satisfy justice, and all this for persons unknown. When any one engages, in a legal way, to become responsible for another in matters of debt or offence; he is always supposed to have some knowledge of the person for whom he engages, so as to distinguish him from all others, who may be in similar circumstances and stand in the same need; and the name of the person, whose cause he undertakes, must also be mentioned in the engagement to render it valid.

Nor does it appear that the design of God in the salvation of sinners, by the incarnation and death of his own Son, could have been certainly answered on any other hypothesis. Supposing, for instance, that it had been the divine purpose to save, by the mediation of Jesus, all who should ever believe; without ascertaining the persons who should thus embrace the Redeemer, it would have remained dubious whether any would be finally saved; because uncertain whether any would ever believe. But if it were certain that some would

---

* 2 Cor. v. 21. Gal. iii. 13

believe, this certainty must arise from the purpose of God; for, on any other foundation, nothing future can be absolutely certain. If it was determined that some should believe, the divine appointment must be considered as extending to every individual whose faith and salvation are supposed to be certain. For faith is a gift of grace, and could not be foreseen in any but these on whom the great Dispenser of every favour had determined to bestow it. Hence we may safely infer, that as the death of Christ was absolutely certain, in virtue of a divine purpose, and the everlasting compact between the Eternal Three; so all the individuals that should ever be saved by the undertaking of Jesus, were chosen of God; were distinguished from others, and consigned to the great Shepherd as his peculiar charge.

It is equally clear that the elect were chosen of God before time began ; for their election is one of the first effects of divine love. This love was from everlasting The love of God to their persons, and their election to complete felicity, must, therefore, be eternal. If, indeed, there had ever been a point in duration, in which the blessed God had no thoughts of a Mediator, nor any designs of manifesting his love to miserable and guilty creatures ; then it might be supposed that there was an instant in which the favoured few, who are called *his elect*, were not the objects of his choice ; but if it was Jehovah's eternal purpose to manifest the riches of his grace by a Mediator ; if the Deity, subsisting in three distinct Persons, and acting under the personal characters of the FATHER, the SON, and the HOLY SPIRIT, did, before all worlds, resolve on the measures to be pursued ; and if a Mediator was appointed, as the grand medium of divine operation in the wonderful work ; then we may safely conclude, that the persons to be interested in this mediation and benefited by it, were fixed upon and chosen. For both reason and revelation concur to forbid our supposing, that the Son of the blessed should engage as Mediator, and act as a Substitute, for he did not know whom ; or that the counsels of Heaven should terminate in mere peradventures. It would be equally incongruous for us to imagine, that a resolution in the Eternal Mind concerning the work of redemption, which is evidently the chief of all the ways of God, should have any other date than eternity.

Expressly in our favour and in proof of the point are the declarations of the Holy Ghost. Thus we read; *God hath, from the beginning, chosen you to salvation —He hath chosen us in him before the foundation of the world.* They were chosen in Christ as their head and representative. Christ and the elect constitute one mystical body. He the head, and they the members; *the fulness of him that filleth all in all. Before the foundation of the world.* This emphatical phrase is evidently expressive of eternity. Before the world was formed, or any creature existed, time did not commence. The commencement of time, and that of created existence, are exactly of the same date. Prior, therefore, to the formation of the universe, duration was absolute eternity. The same infallible writer in the same epistle, speaking of the amazing scheme of man's redemption formed in the mind of God, calls it the ETERNAL PURPOSE, *which he purposed in Christ Jesus our Lord;* which, as we have before proved, necessarily infers the choice of the objects of that redemption.

This truth may be further evinced by considering, that as the inheritance of glory was prepared for its future possessors, before the foundation of the world; so *grace*, and all spiritual blessings that were necessary to fit them for the enjoyment of it, were *given them in Christ Jesus;* were lodged in his hands, as their federal head, as the appointed Mediator, and for their use, *before the world began.** Nor can we conceive of any new determinations arising in the Eternal Mind, or any purposes formed by our Maker, that were not from everlasting, without supposing him defective in knowledge, or mutable in his perfections. Suppositions these, which very ill become the character of Him whose name is JEHOVAH.

But is there any reason assignable, why the elect were

* 2 Tim. i. 9.—Eph. i. 3, 4.

chosen to life and glory, while others were left in their sins to perish under the stroke of divine justice? None, in the creature. For all mankind, considered in themselves, were viewed as in the same situation, and on a perfect level. Notwithstanding, the great Author of all things and Lord of the world condescends to assign the reason when he says; *I will have mercy on whom I will have mercy.* In this the adored Redeemer perfectly acquiesced, as appears from those remarkable words; *Even so, Father, for so it seemed good in thy sight.* In this the penetrating judgment of that wonderful man, who was caught up to the third heaven, rested completely satisfied :* and in the same reason of the divine procedure we ought all to rest, without a murmuring word, or an opposing thought. Nor can we rebel against the sovereign determinations of the Most High, without incurring flagrant guilt; or persist in so doing, and escape with impunity.

But supposing there was no original difference between the objects of distinguishing grace, and those who finally perish; yet, did not the Omniscient *foresee* them as possessed of faith, fruitful in holy obedience, and persevering to the end? and were not these considered by a righteous God as the cause why he chose them rather than others who were viewed as destitute of such recommendations? By no means. For grace *reigns* in the choice of all the elect; and grace, as a sovereign, rejects with disdain every such proud pretence to a claim upon her. She never affords her smiles to any because they are worthy. She ennobles none because they are better than others. So to do would be quite inconsistent with her amiable character; would be utterly subversive of her grand design. Wherever she bestows her kind regards, it is with the condescension of an absolute sovereign. Wherever she interposes her helping hand, it is on the behalf of those who have no other assistance, nor any other plea. But, as a further proof of my negative, I would offer the following arguments.

Faith in Christ and holy obedience are represented by

* Rom. xi. 15, 16.

the unerring Spirit as the fruits and effects of election: they cannot, therefore, be considered as the cause without absurdity in reason, and a contradiction to divine revelation. For it is written; *As many as were ordained to eternal life, believed—He hath chosen us—that we might be holy.* They believed because they were *ordained to eternal life*; not ordained to eternal life, because it was foreseen they would believe. They were chosen, not because they were, or ever would be holy; but that they *might be so.** Those, and those only, partake of faith, who are called by divine grace: but such only are called to faith and holiness, who were predestinated to be conformed to the image of Christ. For *whom he did predestinate them he also called.*† Again: The chosen of God are the sheep of Christ. None but those who are so denominated believe on him, according to his own declaration; *Ye believe not, because ye are not of my sheep.*‡ By which we are taught, that believing in him does not *make* us sheep, or give us a right to the character; but is an evidence that we were so considered in the sight of God, and given into the hands of the great Shepherd to be saved by him. Once more: God *hath called us with an holy calling, not according to,* not in consideration of *our works,* whether past or future; *but according to his own purpose and grace, which he purposed in Christ Jesus before the world began.*§ If, then, we are not called according to our works or worthiness. but according to the everlasting purpose, and free distinguishing grace of Him who *worketh all things after the counsel of his own will;* much less is it to be supposed, that we were chosen according to them, or in any foresight of them.

To illustrate the truth and confirm the argument, it may be further observed, that faith and holiness, in the method of grace, occupy a middle station. They are neither the foundation, nor the topstone, in the spiritual building. Though inseparably connected with election, they are neither its cause nor its consummation. *That*

---

* Acts xiii. 48. Eph. i. 4.   † Rom. viii. 30.
‡ John x. 26.   § 2 Tim. i. 9.

is sovereign grace; *this* infinite glory. Faith and holiness are, as one observes, what stalks and branches are to a root; by which the vegetable juices ascend, to produce and ripen the principal fruit. *By grace ye are saved* THROUGH *faith—chosen to salvation* THROUGH *sanctification of the Spirit and belief of the truth.* Consequently, they are no more the cause of election, than the means necessary to attain any valuable end are the cause of appointing that end; than which nothing can be supposed more absurd. Besides, if men were foreseen as possessed of faith and holiness, prior to their election, and independent on it: it is hard to conceive what occasion there was for their being elected. There could be no necessity for it to secure their final happiness. For the Judge of all the earth must do right: and eternal misery was never designed to be the portion of any who believe and are holy; for peace and salvation are inseparably joined to such a state, and to such characters. To have ordained those to happiness and glory that were foreseen to be thus qualified, would, therefore, have been altogether unnecessary.

Further: Election depends on the mere good pleasure of God, without any motive in us to influence the Divine will. No other cause is assigned by Paul, when stating and defending the doctrine; no other reason is given by his Divine Master. The former asserts, that the King immortal *predestinated us—according to the good pleasure of his will.* That *it is not of him that willeth, nor of him that runneth, but of God that showeth mercy. Therefore hath he mercy on whom he will.* And the latter with joy declares; *I thank thee, O Father, Lord of heaven and earth, because thou hast hid these things from the wise and prudent, and hast revealed them unto babes. Even so, Father, for so it seemed good in thy sight.* That revelation which is here designed, is no other than the *execution* of the Divine purpose in election. And the only reason assigned by Him who is the Wisdom of God, and perfectly acquainted with the counsels of heaven, why the mysteries of the gospel are revealed to some; while others, of superior abilities and greater reputation among their fellow-creatures, are left in absolute ignorance, and suffered to oppose them to their aggravated ruin; is the sovereign pleasure of Him who *giveth no account of any of his matters.*

Much to our purpose are the words of Paul, when professedly defending the doctrine of divine election. *The children being not yet born,* and, consequently, *neither having done any good or evil,* to obtain the approbation or to provoke the resentment of their Creator; *that the purpose of God according to election might stand; not of works,* or worthiness in the objects of it, *but of* the grace of *him that calleth:* it was said concerning Jacob and Esau, as an instance of the divine procedure towards mankind in general, as an evidence of the truth of the doctrine; *the elder shall serve the younger.* And again: *There is a remnant according to the election of grace.* This assertion the sacred disputant proceeds to confirm, by the following nervous argument—an argument taken from the nature of grace, as contradistinguished to all works and worthiness of every kind. *And if by grace, then it is no more of works; otherwise grace is no more grace. But if it be of works, then it is no more grace; otherwise work is no more work.* In this passage the truth under consideration is asserted in the plainest manner, and confirmed by the strongest reasoning. So that if any submission of judgment and conscience be due to the positive dictates of the infallible Spirit; if any regard ought to be paid to a demonstrative argument urged by the Lord's ambassador; here they are due, and here they ought to be paid. For Paul teaches and proves, that our election to eternal glory must be either entirely of grace, or entirely of works; grace and works being directly opposite. They cannot, therefore, unite in producing the same effect, or in promoting the same end. Whoever, then, acknowledges any such thing as an election of sinners to future happiness, must necessarily maintain, either, that the sole reason why they were chosen rather than others, was their own *superior worthiness,* without grace being concerned at all in the choice; and so their election is an act of remunerative justice;

or, that they were *equally unworthy* of the divine regards as any of those that perish; and so their election is an act of sovereign grace. One of these he must hold, in opposition to the other. For if there be any other alternative, the apostle's argument is inconclusive. There is no reconciling expedient that can be devised by the wit of man. We may attempt a coalition between works and grace, but it will be found impracticable; while, in so doing, our pride and folly will be great, and our disappointment certain. For such an attempt would not only bring the greatest confusion into all our ideas about works and grace; but, as far as possible, destroy the very things themselves. Such persons as maintain the contrary hypothesis, may, to save appearances, *say*, that election is of grace; but if it be on a foresight of faith and obedience, there is in reality nothing of grace in it: for grace is *free favour*. On this supposition, election is no other than an *appointment of a reward to its objects, on a foresight of the requisite conditions being prescribed, and performed by them*. But, as such, it is an act of remunerative justice; or, at least, of fidelity and truth; and cannot, without open violence to the common signification of the terms, be denominated an act of mere favour, or of pure benevolence.

That it is the design of Paul, when describing the subject in his epistle to the Romans, to exclude all consideration of human worthiness, and to resolve the election of those who are saved entirely into the grace of God, as infinitely free and divinely sovereign, appears from those *objections* to which he replies. For the objections made, and the answers returned, are of such a nature as would appear quite impertinent, and without the least shadow of reason to support them, on supposition that God, when he chose his people, had any regard to their superior worthiness, in comparison to those who perish The objections suppose that the divine conduct in this affair is inequitable. But such a supposition could not have been made, such a charge could never have been laid against it, by any man of sense, or of the least reflection, if the Almighty, in the decree of election, had proceeded to distinguish between one man and another, according to their personal qualities and moral worth.

The infallible writer having treated about God's distinguishing love to Jacob and his rejection of Esau, starts an objection against the tenor of his arguing and the truth he maintained; an objection, he knew, that was both plausible and common. *What shall we say, then?* what will be inferred as the necessary consequence of our foregoing assertion? Will any one dare to conclude that there *is unrighteousness with God*, because he dispenses, or withholds his favours, according to his own sovereign pleasure? *Far be it!* such a consequence will be held in the utmost abhorrence, by all who revere their Maker. The apostle having rejected the shocking inference, in the strongest manner, proceeds to confirm his assertions and to prove his doctrine. This he does by appealing to the ancient scriptures. *For He*, whose name is JEHOVAH, *saith to Moses; I will have mercy on whom I will have mercy, and I will have compassion on whom I will have compassion.* From which memorable and ancient oracle, he infers the following conclusion: *So, then, it is not of him that willeth, nor of him that runneth, but of God that showeth mercy.* Hence it appears with striking evidence, that it was Paul's design to prove, not only that some of the fallen race were chosen, in contradistinction to others; but also, that those objects of the Divine choice were appointed to glory, not in consideration of any thing which caused them to differ from others; but purely, solely, entirely, because it was the good pleasure of God to make them partakers of that mercy on which they had not the least claim, any more than those who perish. For, on a supposition of the contrary, it does not appear that his quotation from the writings of Moses, and the conclusion he forms upon it, were at all to his purpose; but rather adapted to mislead his reader, and to bias his judgment in favour of error.

The zealous and indefatigable teacher of heavenly truth, in prosecuting his subject, meets with another objection which he is equally careful to obviate. For, after having asserted that Jehovah has *mercy on whom he will, and whom he will, he hardeneth,* it is added; *Thou wilt say then unto me, Why doth he yet find fault* with any of his creatures, or blame their conduct? *for who hath resisted his will,* or rendered his purposes void?—This objection exhibits a faithful mirror, in which every opposer of divine sovereignty may see his face and read his character. The most horrid and shocking consequences that are now charged on the doctrine of eternal, unconditional, and personal election, are here included and reduced to a small compass. This objection, in modern style, reads thus: " According to the Calvinistic doctrine of election, men are mere machines. They are impelled to this or that by a fatal necessity. They are no longer the proper objects of praise or blame, of reward or punishment. Adieu, therefore, to every virtuous action and all praiseworthy deeds. Whether we be righteous or wicked, here; whether we be saved or damned, hereafter; an arbitrary will, and a sovereign, omnipotent decree are the cause of all."—Such persons, however, as are inclined to repeat the stale objection, may do well to consider, in what manner the apostle refutes it; and how he treats the proud opposer of the sovereign prerogative of the great Supreme. The objection is levelled against the sovereignty of God, in making such an immense distinction between persons equally unworthy of Divine clemency. But, though bold and blasphemous to the last degree, the unerring teacher does not refute, or attempt to remove it, by informing the objector, that it was not his design, by the immediately foregoing assertion, to affirm, that the sole cause of that infinite difference which shall subsist to eternity between the state of one man and of another, equally guilty and alike miserable, considered in themselves, was the sovereign pleasure of God. No; he is far from giving any such hint; but immediately recurs to the *supreme dominion* of Him who formed the universe, as a clear consideration of sufficient importance, and sufficiently clear, to establish the point. So far from softening his former assertions, however harsh they might seem, that he at once confirms the truth he asserted, and illustrates the propriety of his language. In doing of which he suggests, that the objection, horrid as it is, cannot have the least force, or pertinency of application, except it were proved that the Majesty of heaven had not an absolute right to dispense his favours just as he pleases. But this the resolute asserter of Jehovah's honour was not willing to grant. This he could by no means allow, without *denying the God that is above.* He, therefore, boldly repels the confidence of the proud objector, by a strong exclamation, and a mortifying query. *Nay, but, O man! who art* THOU *that repliest against God?* Shall a worm of the earth, an insect, an atom, arraign his conduct who is Lord of the universe, and pronounce it unrighteous? Shall impotence and dust fly in the face of Omnipotence? Shall corruption and guilt prescribe rules of equity, by which the Most Holy shall regulate his behaviour toward the rebellious subjects of his boundless empire? Far be it! *Wo to him that striveth with his Maker! Let the potsherd strive with the potsherds of the earth;* but let not the despicable fragment presume to make war upon Heaven; lest Divine wrath, like a devouring fire, break out and consume it.

The zealous and cautious disputant having severely rebuked the opposer's folly and arrogance, proceeds to confirm his assertion, and to illustrate the momentous truth by a familiar instance, and by appealing to the common sense of mankind. *Shall the thing formed say to him that formed it, Why hast thou made me thus?* For example: *Hath not the potter power over the clay, of the same lump to make one vessel to honour, and another to dishonour?* None can deny it. Is this power allowed, by the common consent of mankind, to belong to the meanest artificer; and shall it be denied to HIM, who is the Former of all things? Such a denial would be a monstrous compound of absurdity and blasphemy.—The apostle now proceeds to apply his illustration. *What if God, willing to show his wrath and to make his power known,* having *endured with much long-suffering the vessels of wrath fitted for destruction,* by their own rebellion against him, should, in the end, pour out his vengeance upon them; who shall dare to pronounce his conduct unrighteous? *And*, what if the same sovereign Being, *that he might make known the riches of his glory on the vessels of mercy, which he had afore prepared unto glory,* determined to manifest infinite love in their complete deliverance from deserved destruction, who has a right to complain? Shall the eye of any be evil, because their offended Maker is good? Has he not an eternal right to do what he will with his own? Or, is he a debtor to any of his creatures? If so, they shall be fully recompensed. Shall every petty sovereign, in the kingdoms of this world, be allowed to choose his own favourites; and, in certain cases, to manifest his clemency to some delinquents, while he leaves others to suffer the desert of their crimes, without being subject to the control of his meanest subjects in the performance of those sovereign acts? and shall HE who rules over all be denied the exercise of his supreme royal prerogative? Absurd, in supposition! impossible, in fact!—But though God bestows his favour on whom he pleases, yet, as he is an infinitely wise agent, he must always have the highest reason for what he does. Divine sovereignty, therefore, must not be considered as a blind partiality, or a dictate of mere *will* without wisdom; but as the exercise of an all-comprehensive understanding, and of a will that is inflexibly right, ordering all the affairs of Jehovah's vast empire for the manifestation of his own glorious attributes. To conceive of a sovereign decree, as detached from wisdom and rectitude, is to picture to ourselves the conduct of a Turkish despot; not the appointment of Him that governs the world.

The love of God to his offending creatures must be considered, in the whole of its exercise, as under the direction of his Divine understanding: and as his boundless intelligence comprehends all possibilities, his love must be consummately wise in all its operations. The supreme perfection of Jehovah's nature forbids our supposing, that he can decree without wisdom, any more than govern without rectitude, or punish without justice. Hence the apostle, when discoursing on that profound subject, eternal predestination, concludes thus; *O, the depths!*—of what? An arbitrary will, or an absolute sovereignty, detached from wisdom? far from it. But *of the riches both of the* WISDOM *and* KNOWLEDGE *of God!* To resolve those eternal decrees, which constitute the great plan of Providence, into the Divine will, detached from Divine wisdom; is neither the doctrine of Scripture, nor agreeable to sound reason—is to represent the Supreme Lord under the notion of an eastern tyrant, rather than to give an idea of GOD, ONLY WISE.

If, then, we consider the Almighty as choosing any of the fallen race to life and happiness, we behold him exercising the mercy of a *compassionate Father*, to his miserable offspring. But if we consider him as choosing this person rather than that, when both were equally wretched; we view him as vested with the character of a *sovereign Lord*, and as the sole proprietor of his own favours. If, therefore, the question be asked; Why any were chosen to salvation, when all deserved to perish? The answer is; Because our Maker is merciful. But if it be further asked; Why Paul, for instance, was chosen rather than Judas? The answer is; Because he is Lord of all, and has an indisputable right to do what he will with his own. But if this answer will not satisfy the curious inquirer, he is directed by the Spirit of inspiration to ask the potter, what was the reason of his very different procedure with the same lump of clay; and why he formed the vessels into which it was wrought, for such different and opposite uses? The artificer will readily answer, as directed by common sense; "Not any thing in the clay itself; but my own deliberate and free choice. For it was of the same kind, and possessed the same qualities throughout the whole mass: nor could one part dictate how it would be formed, or for what uses, any more than another." Thus the most ignorant potter, without hesitation, would assert a kind of sovereignty over his clay. And are not mankind in the hand of God, as clay in the hand of the potter? Or, shall Jehovah's sovereignty over his offending creatures, be inferior to that of a puny mortal over passive matter? Reason and revelation forbid the thought. In election, therefore, we have a striking display of Divine grace in its utmost freeness; and of God's dominion in its highest sovereignty. Of the former, toward the vessels of mercy; of the latter, toward all mankind. That, we behold with admiration and joy; this, we revere in silence: well remembering who it is that says; BE STILL, AND KNOW THAT I AM GOD.

Having shown, in the preceding paragraphs, that election is an act of sovereign grace; I now proceed to consider the great *end* which the Supreme Lord intended by it. The ultimate end is his own eternal glory; and, subordinate to it, the complete happiness of all his people. The glory of the Supreme Being is, as before observed, the final cause of all the eternal counsels, and of all Divine operations; especially of those which respect the salvation of sinners. They were all designed for the PRAISE OF HIS GLORIOUS GRACE.

Too ready we are to imagine, that the purpose and pleasure of God terminate in the happiness of those that are chosen, and in the misery of those rejected; as though the eternal felicity, and the everlasting torment of sinful creatures, were the final cause of the Divine decree. But this is a great mistake, and represents the doctrine of predestination in a very false, as well as unfavourable light. For as it would be pregnant with blasphemy to suppose, that He who is supremely blessed and supremely good, should take delight in the infinite misery of a rational being, without reference to a further and nobler end;* so we cannot conceive, on any principles of reason, or of Scripture, that he should propose any thing short of his own glory in the wonderful economy of human

---

* It is indeed said, *I will laugh at your calamity; I will mock when your fear cometh.* But then, as the learned VITRINGA observes; "Quod de Deo *anthropopathos* dictum prudenter intelligi debet; non vere, ac si exitium hominis miseri, et stultitia sua voluntaria pereuntis, Deo delectationem adferat; sed quod mala, quæ gravissimi peccatores juste perserunt, maxime conveniant rationibus Divinæ justitiæ, in cujus exercitio Deus acquiescit, et sibi placet." *Comment. ad Canticum Mosis*, p. 133.

salvation. For as it would be highly injurious to the Divine character to suppose that the misery of apostate creatures is the ultimate end at which the eternal Sovereign aims, in the damnation of those who perish; or that any thing short of his own glory, in the displays of his spotless purity and inflexible justice, was the end which he had in view; so it would be greatly unworthy of his infinite wisdom and boundless perfection for us to imagine, that the glory of his own grace, and the everlasting honour of all his adorable excellencies, were not his supreme design in the free election and complete felicity of all his people. Does he execute vengeance on any of the works of his hands? it is to demonstrate the infinite opposition of all his perfections to moral evil, and for the honour of his eternal justice, as a righteous Governor. Does he spare any of the rebellious subjects of his vast dominions, and save them from the death they deserved? it is to display his mercy in connexion with truth and righteousness, and for the glory of all his unchangeable attributes. We may therefore conclude with Paul, that the great end of election, and of all its consequent blessings, is no other than to *make known the* RICHES OF GOD'S GLORY *on the vessels of mercy.*

As the eternal glory of God, in the consummate happiness of all his chosen, is the exalted end of the decree of election; so the *means* appointed to accomplish the wonderful design, are equally worthy of infinite wisdom. They are such as proclaim *the just God and the Saviour;* such as demand the testimony of conscience, that *the Lord is holy in all his ways, and righteous in all his works.* The principal of these means undoubtedly are, the incarnation of the eternal Son, and his Divine mediation; the sanctification of the Spirit, and belief of the truth. For thus we read: *God hath appointed us to obtain salvation by our Lord Jesus Christ—He hath chosen you to salvation, through sanctification of the Spirit and belief of the truth.* Redemption by the blood of Jesus, and sanctification by the Spirit of God, are equally necessary to accomplish the great design. For as there is no remission *without shedding of blood;*

so, without holiness, *no man shall see the Lord*. As none shall be condemned to final perdition, but those who did such things as were *worthy of death*, so none shall enjoy the inheritance of glory, but those whom impartial justice shall entirely acquit, and immaculate holiness completely approve. And as none of the damned shall ever be able to assign any other cause of their infinite punishment, but that sin which they freely committed so all the elect shall ascribe their salvation to the grace of God and the work of Immanuel. We may therefore conclude, that though Christ and his mediation were not the cause of election, yet his obedience and death were the grand means appointed for the execution of that gracious purpose. And though the Almighty chose no man to glory, because of his future faith and obedience, yet provision was made, in the sovereign decree, for the sanctification of all its objects, prior to their enjoyment of blessedness.

The purpose of God in election is *immutable*, and *infallibly connected* with the eternal felicity of all its objects. That this decree is unchangeable, appears from the immutability of the divine purposes in general. For there is the same reason that the appointment of God, in the choice of his people, should unchangeably stand, as there is for any other of his eternal designs; and that immutability is stamped upon the divine decrees in general, the Scriptures abundantly show. Thus it is written: *The Lord of Hosts hath purposed, and who shall disannul it?—My counsel shall stand, and I will do all my pleasure—He is in one mind, and who can turn Him? And what his soul desireth, even that He doth—To show unto the heirs of promise the immutability of his counsel—Who hath resisted his will?—That the purpose of God according to election might stand—With whom is no variableness, neither shadow of turning.**

Nor can we suppose that God should reverse his de-

---

* Isa. xiv. 27, and xlvi. 10. Job xxiii. 13. Heb. vi. 17. Rom. ix. 11. 19. James i. 17.

crees, or alter his purposes, without impeaching, either his omniscience, as though he did not *foresee* the events that would happen ; or his power, as if he were not *able* to execute his own designs : neither of which can possibly attend that infinite Being, whose will is fate, and whose word is the basis of the universe. If God were to change his mind, it must be either for the better, or for the worse. If for the better, he was not perfectly wise in his former purpose. If for the worse, he is not wise in his present resolve. For there can be no alteration without a tacit reflection, either on the past, or on the present determination. If a man change his resolution, he is apprehensive of some defect in his former purpose, which moves him to such a change : and this must arise, either from a want of capacity to foresee, or from not duly considering the object of his counsel. But neither of these can be supposed of Him who is supremely wise without denying his Deity. A change of purpose may, indeed, be an act of wisdom in the rational creature ; but it supposes folly in his former conduct, which is inconsistent with consummate perfection. *The only wise* God had no occasion for second thoughts. As he is wise to perfection, he sees no cause of reversing his purposes. As he is boundless in power, he is subject to no control in executing his will, or in making his people partakers of those blessings he designed for them. To suppose, therefore, that any who were chosen to eternal glory should finally fail of enjoying it, is an imagination absurdly impious ; as it suggests a charge of palpable imperfection against JEHOVAH, and would make him *altogether such an one as ourselves.*

That election is infallibly connected with eternal happiness, appears from the following remarkable passage : *Whom he did predestinate, them he also called; and whom he called, them he also justified; and whom he justified, them he also -glorified. What shall we then say to these things?—If God be for us, who can be against us?* If the purpose of God in election be not immutable ; or if the objects of it might possibly fail of the glorious end ; there would be no certain connexion between the several blessings that are here mentioned. On such a supposition, to argue, as the apostle does, from the past election of any persons, to their future glorification, would be exceedingly weak, and the inference a gross inconsequence. Nor would there have been any propriety in his joyful exclamation; *What shall we then say to these things?* nor any solid foundation for this bold conclusion; *If God be for us, who can be against us?* For, admitting that God may possibly change his purpose; or, that his decree may prove weak and ineffectual, so that in any instance the event designed by it may not be produced; there was but little reason for Paul thus to exclaim in admiration and joy, or with confidence thus to conclude upon his everlasting happiness, from the consideration of God's electing love. To impute such unmeaning and inconclusive argumentation to him, would be an high reflection upon him, as Gamaliel's pupil; would be absolutely inconsistent with his more exalted character, as an amanuensis to the Spirit of wisdom. We may, therefore, safely conclude that election to future happiness, and the certain enjoyment of it, cannot be separated. For, *Whom he did predestinate— them he also glorified.*

Having considered this important truth under the several foregoing views, I shall now proceed to show that it is a *doctrine according to godliness;* and that it is nobly adapted to promote the holiness and comfort of true Christians. As an article of that faith which was once delivered to the saints; as an infallible truth of the gospel, its tendency must be salutary, its influence must be sanctifying, on all who cordially embrace it. Such will ever find, that it wears the most friendly aspect on their progress in real holiness, and on their enjoyment of substantial peace. Could it be proved that it has no influence on these, we might venture, without hesitation, to renounce it as an error, and to abhor it as an enemy. For that is no part of evangelical truth, which, in its genuine tendency, is not adapted to promote the happiness of real Christians, and to advance the interests of true holiness. This, however, is not the case with the doctrine under consideration. For a frequent and devout meditation upon it, by those who are taught from above, and who view it in its proper connexions, is evidently calculated to humble their souls in the dust before the eternal Sovereign; to inflame their hearts with love to his adorable name; and to excite their gratitude for benefits received and blessings expected. Consequently, their holiness and comfort must be advanced by it: for humility, love, and gratitude, are the vitals of real religion. As these abound in the heart, our spiritual joys are increased, and our Maker is glorified. As these abate, we lose the savour of divine things, and the interests of religion decline. Where these have no existence, the most extensive round of duties, the most costly and shining performances, are of no esteem in the sight of God.

This doctrine is adapted to promote *genuine humility*. For it shows that all mankind, in their natural state, are equally obnoxious to wrath and exposed to ruin; and, exclusive of that grace which appears and reigns in election, that their condition is absolutely desperate. It allows not the least liberty for any of the sons of men to claim superior worth, or to glory over their fellows. When self-admiring thoughts arise in the Christian's breast, it stops them short with needful and sharp rebuke; *Who maketh thee to differ? and what hast thou that thou didst not receive? Now if thou didst receive it, why dost thou glory as if thou hadst not received it?* Those therefore, who are the favoured objects of distinguishing love, and who look for salvation by it; discovering that their persons are alike sinful and their state equally wretched, considered in themselves as the persons or state of those that finally perish; cannot, according to the genius of this doctrine, but lie low in humility before God. Being fully convinced that the eternal choice of their persons was not on account of the least possible difference between themselves and others; and that the whole reason of their hope centres in that grace which might have been manifested to others, had the great Sovereign so determined; they are at all times free to acknowledge, that the chief of sinners, and the most worthless objects, are their proper characters. The influence of this humbling truth they feel in their consciences, and their ardent desire is to express it in their lives.

Let us attend the believer in his secret retirements: let us behold him on his bended knee, and hear him pouring out his soul to God. In his intercourse with Heaven, at the throne of grace, his language will be to the following import. " Thou GREAT SUPREME, who art glorious in holiness, and the infinite Sovereign of all worlds; who humblest thyself to behold the things that are in the highest heavens; whose condescension is unspeakably great, in deigning to regard the persons or services of the most holy and exalted creatures; didst thou consider *me* in my low estate, as a fallen creature and a miserable sinner? Did thy everlasting love fix on *me* as its object, when I might, with the greatest equity, have been marked out as a victim for eternal justice? Is not my person polluted, and my state by nature damnable? Was not my original depravity as great, and are not my actual transgressions as numerous as any which can be found among the apostate sons of Adam? And hast thou determined to make *me* an everlasting monument of sparing mercy, while millions are left to suffer the awful desert of their crimes? Nothing in me couldst thou behold, but a shocking compound of impurity and folly, of guilt and wretchedness. Nothing in my conduct couldst thou foresee, but what was adapted to provoke thy abhorrence, rather than to obtain thy regard. O, thou majestic Being! why such mercy to a hardened rebel? why such love to an inveterate enemy? Obliged I am, in the court of conscience, to plead guilty to the complicated charge which thy own righteous law exhibits against me. Motive, or cause, of thy tender regards, I can find none in myself. Thy own sovereign will, thy own free pleasure; these are the only cause why mercy is manifested to me, of sinners the vilest. For should a wretch who is now in hell advance a claim on thy favour, grounded on his own worthiness, I must acknowledge it as well founded as any to which I can pretend. *Pride!* thou most detestable of all tempers, forever depart from my breast! *Humility!* thou fairest flower of heavenly origin, thou brightest ornament of the Christian character; be thou my constant companion ; be thou the livery in which I shall always appear ! Shall a miscreant, who might have been justly doomed to damnation; shall a worthless worm, that is beholden to grace for his all, entertain aspiring thoughts, or assert his own importance? as well might Lucifer himself challenge a seat in paradise. O, my God, let me but view thy electing love in all its freeness, and thy distinguishing favour in all its sovereignty, and I shall be truly humble. Then shall my soul lie low in the dust, and reigning grace shall have the glory of all my salvation. Whatever blessings I now possess, whatever enjoyments I hereafter expect, I freely acknowledge the unrivalled honour belongs to Thee."

Nor is the doctrine maintained less adapted to inflame the heart with sacred *love*. *Love is of God ; he, therefore, who dwells in love, dwells in God, and God in him.* " Didst Thou, who needest not the services of angels ; who art infinitely perfect and infinitely happy in thy own eternal Self," will the elect and regenerate soul say, " didst THOU entertain thoughts of love towards me, before the foundations of the world were laid ? Did thy purposes of communicating bliss terminate on a worm so mean, on a wretch so vile ? *How precious are thy thoughts unto me, O God! how great is the sum of them!* Didst thou record my worthless name in the book of life, and constitute me a member of that mystical body of which Christ is the head ? Were my person and all my immortal interests consigned over, by an irreversible grant, into the hands of thy only Son, as the appointed Mediator in order to secure my eternal happiness beyond the possibility of a failure ? Didst thou, my God, in the original plan of salvation, provide for the honour of thy justice, as well as the glory of thy grace, by appointing a Surety to perform the obedience to which I am bound, as a creature ; and to suffer the punishment that I deserve as a criminal? And, in order to effect the amazing design, didst thou determine, before 1 had a being or time commenced, to deliver up the Son of thy love, clothed in humanity, to the stroke of incensed justice, and to the execrable death of the cross? and all this to rescue and save, to ennoble and dignify—what? be astonished, O ye heavens, at this!—*a rebellious worm, a despicable insect?* elated with pride, and replete with enmity against Thee, thou greatest and best of Beings! Stupendous goodness! Marvellous grace! O, my God! was I the object of thy eternal choice when viewed by Omniscience as fallen under guilt, and sunk in ruin; loathsome as the dunghill, and abhorrent as hell? and shall not my best affections and warmest love be devoted to Thee? Didst Thou number me among the objects of grace, when thou mightest with honour to thy crown and dignity, as a righteous Governor, have consigned me over to endless perdition; and shall not my heart flame with love to thy adorable name? Didst Thou love and choose me, when deformed and filthy, possessed of dispositions partly brutal, and partly diabolical? Art thou infinitely amiable in all thy perfections, and completely righteous in all thy ways, and shall not my very soul love and adore Thee? Hast Thou, of thy mere grace, distinguished me as an object of thy complacential regards; and shall not Thou be the object of my warmest passions and most intense desires? Yes, blessed Lord! Come, possess my heart, and sway my affections! Thine they are, and thine, through grace, they shall ever be. Depart from me, ye rivals of my God! Ye idols of unregenerate hearts, pleasure, wealth, pomp, and power, get you hence! Address me no more with your soft solicitations; entice me no more with your gilded baits. JEHOVAH has condescended to take me for his own: I choose him for my portion, I love him as my all."

·A devout consideration of this momentous truth is also a noble incentive to *gratitude*. Gratitude is a delightful disposition, and an amiable temper. It burns in heavenly bosoms, tunes the harps of celestial choirs, and gives the sweetest accent to all their songs. Love to the infinitely amiable God, and gratitude to him for his boundless beneficence; these enter into the essence of all religion; these are the very life and soul of all intellectual happiness. In proportion, therefore, as these are promoted, the holiness and comfort of mankind are advanced. That an interest in the election of grace, and a sense of it warm on the heart, are a powerful incentive to the most generous gratitude, we may boldly assert, as we have an authority which none can dispute. Paul, we find, when contemplating the riches of grace in eternal election, breaks out in the following language. *Blessed be the God and Father of our Lord Jesus Christ, who hath blessed us with all spiritual blessings in heavenly places in Christ;* ACCORDING AS HE HATH CHOSEN US IN HIM, BEFORE THE FOUNDATION OF THE WORLD. Again: *We are bound to give thanks always to God for you, brethren, beloved of the Lord;* BECAUSE GOD HATH FROM THE BEGINNING CHOSEN YOU TO SALVATION. Such are those grateful acknowledgments the apostle makes, on the behalf of himself and his brethren, to the Author of all good, in reference to their election: and similar will be the sentiments of gratitude in every regenerate heart, in proportion as this important truth is known and experienced.

Let us once more listen to the devout addresses and humble acknowledgments of the believer, when bending the supplicant knee before his Father. O Thou, that art infinitely exalted above all blessing and praise! what shall I render to Thee for all thy benefits? Hast Thou, my Father, and Thou, my God, chosen me to holiness, chosen me to eternal life, and that of thy mere grace; and shall not thy glory be the end of all my actions, while I possess either breath or being? Didst Thou enter into an everlasting covenant with the Son of thy love, to save me from final ruin and bring me to immortal bliss; and shall not I freely engage with hand and heart to be thine forever? Thine I am, by right of creation; thine I am, by electing love; and thine I would eternally be, in the performance of every duty, and in the exercise of all my powers. Were the treasures of infinite wisdom displayed in contriving the way, and in appointing the necessary means for my complete felicity; were the stores of unbounded mercy and the riches of sovereign grace, laid open in the eternal counsels of peace on my behalf; and shall not my life, my soul, my everlasting all, that are saved at such an expense, be devoted to Thee? Bind me, O blessed God! for ever bind me to thyself, with the delightful cords of love; that I may never desert thy service, that I may never dishonour thy name. *Dishonour* THEE? painful thought! May I ever choose to die a thousand deaths, rather than act a part so disingenuous. Hast thou chosen me out of the world? didst thou pity and spare my guilty soul, while numbers were left in their perishing state; and, do not reason and conscience, do not all the sentiments of honour and gratitude of which the human heart is susceptible, conspire with divine revelation to show, that I am laid under infinite obligations to admire thy goodness, and continually to speak thy praise? Such an everlasting and immense distinction as Thou hast made in election, between creatures equally deserving of punishment, challenges from the objects of discriminating love all possible thankfulness. Lord, here I am thy devoted servant! To love and adore thy perfections, to know and peform thy will, be all my delight and all my employ. I bow before thee, and acknowledge myself entirely thine. I give myself entirely to thy disposal, as my only and sovereign Lord. As unformed clay in the hand of the potter, to be moulded and fashioned according to thy own will, I commit myself and all my concerns to Thee."— Such is the salutary tendency of this doctrine, and such the language of all that are truly acquainted with it, in proportion as faith is in exercise.

But, however comfortable this truth may be, to such as are persuaded of their interest in the love of God; is it not adapted to discourage the inquiring soul, and to overwhelm the awakened sinner with desponding fears? Does it not administer abundant occasion for the anxious mind thus to reflect? I know not whether Christ and his salvation be *free* for me. If I be not of the number of God's elect, I have evidently no interest in him, nor in any thing that he has done. Consequently, how much soever I may desire to believe and be saved by him, I never shall, if not ordained to eternal life." This objection, however plausible it may seem, or however much the conscience of an awakened sinner may be harassed by it, is weak and impertinent. It supposes that a person must know the divine appointment concerning him; that he must, as it were, peruse the eternal roll of God's decrees, and read his name in the book of life, before he can upon solid grounds apply to Christ for salvation. But this is a grand mistake.

Let me illustrate the point. When food is presented to a person pinched with hunger, would it be wise, would it be rational for him to hesitate about the propriety of using it, because he does not know whether his Maker has appointed that he shall be nourished by it? though at the same time he well remembers, that *man does not live by bread alone, but by every word which proceedeth out of the mouth of God:* and therefore supposing he eat it, without the concurrence of Providence, it will be of no service to him. Would he not rather say; "Meat was made for the use of man: I feel my need: I will endeavour to use it, therefore, as the appointed mean of satisfying my craving appetite, and of supporting my animal frame?"—Now Christ is the bread of life, and the food of our souls. This heavenly food was provided by grace, is exhibited in the gospel, and freely presented to all that hunger, without any exception. What, then, has the awakened sinner to do, but, as the Lord shall enable him, to take, and eat, and live forever? It is very evident, that he has no business to inquire about any further right to partake; since it was not provided for sinners, nor can be of use to them, under any other character, or considered in any other light, than that of miserable objects who are *starving* for want of spiritual food.

According to this doctrine, complete provision is made for the certain salvation of every sinner, however unworthy, who feels his want and applies to Christ. The gospel is not preached to sinners, nor are they encouraged to believe in Jesus, under the formal notion of their being elected. No: these tidings of heavenly mercy are addressed to sinners, considered as *ready to perish;* and all the blessings of grace are displayed for their immediate relief, as convinced that such are their state and character. All, without any exception of persons, or any regard to worthiness, who apprehend their danger and feel their want, are invited by the Lord Redeemer to a participation of spiritual blessings, previous to any inquiries about their election, that being a following consideration. The order established in the economy of grace, and in reference to this affair, does not require perishing sinners to prove their election before they are permitted, or have any encouragement to trust in Christ for complete deliverance: but, seeing their state, they have all the encouragement which the word of Jehovah can give, without hesitation to rely on the Saviour; and all the assurance which the oath of God can impart, that in so doing they shall obtain pardon for their sins and peace for their consciences; a freedom from wrath, and the enjoyment of glory. These things are evident from the tenour of divine revelation; and to conceive otherwise proceeds on a mistake of the doctrine, and is followed by an abuse of the truth. Consequently, it administers no real occasion of discouragement or fear, to the inquiring soul or the sensible sinner—to none of the human race, in whose esteem a Saviour from the guilt and power of sin would be precious or welcome. As to those who are dead in sin and unconcerned about their souls, or that have an high opinion of their own righteousness; the Redeemer with all his glory, and the gospel with all its blessings are despised by them, so that they must be out of the question.

But may it not be inferred, "that this doctrine is calculated to countenance spiritual sloth, and to encourage licentious practices, in those who conclude that they are in the number of the favoured few?" That none who are so persuaded will find themselves deceived in their expectations, I dare not assert. I will not therefore affirm, that there are no instances of persons *professing* to believe the evangelical doctrine, and *pretending* to an interest in the heavenly blessing; who do not abuse the former, and who may not fall infinitely short of the latter. But this I will boldly affirm, that whoever, from such a persuasion, encourages himself in spiritual sloth, or licentious practices, is guilty of basely abusing the doctrine of grace, which, in its own nature, has a directly contrary tendency; and marks himself out as a vessel of eternal wrath, rather than an object of sovereign mercy.

Nor can this objection have any force, except it were proved, that the infinitely wise God has appointed the *end*, but entirely forgotten the *means* which are necessary to attain and enjoy it. A supposition this, highly unworthy of his character, and contrary to his express declarations. For though the eternal Sovereign had no respect, in the choice of his people, to any thing in them that was worthy of his regard, or to any good works foreseen; yet his professed design in their election was, *that they might be holy and without blame before him in love.* This being the design of God respecting his chosen, it would be strange indeed, strange to a wonder, if the revelation of his immutable purpose should have a tendency to make them quite the reverse, and prove an incentive to their vilest lusts!—It is written, *God hath from the beginning chosen you to salvation.* How? According to this bold objection one would suppose it was in such a way, as allowed them larger scope and greater liberty for gratifying their licentious passions and lawless appetites, than corrupt nature could otherwise have enjoyed—in such a way as pays no regard to the interests of holiness; as makes no provision for the honour of God in a Christian conversation. If this could be proved, the doctrine would deserve the utmost abhorrence: but it is far from being the case. For the objects of this gracious purpose, we are expressly informed by the oracle of heaven, were chosen to salvation THROUGH SANCTIFICATION OF THE SPIRIT, *and belief of the truth. Sanctification of the Spirit* may be considered not only as an appointed and *honourable mean* of attaining that exalted end, the salvation of the soul and the glory of God; but also as an *essential part* of that salvation to which they were chosen, which is begun on earth and completed in glory. Taken in either view, it is obvious that this instructive and important text is a full proof that the objection alleged is quite impertinent, and entirely void of truth to support it. Consequently, that those who make it are influenced either by gross ignorance or inveterate prejudice. For hence it appears, that the holiness and the happiness of God's people are equally secured by the Divine purpose. Besides, those, and those only, who live by faith on Jesus Christ, and walk in the ways of obedience, have any evidence that they are the elect of God. In proportion, therefore, as they lose sight of the glorious object of their dependence, and deviate from the paths of holiness, they lose sight of their interest in distinguishing love. So that their inward peace and spiritual joy are greatly concerned in a pious conduct.

Nor is the following objection, so frequently and violently urged, any more to the purpose. "If this doctrine be true," say our opponents, "there is little or no occasion for the use of means, in order to attain salvation. For if we are elected, we shall be saved without them; and if not, they will prove abortive. On such a supposition, all our prayers, and tears, and strivings; all our circumspection and self-denial, will be of no avail. We may, therefore, as well take our ease and rest contented. A profession of religion is an useless thing: for the final event is fixed by a predestinating God, and who shall reverse it?" This objection agrees with the former, in supposing that the end is decreed without regard to the means. A palpable fallacy, and pregnant with great absurdities. Let us apply the principle, on which the objection proceeds, to the common affairs of life. I take it for granted, that there is a superintending Providence over all human affairs, over all our minutest concerns. If so, either the great Ruler of the world from everlasting *determined* what he would do, in all that infinite variety of circumstances in which any of his creatures should ever exist, or he did not. If not, innumerable millions of new determination must have arisen in the eternal Mind since the world began, respecting his conduct toward his creatures; or he must have acted without any prior determination at all, and so without a plan ; neither of which

corresponds with our ideas of an infinitely perfect Agent.
If he did, from eternity, determine upon his conduct, and
form the extensive plan of his future operations respecting rational creatures; then, it is evident, the objection
lies with equal force against our using means, or exerting
endeavours, in order to obtain any promising advantage,
or to avoid any threatening evil in common life, as it
does against making use of means in the important concerns of our souls, and in reference to a future world.
For it is absurd to suppose, that the Divine purpose can
be made void, any more in the one case than in the other.
According to this way of arguing, trade and commerce,
the labours of husbandry, and all the employments of life,
must be at a stand. For who, among all the busy mortals
on earth, can foretell the event, or ascertain success?
Who can tell, however promising the prospect, but Jehovah's purposes may render all his contrivances and all his
painful industry entirely fruitless? Nay, further, upon
this principle, we must not eat our common food, nor
seek the needful refreshments of sleep; for it must be
confessed, that we are absolutely ignorant what the purposes of God may be, as to the event, in either case. If
it be his determination that we shall enjoy health and
vigour, what occasion for the one or the other? and if
not, what good will they do us? For *his purpose shall
stand, and he will do all his pleasure.* But who, notwithstanding this, ever took it into his head to adopt the
principle, and thus to apply it, in affairs of the present
life? None, surely, but a fool, or a madman. While
we have our sober senses in exercise, however firmly we
may believe the existence of eternal decrees; or however
clearly we may discern the interposition of providence,
on ten thousand different occasions; we never suppose
that those everlasting purposes, or these providential interpositions, were designed to supersede the use of means,
or had, as to the concerns of time, any such tendency.
Why, then, should we strive to separate the end from
the means, in things of infinitely greater importance?
The dictates of inspiration, the maxims of philosophy,
the principles of common sense, and the general conduct

of mankind, all unite in utterly disavowing such a procedure, as irrational and absurd to the last degree.

This objection militates no less against the infallible *foreknowledge* of God, than against his purpose. For Jehovah is perfect in knowledge. That knowledge which is absolutely perfect can admit of no increase. All the volitions, therefore, of moral agents, and all the events consequent upon them, were from eternity present to the Divine Mind, and open to his omniscient eye. And as every thing future was included in his all-comprehending view, before the world began; so it would be absurd to suppose that any event should ever take place, otherwise than as He foresaw it. With equal reason, therefore, might the objector infer from the Divine prescience, that the use of means to attain any end is vain, as from the doctrine of predestination. For between the foreknowledge and the purpose of God there is a close and inseparable connexion. To illustrate the point, and to apply the argument. Admitting the perfect foreknowledge of God, the objector may thus argue against the use of means, respecting his eternal state, "The foreknowledge of God is perfect. From eternity he viewed my final state. Either he foresaw me seated on a throne of bliss, and exulting in a sense of his favour; or loaded with chains of darkness, and groaning in the agonies of endless despair. As he from eternity viewed me, so it must inevitably be; for perfect foreknowledge is infallible. My eternal state is therefore a fixed point with the Deity. What need then of the use of means to avoid punishment, or to obtain felicity? Prayer and watchfulness, all the exercises and all the duties of a painful profession, are entirely in vain. If the Omniscient foresaw me happy in the future world, I cannot be miserable. If he foresaw me miserable, I shall not, I cannot be happy; though all the angels in heaven, and all the men upon earth, were to afford me their united aid."

This argument, I humbly conceive, wears the face of probability to as great a degree, and infers the objection I am now refuting with as much propriety and force, as that which is formed, and the inference from it, against the decree of election. But the truth is, neither that nor this has the least force or propriety. For as Jehovah, when he decreed the end, appointed the means and the application of them to their respective objects; so, in his eternal prescience, he not only viewed the end, but also foresaw the means, with their application and use, as connected with the final event. As he foresaw none in the abodes of darkness, but those whom he viewed as guilty, and as walking in the ways of destruction; so he determined to bring none to glory, except in a way becoming himself as perfectly holy, and by the use of means which grace should render effectual. Hence it appears, that the objector must either give up his argument, or deny that his Maker is perfect; which would be to undeify *the God that is above.* This, indeed, with a bold impiety many have done, in order to support their favourite notions about free-agency and the liberty of the human will, in opposition to the doctrine of sovereign grace, and of Divine predestination: being well aware, that whoever allows the eternal and perfect foreknowledge of God, cannot consistently deny his decrees respecting the final state of men. This the Socinians have freely acknowledged. " Admitting, say they, the infallible prescience of all future contingencies, CALVIN's doctrine of the predestination of some, by name, to life, and of others to death, cannot be refuted."* They therefore do their utmost endeavour to prove (horrid to think!) that He who formed and governs the universe, is not possessed of such a foresight, in other words, that he is not God. This they do, by much the same arguments that others use, in opposition to the doctrine here maintained.

To the foregoing objections some, perhaps, may be ready to add, with an air of confidence; " Does not this doctrine, in its inseparable connexions, represent the Most High as partial in his conduct towards his creatures, and as a *respecter of persons?* as dealing hardly, if not unjustly, with far the greater part of mankind?" In answer to which I observe, that as to the charge of

* Apud WITSIUM, *Œcon. Fœd.* l. iii. c. iv. § 12.

partiality and respect of persons, here exhibited against the Divine conduct, it is entirely void of the least foundation. For wherever such a charge may be advanced with propriety against the conduct of any one, it must be in the affairs of remunerative, or of punishing justice, and where the rules of equity are more or less transgressed; but cannot possibly have place in matters of sovereign favour and mere bounty, of which kind is election. For instance: if we consider a person in the capacity of a *magistrate*, as invested with the executive power of the criminal laws of his country, and behold him inflicting upon such offenders as are poor, and mean, and of little account in the world, the penalties annexed to their respective crimes; while he suffers others of nobler birth, of more elevated rank, and of affluent circumstances, to escape with impunity; we have great reason to remonstrate against such a procedure, as a culpable partiality, a criminal respect of persons, and as no other than a perversion of justice. But if we consider the same person under the character of a benefactor, and behold him dispensing his favours among his indigent neighbours, in order to relieve their wants and render them happy; we never imagine that he is under any obligation to show an equal regard to all that are distressed with poverty. Supposing he distribute his bounty in great variety to the favoured objects of his beneficence; nay, supposing he indulge some with favours, while others, who stand in the same need, are entirely overlooked; shall we arraign his conduct, and call him a *respecter of persons?* By no means. For were that the case, there would be nothing indecent, if, after he had manifested his beneficent regards to some, others were to come with a commanding voice, and *require* his assistance in the same way, and to the same degree; than which nothing can be more impertinent. Besides, though men are under obligation to love and assist one another; though, being only stewards of what they possess, they are accountable to the Supreme Judge for the manner in which they use their faculties, their time, and all their talents; yet God has the most perfect right to *do what he will with his own.* For no creature, and especially no *offending* creature, has any claim upon his bounty.

If Jehovah must be denominated a respecter of persons, and his conduct pronounced partial on supposition that he loved and chose some to everlasting happiness, while he rejected others and left them to perish under his righteous curse; if the equity of his proceedings, in the affairs of grace, must be called in question, because he bestows eternal blessings on some, and entirely withholds them from others; how shall we vindicate the methods of Providence in ten thousand different instances? Does not God, as to the concerns of religion, afford those means of grace, his word and ordinances, to some, while they are entirely withheld from others? and where they are enjoyed, does he not regenerate and sanctify some by the Spirit of truth, while others, who have the same external means, continue in spiritual darkness, and finally perish? If, then, the uncontrollable God may do that in time for some, which he is under no obligation to do for any; none can doubt whether he might from eternity form such a resolution: for Divine Providence is nothing but the execution of God's eternal purpose. Similar to this is the conduct of God toward mankind, as to temporal things. For nothing is more evident, than that the Supreme Governor of the world is liberal in communicating enjoyments of every kind to some; while others, not more unworthy, are all their lives exposed to the greatest distresses. And though there is a vast disparity between temporal and eternal blessings, yet, if to distinguish between his creatures, in bestowing or in withholding the latter, would any way impeach his character; it must in proportion do so in the former. For the Judge of all the earth must do right. And as none can, without open blasphemy, quarrel with the sovereign dispensations of Providence, on account of that difference which subsists between one man and another in the present life: so none should indulge a captious humour in finding fault with the methods of grace, because their Maker does not manifest an equal regard to all.

Nor can it be inferred from any thing implied in this

doctrine, that our eternal Sovereign deals hardly, much less unjustly, with any part of mankind. Here let me ask the objector, and let him ask his own conscience; Have all mankind sinned? Is sin a transgression of Divine law? Is the law they have broken, righteous, just in its requisitions, and equitable in its penalty? If so, every man is guilty before God, and every mouth should be stopped: for all have deserved to die; to perish; to be destroyed with an utter destruction. Either these things are acknowledged as undoubted truths, or the authority of the Bible is rejected. These truths being admitted, reason itself must allow, that if all mankind had perished under a curse, the honour of their Maker, as the Supreme Governor and righteous Judge, must have been unimpeached. But if so, it is impossible to conceive how his choosing some to life and happiness, and his rejecting others, can afford the least occasion for the charge suggested in the objection. For the election of those whom God determined to save, does not injure the non-elect. Their situation would not have been at all the better, if none had been chosen, nor any saved. For non-election is not a punishment; it is only the withholding a free favour, which the sovereign Lord of all may bestow on whomsoever he pleases.

When the whole world is considered as *guilty before God*, we must allow that he had an unlimited right to determine about the final state of men. He was at perfect liberty to determine whether he would save any, or not. He might have left all to perish, or he might have decreed the salvation of all. Or, he might purpose to save some, and reject others: and, so determining, he might love and save, he might condemn and punish, whom he pleased. Surely, then, it cannot be absurd in reason, or inconsistent with the Divine character, to suppose that he actually has chosen some to infinite glory, and determined to punish others according to their demerit. To acknowledge that all have sinned against God, forfeited his favour, and deserve to perish; and at the same time to suppose, that he might not leave what number he pleased to condemnation and wrath, imply a contradiction. For those who might not be rejected, whether more or fewer, must have a claim on Jehovah's favour; consequently, not justly liable to perish, which is contrary to the supposition.

It is eternally fit that God should order all things according to his own pleasure. His infinite greatness, majesty, and glory, certainly entitle him to act as an uncontrollable Sovereign, and that his will should in all things take place. He is worthy, supremely worthy, of making his own glory the end of all that he does; and that he should make nothing but the dictates of his own wisdom, and the determinations of his own will, his rule in pursuing that end, without asking leave or counsel of any creature, and without giving *an account of any of his matters*. It is quite agreeable, that He who is infinitely wise and absolutely perfect, should order all things according to his own will; even things of the greatest importance, such as the complete salvation, or the eternal damnation of sinners. It is right that He should thus be sovereign, because he is the first, the eternal Being, and the fountain of existence. He is the Creator of all things, and they are universally dependent upon him; it is, therefore, entirely consistent with his character, that he should act as the Sovereign Lord of heaven and earth.

If the objection under consideration were founded in truth, God could not exercise mercy in his own right, nor would the blessings of grace be his own to give. For that of which he may not dispose as he pleases, is not his own, he cannot make a present of it to any of his creatures, they having a claim upon it; for it is absurd to talk of *giving* to any one that to which he had a right in equity. But what would this objection make of God? Must the High and Lofty One be so circumscribed in the exercise of his grace, that he cannot manifest it at his own pleasure in bestowing his gifts; but if he dispense them to one, must be obliged to give them to another, or be obnoxious to the charge of partiality and cruelty? Shocking to think! The very thought is blasphemy. This impious imagination arises, absurd as it is, from the high opinion we form of ourselves, and the diminutive thoughts we entertain of our Maker.

But why should the objector be so much concerned about the honour of Divine justice, in the conduct of God toward mankind, on supposition that he has chosen some and rejected others? Why should he not be as much concerned lest the glory of his Maker should suffer a stain, by the final rejection of all the angels that sinned and fell from their first estate? Certainly, there is equal, if not superior reason. Why, then, does he not plead the cause of those old apostates, those damned spirits, and quarrel with God because he hath shown more regard to fallen men than to fallen angels? Yet he is under no pain on their account; nor does he suspect that the Divine character will lose any part of its glory, because they are all, without one exception, the objects of Jehovah's eternal vengeance—but, very likely, he concludes that *they* deserve to be damned. True: and is it not so with men? If not—how shall I speak it? the law of God is unrighteous, for it denounces damnation as the desert of sin: the vicarious death of Christ was an unnecessary and shocking event; the capital parts of the Bible are unworthy of the least regard, and the distinguishing doctrines of Christianity are no better than a dream, a fable—a gross imposition on all who believe them. Without admitting this fundamental truth, that men, considered as guilty creatures, *deserve to perish forever;* we can behold neither equity in the law, nor grace in the gospel. The eternal rectitude of the great Lawgiver, and the amiable glories of the wonderful Saviour, are quite obscured; while the whole economy of redemption, as revealed in Scripture, is thrown into the utmost confusion. Consequently, the objector has no alternative, but either to give up his point, or blaspheme his Maker.

The truth maintained may now be considered by way of improvement, as it respects the careless sinner and the real Christian.—As it respects the *careless sinner.* Is this your character, reader? If so, it is happily adapted to strike your conscience and alarm your fears; to arouse your lethargic soul, and awaken your inquiries after eternal blessedness. You have seen that it is a righteous thing with God, to execute justice on all who are guilty; and that, if he had left all mankind to perish, none would have had any reason to complain. Now, though he has, of his mere goodness, chosen a number of the fallen race, and determined to bring them to glory; yet millions are left to suffer the awful desert of their crimes. How, then, do you know but this may be your case? Remember, thoughtless mortal! that if you be rejected of God, you are lost forever. And are you still unconcerned about your soul? then the sentence of a broken law, and the wrath of an awful Judge, abide upon you. You are in the hands of an offended God, and, shocking to think! you are at a dreadful uncertainty what he will do with you. You are, it may be, sometimes afraid what will become of you; afraid lest you should have your portion in the lake which burns with fire and brimstone. Yes, and be it known to you, that while you are habitually careless about your eternal interests, and a lover of pleasure more than a lover of God, you have reason to fear. Your apprehensions of eternal punishment have a real foundation. You have reason to tremble every moment. But you will do well to remember, that though you be ever so much afraid of the final event; though everlasting damnation be ever so dreadful, yet it is what you have deserved. Your injured Maker and affronted Sovereign may inflict it upon you, and be righteous, and holy, and glorious in it. However dreadful it now is, in your apprehension; or however intolerable it would be to you in the execution; yet, in regard to God, neither the one nor the other can render it the less righteous. You should remember, sinner, that your Maker sustains the character of a universal Sovereign, and of a righteous Judge. His honour, therefore, is deeply concerned in punishing the guilty. Though damnation be worse than the loss of being, yet you have no reason to complain of injustice; except you can form a perfect estimate of what degree of guilt attends innumerable acts of rebellion against unlimited authority, infinite majesty, and boundless perfection, and, upon a just comparison of the degree of guilt, with the intenseness and duration of the punishment, pronounce them unequal. But who can tell to what an enormous height the guilt of one single act of rebellion against infinite Majesty must arise in the boundless empire of God? We may boldly affirm, that none but the omniscient—none but he who is possessed of that peerless majesty, can solve the question. Meditate on these awful truths; and may the Lord enable you to *flee from the wrath to come!**

Does my reader profess to believe and embrace this divine truth? Has he tasted that the Lord is gracious and is he a *real Christian?* This doctrine informs him whence his happiness flows, and to whom the glory is due. Hence he learns, that grace is an absolute sovereign; that she dispenses her favours to whomsoever she pleases, without being subject to the least control. Here she appears, maintaining her rights and asserting her honours, with a grandeur becoming herself. Yes, reader, this doctrine presents you with GRACE ON THE THRONE; while, as an herald, with a friendly importunity and a commanding voice, it cries in your ear, BOW THE KNEE! And as this doctrine presents you with a view of grace in its sovereign glory; so it points out the objects of eternal love as in a state of the utmost security. For *who shall lay any thing to the charge of God's elect?* To know your interest in the election of grace, is therefore a matter of great importance: and that such knowledge is attainable, is evident from that exhortation of the Holy Ghost: *Give all diligence to make your calling and election sure;* sure to your own mind, and satisfactory to your own conscience. That such a persuasion, grounded on truth, is intimately connected with a Christian's peace and joy, is beyond a doubt. Nor is there any other diffi-

---

* Hence it appears, that as the doctrine of God's general and equal love to mankind, and the sentiment of universal redemption, are too evidently calculated to lull the conscience asleep, under a false presumption of interest in the Redeemer and of happiness by him, where there is no evidence of love to God and his ways; so the doctrine of distinguishing grace, and of the Mediator's substitution in the stead of his chosen seed, has an obvious tendency to alarm the careless sinner and to awaken the drowsy formalist.

culty in attaining the certainty, than what attends a well-founded persuasion of our being called by grace. Whoever has reason to conclude that he is called by the gospel and converted to Christ, may, from the very same premises, infer his election. For none but those that were chosen to life and happiness are born of God, or believe in Christ. If then you espouse the doctrine, you should not be satisfied with merely avowing the sentiment as an article of your belief; but should consider it as a truth according to godliness, and seek the advantage resulting from it. For you will find it of little avail, that you have adopted the sentiment into your theological system, if you experience no benefit from it, in a way of humility and love, of consolation and joy. Viewed in such a connexion with experimental religion, you should meditate on it: considered as thus important, you should endeavour to vindicate it from the hateful charges of the sons of pride.

Are you, on divine authority, not only convinced that the doctrine is true, but also persuaded of your interest in the love it reveals? Remember the exalted privileges to which you are chosen. Chosen you are, to a participation of grace, with all its immense donations to the fruition of glory, with all its eternal felicity. Regeneration, justification, adoption, sanctification, and perseverance in faith; these, Christian, with all that inconceivable bliss which results from the enjoyment of God himself, are the blessings designed for you in the decree of election. Surely, then, with such blessings in hand, and such prospects in view, it is but reasonable that you should be entirely devoted to God, and live his obedient servant. If gratitude have any persuasive energy, or if love have any constraining influence, here they should operate with all their force. Henceforth the glory of God and the honour of that adorable Person, by whose mediation you come to enjoy these wonderful favours, should be your main concern, and the end of all your actions. Remember the honourable character conferred upon you in the sacred writings. Among those names of distinction which the people of God bear, that of *the elect* is none of the least remarkable. Of this character the Spirit of wisdom reminds believers, when he urges upon them the duties to which they are called. *Ye are a chosen generation, a peculiar people.* Would we know to what end they are chosen, and why they are a people distinguished from others, as God's peculiar property? the following words inform us. *That ye should show forth the praises of Him, who,* as a fruit of his electing love, *hath called you out of darkness into his marvellous light.* Here is the Christian's duty in general, and to perform it should be his constant business: for he was *chosen in Christ, that he might be holy and without blame before him in love.*

Or, is my reader one of those to whom the remark would be applicable; " This man entertains high notions in religion, and pretends to sublime attainments in knowledge. *Eternal* purposes and *absolute* sovereignty, *unchangeable* love, and *distinguishing* grace, are his favourite topics : yet he lives in open neglect of the plainest precepts, and of the most important duties. While pride and covetousness, wrath and malice, with various other unsanctified tempers, govern his conduct and render him a scandal to Christianity." The very thought of such a reflection is grieving to godly persons : for lamentable is the state of that professor to whom it may be justly applied! You may dispute as long as you please, in vindication of divine sovereignty in the affairs of grace ; but it will be to little purpose, as to yourself. Because it is plain that you are an enemy in your heart, and a rebel in your life against that infinite Sovereign whose rights you pretend to maintain. By such a neglect of his precepts and such a transgression of his laws, you virtually deny his absolute authority, and renounce his supreme dominion. Sinful appetites are the law you obey, and carnal pleasure the end you pursue ; while your Maker and Lord has neither the affection of your heart, nor the service of your hands. May that omnipotent, sovereign grace, of which you talk without any experience, deliver and save your sinking soul! For, verily, it would be hard to find a more shocking character out of hell.

CHAPTER IV.

OF GRACE, AS IT REIGNS IN OUR EFFECTUAL CALLING.

We have seen in the preceding chapter, that grace presided in the eternal counsels, and reigned as an absolute sovereign in the decree of election. Let us now consider the same glorious grace, as exerting its benign influence in the regeneration and *effectual calling* of all that shall ever be saved. Election makes no alteration in the real state of its objects. For, as they were considered, in that gracious purpose, in a sinful, dying condition; so they continue in that situation, till the energy of the Holy Spirit, and the power of evangelical truth, reach their hearts. The means being decreed as well as the end, it is absolutely necessary, to accomplish the great design of election, that all the chosen in their several generations, should be born of the Spirit and converted to Jesus; called of God, and bear his image.

That important change which takes place in the mind and views of a sinner, when converted to Christ, is frequently signified in the infallible word, by being *called of God; called by grace; called by the gospel.* In performing this work of heavenly mercy, the eternal Spirit is the grand agent, and evangelical truth the honoured instrument. Are men, in their natural state, considered as asleep in sin and dead to God? when they are called, their minds are enlightened, and spiritual life is communicated. The Spirit of God, speaking to the conscience by the truth, quickens the dead sinner, shows him his awful state, and alarms his fears. *The dead shall hear the voice of the Son of God, and they that hear shall live—Awake thou that sleepest.* Are they considered as having departed from God, and at a distance from him; in the way of destruction, yet afraid to return? then the language of the gospel is, *Return to the Lord, and he will have mercy upon you; and to our God, for he will abundantly pardon. Him that cometh to me, I will in no wise cast out.* Such a revelation of grace being made in the gospel, and such invitations being addressed to perishing sinners, the Spirit of truth in effectual calling gives them encouragement from these declarations to return to God, and enables them to look for salvation from the hand of Him against whom they have sinned, and from whom they have so deeply revolted. Such, in a general view, is the nature of, that heavenly blessing which is the subject of our present inquiry.

That any sinner is *called out of darkness into marvellous light*, is entirely owing to divine grace. *God called me by his grace*, is the language of Paul ; nor do the saints ascribe their conversion to any other cause. Man, being by nature dead in sin, unacquainted with its evil, and elated with a fond conceit of his own abilities ; looks upon his offences against God, rather as pitiable failings than shocking crimes. He extenuates his faults, and magnifies his duties. He depreciates the work of Christ, and relies on his own supposed good performances. Being entirely ignorant of his moral weakness, the total corruption of his nature, and the extensive demands of divine law ; he endeavours, if at all concerned about his soul, to establish his own righteousness, as the principal ground of his acceptance with the high and holy God. He trusts in some general mercy, to be exercised toward him through Jesus Christ, to make up the deficiencies attending his own sincere attempts to perform his duty. In case of a relapse into open and scandalous offences, he flatters himself with the hopes of pardon, and of having an interest in the love of God, if he do but forsake his past transgressions, be sorry for them, and amend his ways for the future. This, he thinks, is the obvious and easy way of placating an offended God, and of obtaining the divine favour. On such a sandy foundation are the hopes of men commonly built. Thus we lie, asleep in sin, and dreaming of happiness ; on the verge of a dreadful precipice, yet unapprehensive of danger, till reigning grace exerts her influence to recover us from our native ruin.

But when the Spirit of God convinces of sin by the holy law, and manifests its extensive demands to the conscience of a sinner; when he is informed that every sin subjects the offender to a dreadful curse; then his fears are alarmed and his endeavours are quickened. Being aroused from his spiritual slumber, he is more earnest and punctual in the performance of religious duties, in endeavours after holiness, and in the pursuit of happiness. He is not content with that careless and superficial way of performing devotional services, which before satisfied his conscience and gratified his pride. For now, guilt burdens his soul, and conscience sharpens her sting; while the terrors of the Almighty seem to be set in array against him. The duties he has neglected, the mercies he has abused, and the daring acts of rebellion he has committed against his divine Sovereign, crowd in upon his mind and rack his very soul. The justice of the Lawgiver appears ready to vindicate the law, as holy and good; and, like an incensed adversary, unsheaths the sword and makes a loud demand for vengeance. In such a situation, he cannot but earnestly seek to escape impending ruin. But yet, his heart being deeply leavened with legal pride, and unacquainted with the divine righteousness, he labours to obtain salvation, *as it were, by the works of the law.* When, by the Spirit and word of truth, he is further made sensible of his natural depravity, and of the defects attending his best performances; when he considers how very imperfect they shall appear in his own eye, and that a perfect righteousness is absolutely necessary to his acceptance with the eternal Judge; then his hopes of salvation by his own obedience vanish, and his apprehensions of eternal punishment increase. Thus, *when the law comes*, shining in its purity and operating on his conscience with power, *sin is revived;* a sense of deserved wrath possesses the soul, and his former self-righteous hopes expire.

He now reflects on his past ignorance and pharisaica pride, with the greatest amazement and the deepest self-abhorrence. However reluctant, he is obliged to give up his former exalted notions of his own moral excellence;

and is compelled, with the polluted leper, to cry, *Unclean! unclean!* Now he perceives a propriety, now he feels an energy in those emphatical Scripture phrases, which describe the state of a natural man, by a filthy sow wallowing in the mire ; by a dog in love with his vomit ; and by an open sepulchre emitting the abhorred stench of a putrefying carcass. These objects, he is fully convinced, are infinitely less offensive to the most delicate person and the keenest sense, than that moral pollution is, which, in the sight of an holy God, has defiled his whole soul. Now he freely acknowledges, that what he used to look upon as trivial offences, are shocking crimes. He is thoroughly convinced that the various transgressions of his life, however vile and enormous, are so many streams from a corrupt fountain within ; that they proceed from a desperately wicked heart. He is amazed, he is confounded, when he reflects on his inbred corruptions, and views his native depravity. His eyes being opened to behold the spirituality and vast extent of the divine law, he considers his whole life as one continued scene of iniquity. For instead of living every moment of his time in the uninterrupted and most fervent love of God, as the law requires ; he finds, to his grief and shame, that he has lived in the love of self and sin ; self-love having been his law; self-pleasing all his end. Viewing the holy law as a transcript of divine purity, he plainly sees that he is no less obliged to love God with all the powers of his soul, for the sake of his infinite excellencies, than he is to avoid the horrid crimes of murder and adultery. In a word, he considers himself as the *chief of sinners.* The sentence of the law, though terrible to the last degree, he allows to be just. The execution of it he cannot but dread ; yet from his heart he acquits both the law and the lawgiver of any unrighteous severity, though he never should taste of mercy. His language is, The law is just, and death is my due.

Methinks I behold the awakened sinner, sobbing with anguish and bathed in tears ; fixed in thought and indulging reflection about his state and his danger. "The law, how holy, which I have transgressed! the curse, how awful, that I have incurred! My crimes, how numerous! Their aggravations, how dreadful! How ineffably wretched my state! for my soul, my immortal *all*, is in the utmost jeopardy. What shall I do? Whither shall I flee for refuge? Shall I look for relief to carnal enjoyments and sinful pleasures? Shall I quaff the sparkling bowl, or frequent the circles of polite amusement? Such a procedure would enhance my guilt and increase my torment; would be like seeking an asylum in hell. Shall I plead with my Sovereign and Judge, that I have not been so wicked as others? But how shall I prove the fact? or if I could, the debtor that owes but fifty pence, having nothing to pay, is equally obnoxious to an arrest and a prison, with one that owes five hundred. For Jehovah declares, *Cursed is every one that continueth not in* ALL *things which are written in the book of the law to do them.* But have I performed no good works, nor any obedience, from which I may extract some comfort, on which I may build my hope of acceptance? Here, alas, I am entirely destitute. Conscious I am, that I have not loved God, that I have not sought his glory; and without these there is no acceptable obedience. My very prayers need an atonement, and my tears want washing. Shall I promise amendment, and vow reformation, if He, to whom I have forfeited my life, will be pleased to spare it? Shall I say, with him, in the parable that owed ten thousand talents, *Have patience with me, and I will pay thee all?* This would be an evidence of superlative pride, and an instance of the greatest folly. My debt, like his, is enormous; and would my Creator compound for the widow's two mites, I should still be insolvent. I now find by experience that I am utterly without strength. But supposing I possessed abilities, and were to perform a perfect obedience in future; this would make no amends for my past transgressions: the old and heavy score would still stand against me. Had my offences been committed against a fellow-creature, I might possibly have been able to make compensation. But they are against my Maker; to whom I owe my time and talents; all that I have and all that I am. *If one man sin against another, the judge shall judge him: but if a man sin against the Lord, who shall entreat for him;* or how shall the offender atone for his crime? It is the infinite JEHOVAH against whom I have sinned: it is the eternal Sovereign of all worlds against whom I have rebelled. Who, then shall entreat for me! Yes, I have trampled on infinite authority. The language of my stubborn heart and abominable conduct has been, *Who is the Lord, that I should obey him?* As the universal Governor, I have renounced his dominion, and seated self on the throne; as my constant Benefactor, I have abused his mercies to his dishonour. Infinitely perfect and supremely amiable as he is in himself, I have neither loved nor adored him: I have treated him as though he deserved neither affection nor reverence. I have—shocking impiety!—I have preferred the vilest lusts, and the gratification of the worst appetites, to his honour and service. How have I neglected the divine word and sacred worship? I have treated the Bible as if it were not worthy of a serious perusal, and in so doing have been a practical Deist. The assemblies of the saints, my closet, my conscience, all bear testimony against me, that I have lived, as *without God in the world.* Or, if at any time I have attended religious worship in public or private, how have I mocked my Maker? I have behaved myself in his awful presence, as though he had been a senseless idol; one who neither knew nor cared how he was worshipped. When I pretended to acknowledge my sins, my confessions froze on my formal lips: and if I asked for heavenly blessings, it was as though I had little or no necessity for them. With delight and avidity I have pursued transitory pleasures and vicious enjoyments; but as to the worship of God, I have been ready to cry, *O, what a weariness is it!* I have said to God, it has been the language of my heart and conduct, *Depart from me; for I desire not the knowledge of thy ways. What is the Almighty, that I should serve him? and what profit shall I have if I pray to him?* Can I doubt, then, can I question for a single moment, whether I deserve to die, deserve to be damned? DAMNED! dreadful punishment! Imagination recoils at the thought. The idea chills my blood. Heaven avert the impending, the righteous vengeance! But God is just; and justice requires that sin should not escape with impunity. Does it not follow, then, that my eternal misery is inevitable? In what other way can the rights of the Godhead, the honour of divine holiness, truth, and justice be maintained? If no other way can be found, wretch that I am! I am lost forever." Thus he lies at the feet of sovereign mercy.

As a rebel against the Majesty of heaven, and conscious that he deserves to perish, he lies deep in the dust of self-abasement, and low at the footstool of divine grace. But his ALL being at stake for eternity, and not being sunk into absolute despair, he ventures to address the blessed God; being well persuaded that if his request be granted and his person accepted, his soul shall live; and that if his prayer be rejected, and his person abhorred, he can but die. With trembling hands and a throbbing heart; with downcast looks and faltering lips, he therefore thus proceeds: " Offended Sovereign! I am justly under sentence of death, and should I eternally perish, yet thou art righteous. My mouth must be stopped: I have no right to complain. But is there nothing in thy revealed character that may encourage a miserable creature and a guilty criminal, to look for mercy and hope for acceptance? Art thou not a compassionate Saviour, as well as a just God? Is not Jesus thy only Son, and hast thou not set him forth as a *propitiation through faith in his blood?* To Him, therefore, as my only asylum from divine wrath, I would flee. Yet if repulsed, I dare not, I cannot object; for I have no claim on thy mercy. Only, if it seem good to thee to save the vilest of sinners, the most wretched of creatures; if it please thee to extend infinite mercy to one who deserves infinite misery, and is obliged to condemn himself, the greater will be the glory of thy compassion. However, as a supplicant at the throne of grace, as a perishing sinner who has no hope but in sovereign mercy and in the blood of the cross, I am resolved to wait until freely received, or absolutely rejected. If rejected, I must bear it as my just desert; if accepted, boundless grace shall have the glory.* Thus the name and the work of Jesus forbid despair, and shed a beam of hope on his benighted soul.

One would imagine that the gospel of reigning grace, that the tidings of a free Saviour and a full salvation, would be embraced with the utmost readiness by a sinner thus convinced. One would suppose that, so soon as he heard the divine report, he could not forbear exclaiming, in a transport of joy, " This is the Saviour I want! This salvation is every way suitable to my condition. Perfect in itself, and free for the unworthy sinner. Wonderful truth! Astonishing grace! What could I have, what can I desire more? Here I would rest; in this I will glory." But alas! this is not always the case. Observation and experience prove, that the awakened sinner is frequently backward, exceedingly backward, to receive comfort from the glorious gospel.

* Let none of my readers imagine that the process of conviction here described, is designed as a standard for their experience; or that I would limit the Holy One of Israel to the same way and manner of working on the minds of sinners, when he brings them to know themselves, their state, and their danger. I have no such intention; being well aware that God is a Sovereign, and acts as he pleases in this, as in all other things. For though every sinner must feel his want, before he will either seek or accept relief at the hand of grace; yet the Lord has various ways to make his people willing in the day of his power. Some he enlightens in a more gradual way, and draws them to Christ by gentler means, as it were with the cords of love: while he strikes conviction in the minds of others, as with a voice of thunder, and sudden as a flash of lightning. They are brought to the very brink of despair, and shook, as it were, over the bottomless pit. Nor have we any business to inquire into the reasons of this difference in the Divine conduct. As the Lord saves whom he will, so he may bring them to the knowledge of his salvation, in what way, and by what means he pleases. If any one doubt whether his convictions be genuine, let him remember that the questions he should ask himself, in order to attain satisfaction, are not: "How *long* did I lie under them? To what a *degree of terror* did they proceed? By *what means* were they wrought?" But, "Does it stand true in my conscience, that I have sinned and deserve to perish? Is it a fact that nothing but the *grace of* God can relieve me? These are the questions which demand his notice, and a suitable answer solves the query.

This arises, not from any defect in the grace it reveals, or in the salvation it brings; not because the sinner is under any necessity, or in any distress, for which it has not provided complete relief; but because he does not behold the glory of that grace which reigns triumphant in it, and the design of God, in making such a provision. He wants to find himself some way *distinguished*, as a proper object of mercy, by holy tempers and sanctified affections. This is a bar to his comfort, this is his grand embarrassment. In other words, he is ready to fear that he is not sufficiently humbled under a sense of sin; that he has not a suitable abhorrence of it; or, that he has not those fervent breathings after Christ and holiness which he ought to have, before he can be warranted to look for salvation with a well-grounded hope of success.* Thus the sinner, even when his conscience is oppressed with guilt, and earnestly desirous of salvation, opposes the true grace of God, by desiring some worthiness of his own. Whence it appears, that the genuine self-denial of the gospel is the hardest sacrifice to human pride.

But grace reigns. The Spirit of truth, a principal part of whose business it is, in the economy of salvation, to testify of Christ and of sovereign mercy by him; still calls the poor alarmed wretch by the gospel. Evidencing to his conscience, not only the all-sufficiency, but also the absolute freeness of the glorious Redeemer. Manifesting that there are no good qualities to be obtained; no righteous acts to be performed, either to gain

---

* Here it should be well observed, that deep distress, arising from the fear of hell, is not required of any, in order to peace with God; for such distress does not belong to the precepts of the law, but to its curse. Terrifying apprehensions of eternal punishment are no part of that which is required of sinners, but of what is inflicted on them. There is indeed an evangelical sorrow for sin, that is our duty; which is commanded, and has promises annexed to it: but legal terrors, proceeding from the curse of the law, not from its precept; expressing a sense of danger *from* the law, rather than of having done evil *against* the law; are no marks of love to God, or of an holy temper. An awakened sinner, therefore, wishing for distresses of this kind, is a person seeking the misery of unbelief, that he may obtain a permission to believe. See Dr. Owen *on the Holy Spirit*, p. 306.

an interest in him, or to qualify for him. Showing, yet further, that convictions of sin, and a sense of want, are not to be accounted conditions of our acceptance with Christ and salvation by him; nor ought they to be esteemed previously necessary to our believing in him, on any other account, than as a sensibility of our spiritual poverty and wretchedness, renders relief in a way of grace truly welcome. This is needful, not as inclining God to give, but as disposing us to receive. A sinner will neither seek nor accept the great atonement, till sensible that Divine wrath and the damnation of hell are what he deserves; and what, without the propitiation of the adorable Jesus, he must unavoidably suffer.

I take it for granted we must come to Christ under that character by which he calls us. Now, it is evident, he invites us by the name of sinners. As sinners, therefore, miserable, ruined sinners, we must come to him for life and salvation. The gospel of peace is preached to such, and them the gospel calls; even those who are not conscious that they are the objects of any good disposition. Yes, disconsolate sinner, be it known to you, be it never forgotten by you, that the gospel with all its blessings, that Christ with all his fulness, are a glorious provision made by the great Sovereign, and by grace as reigning, for the guilty and the wretched—for such as have nothing of their own on which to rely, and utterly despair of ever being able to do any thing for that purpose. The undertaking of Jesus Christ was intended for the relief of such as are ungodly, altogether miserable, and without hope in themselves. Such was the beneficent design of God, and such is the salutary genius of his gospel. Delightful, ravishing truth! enough, one would think, to make the brow of melancholy wear a smile. Let me indulge the pleasing thought, and once more express the charming idea. The blessings of grace were never designed to distinguish the worthy, or to reward merit; but to relieve the wretched and save the desperate. These—hear and rejoice!—these are the patentees in the heavenly grant. Yea, they have an exclusive right. For as to all those who imagine themselves to be the better sort of people who depend on their own duties, and plead their own worthiness; who are not willing to stand on a level with publicans and harlots; Christ has nothing to do with them, nor the gospel any thing to say to them. As they are too proud to live upon alms, or to be entirely beholden to sovereign grace for all their salvation; so they must not take it amiss if they have not the least assistance from that quarter. They appeal to the law, and by it they must stand or fall.

He, therefore, who believes in Christ, relies on him as the *justifier of the ungodly.* Nor does he consider himself in any other light, or as bearing any other character, in that very moment when he first believes on him: if he did, he could not believe on him as the justifier of such. The only encouragement a sinner has to apply to Christ for all that he wants, consists—not in a consciousness of being possessed of any pious disposition, of having come up to terms, performed any conditions, or as being any way different from what he was before—but, in that grace which reigns, and is proclaimed in the gospel. Yes; the free declarations of the gospel concerning Jesus, contain a sufficient warrant for the vilest sinner, in the most desperate circumstances, to look for relief at the hand of Christ. Such as, *I came not to call the righteous, but sinners to repentance*—*The Son of man is come to seek and to save that which was lost*—*Look unto me, and be ye saved, all the ends of the earth*—*Come unto me, all ye that labour and are heavy laden, and I will give you rest*—*Him that cometh to me, I will in no wise cast out*—*Whosoever believeth in him, shall not perish, but have eternal life.*

In these, as in similar passages of holy writ, the sinner is encouraged to look to the Lord Redeemer, with assurance that in so doing he shall not be disappointed; to look to Him; not as one whose character and state are different from those of the world in common; but as a guilty creature and ready to perish. These free declarations are founded on the glorious undertaking and finished work of Christ, who *suffered for the unjust;* who died for men, while *sinners* and *ungodly;* and who *reconciled them to God, when they were enemies.* So that *all things are now ready* for the sinner's enjoyment and happiness; here, in a life of faith and holiness; hereafter, in the fruition of glory. These divine testimonies are only a specimen of what might be produced on the occasion; and they, together with others of the same import, are the proper ground of our faith in Christ, or dependence on him, for everlasting salvation.

Hence it appears, that the sinner who is effectually called of God, is not led by the Holy Spirit to believe in a dying Redeemer under a persuasion of his being now distinguished from his ungodly neighbours and former self; or, in other words, of his being a much better man than he was before, in virtue of any good habits or qualities; nor does his comfort arise from any such supposed alteration. No: the Divine Spirit does not bear witness to our spirits, concerning our own inherent excellencies, or inform us how much we are superior to others; but, concerning the all-sufficiency, suitableness, and absolute freeness of Christ, and of all the blessings included in his mediation. The basis of a believer's hope, and the source of his spiritual joy, are—not a consciousness that he has *done* something toward his own salvation, (call it *believing*, or what you will,) but the *truth* he believes and the *Saviour* on whom he relies: which truth, possessed in the heart, is also the spring of his holiness.

A sinner being brought, under the influence of the blessed Spirit, and by the instrumentality of the gospel, to renounce every false confidence and legal hope, and, as to acceptance with the Most High, to pour contempt on every righteousness which is not in all respects perfect; leans on Christ, as the rock of ages; cleaves to him as the only hope of the guilty, and rejoices in him as *able to save to the uttermost* all, without exception, *who come to God by him.* Now a new scene of things opens to his view. He beholds with amazement how God can be just, and yet the justifier of the ungodly. The just God and the Saviour appear in the same point of light. Now the everlasting covenant unveils its infinite stores to his ravished sight, and the gospel pours its healing balm into his wounded conscience. Jesus Christ, and his righteousness, are now his only hope. He finds a sufficiency in the glorious Immanuel, not only to supply all his wants, but to make him infinitely rich, and eternally happy; and in him he rests completely satisfied. He who, but a little before, stood trembling and confounded at the tribunal of conscience; who could scarcely imagine that God would be righteous if he did not pour out his vengeance upon him; finds the work of the heavenly substitute a full vindication of the rights of justice, and an everlasting foundation for his strongest confidence. This wonderful expedient, so well adapted to glorify God and save the sinner, he beholds with astonishment, and contemplates with rapture. Yes, beholding *Grace on the throne*, he bows, adores, and rejoices. Gratitude abounds in his heart, and praise flows from his lips.

When he reflects on his present unworthiness and former state, beholding what enmity he cherished in his bosom against his Maker; when he considers how carnal his affections, how stubborn his will, how proud his heart; how often he had, in his conduct, adopted the language of those who say to the Almighty, *Depart from us; for we desire not the knowledge of thy ways;* he is amazed that he was not long since transmitted to hell. When he further considers how loth he was to acknowledge Divine sovereignty, and bow to heavenly mercy; how long he resisted the calls of Providence; how often he stifled the remonstrances of conscience; and that, if less than an infinite Agent had been employed in reducing an obstinate rebel to obedience, he had been finally obdurate and eternally miserable—when he thus reflects, he is filled with pleasing astonishment. On a comparison between what his offences deserved, and what God has bestowed, he cannot forbear exclaiming, " What hath God wrought! What a miracle of mercy !" He is convinced to a demonstration, that his *calling* must be ascribed to reigning grace. He is fully persuaded that God was the first mover in this, as well as in every other blessing bestowed, in every other benefit enjoyed or promised. When he meditates upon his calling, his language is, " I am found of Him, whom I neither loved nor sought. He is manifested to me, after whom I did not inquire." He will say, "I am *known* of God; I am *apprehended* of Christ:" rather than "I *know* God; I *apprehend* Christ."*

Thus to be called of God is an instance of reigning grace, and an evidence of distinguishing love. Happy are you, reader, if you know by experience what it is to be called by grace. If such be your state, it becomes your indispensable duty to *walk worthy of your calling*, for it is high, holy, heavenly. Yes, believer, your calling is truly noble. You are *called out of darkness into marvellous light;* and out of worse than Egyptian bondage, into the glorious liberty of the sons of God. You are called out of the world, into fellowship with Jesus Christ. Called, you are, out of a state of open rebellion against God, and painful anxiety of mind, into a state of reconciliation and friendship, of conscious peace and heavenly joy. What shall I say? you are called from the slavery of sin, to the practice of holiness; into a state of grace here, and to the enjoyment of glory hereafter. In short, it is the High God that called you; it is the way of holiness in which you are called to walk, and it is an unfading inheritance, an eternal kingdom, you are called to enjoy. Here is your blessedness, and here is your duty. The consideration of these things, as a noble incentive to obedience, should fire your mind with godly zeal; should fill your heart with Christian gratitude; should direct your feet in the paths of duty, and manifest its constraining influence through your whole conduct.

To you that are *uncalled*, what shall I say? Your state is awful. For, leaving the world in your present situation, you are lost forever; you die to eternity. For none shall be glorified hereafter, but such as are called here. If death should summons you hence, before you are converted to Christ, what will become of you? as dry stubble you must fall into the hands of Him who *is a consuming fire*. You may entirely neglect the concerns

---

* Luke xv. 4, 5   Rom. x. 20.   Gal. iv. 9.   Phil. iii. 12.

of your soul; you may, for a season, trifle with the affairs of religion, and hear the gospel with a careless indifference; but, if grace should not interpose for your rescue, dreadful will be the issue. The word of God and the gospel of Christ, will be a swift witness against you another day; will be *the savour of death unto death* to your soul: while God, even G`OD` himself, will be your eternal enemy. *Consider this, ye that forget God, lest he tear you in pieces, and there be none to deliver.*

If you attend on a preached gospel and frequent the house of God, do not take it for granted that you must needs be a Christian, because you make a public profession, and yield a cool assent to the truth. This thousands have done, this you may do, and yet perish forever. If not divorced from the law, if not renewed in your mind and enabled to believe in Christ, as a miserable helpless sinner, it will soon appear that you have only chosen a more decent, though less frequented path, to the regions of darkness; and that you are damned with the single advantage of having left a respectable character amongst your fellow-sinners. A poor compensation this for the loss of an immortal soul, and an awful issue of a religious profession! God grant it may not be the case with my reader!

Nor let any one mistake a set of evangelical notions, received by education, or imbibed under a gospel ministry, for true conversion and faith in the great Redeemer. A mistake here is fatal, and has been the ruin of multitudes. A professor may be wise in doctrinals, and able to vindicate the truth against its opposers; while his heart is entirely carnal, cold as ice, and barren as a rock. *Though I understand all mysteries and all knowledge, and have not charity*, love to God and love to his people, *I am nothing.* Vain, then, are the pretensions of all those, whatever knowledge they may have of the gospel, who live in sin, who love not God, nor seek his glory. They may shine in religious conversation; they may display their talents and feed their vanity, by defending truth and refuting error; and, conscious of superior abilities, may look down with a solemn pride on persons of meaner parts and less understanding in the doctrines of grace, but their superior knowledge will only aggravate their future wo, and render damnation itself more dreadful.

CHAPTER V.

OF GRACE, AS IT REIGNS IN A FULL, FREE, AND EVERLASTING PARDON.

PARDON of sin is a blessing of superlative worth, because absolutely necessary to present peace and future salvation. Without it, no individual of Adam's race can be happy. When the conscience of a sinner is wounded with guilt, and oppressed with fears of Divine wrath, it is sought with ardour, as the most desirable thing; it is received with joy, as the first of all favours.

But great and necessary as the blessing is, had it not been for that revelation contained in the Bible, mankind would have lain under a sad uncertainty, whether there was any such thing as *forgiveness with God*. Being conscious of guilt, yet partial in their own favour, they might have pleased themselves with conjectures, that he would not finally condemn all his offending creatures: but they could never have arrived at certainty. For by whatever medium they might have come to the knowledge of God, as the Author of nature and Sovereign of the world, by the same mean they must have known that perfection is essential to the Divine character; and, consequently, that the Deity must be infinitely opposite to moral evil. But whether such as had rebelled against their eternal Sovereign might be forgiven, consistently with his perfections and purposes, and without impeaching his honour as a righteous governor; this unassisted reason could not have determined. Under what obligations then are we laid, to adore the condescension and goodness of God, who has not left us to grope in the dark, and to form a thousand wild conjectures about an affair of such vast importance! For, possessing a divine revelation of the richest grace, we are taught with absolute certainty, that *there is forgiveness* with our Maker and Sovereign. This revelation of mercy is of great antiquity, and almost coeval with time itself. It was known to the patriarchs; it was exhibited in a clearer manner under the Mosaic economy. But, by the incarnation and work of the Son of God, it has received the highest confirmation, and shines in all its glory. Jehovah's pardoning goodness was loudly proclaimed to Moses, and makes a conspicuous figure in that sacred name, by which the God of Israel was known to the church in the wilderness: *As the Lord descended in the cloud and stood with him there, and proclaimed* THE NAME OF THE LORD. *And the Lord passed by before him, and proclaimed,* THE LORD, THE LORD GOD, *merciful and gracious, long-suffering, and abundant in goodness and truth; keeping mercy for thousands,* FORGIVING INIQUITY, TRANSGRESSION, AND SIN. Yes, to the eternal Sovereign *belong mercies and forgiveness, though we have rebelled against him.*

This capital blessing of the new covenant is represented in the book of God by many strong metaphors, and in a rich variety of language; yet all in exact correspondence to the different views which are there given of the dreadful nature and complicated evil of sin. Is the sinner described as all over *defiled*, and *loathsome* with hateful impurity? his pardon is denoted by the *perfect cleansing* of his person, and by the *covering* of all his filth.* Is he compared to a wretched *insolvent*, and his offences to a debt of *ten thousand talents?* his pardon is represented by *blotting out* of the debt, or by a *non-imputation* of it.† Is he likened to a person who labours under the weight of a *heavy burden*, that galls his shoulders and sinks his spirits? his forgiveness is represented by *lifting up*, and by removing the painful encumbrance.‡ Are his transgressions, for their nature, number, and effects, represented by *clouds;* black, lowering, low hung clouds,

---

* Psalm xiv. 3, xxxii. 1, and lxxxv. 2. 1 John i. 7. Rev. i. 5
† Psalm xxxii. 2, and li. 1. 9. Matt. xvii. 24.
‡ Psalm xxxviii. 4, and xxxii. 1. Matt. xi. 28.

that are just ready to burst in a storm and to deluge the country? his pardon is described by their *total abolition*, by *blotting them out* from the face of heaven, so that no trace of them shall be found, nor any mortal be able to tell what is become of them.* Is disobedience to the Divine law pronounced *rebellion* against the Majesty of heaven, and the sinner considered as a *convict* under the sentence of death? forgiveness consists in *reversing the sentence*, and in *remitting the penalty* due to his crimes. Under this consideration, which is the proper notion of pardon, the language of a gracious God is, *Deliver him from going down to the pit; I have found a ransom.* The Lord is pleased to represent the same invaluable blessing, by *casting our sins behind his back;* by *casting them into the depths of the sea;* by *removing them as far from us as the east is from the west;* by *remembering them no more;* and by making *scarlet* and *crimson* offences, *white as wool,* yea, *whiter than snow.*

In this forgiveness grace reigns, and the riches of grace are displayed. It is an absolutely perfect pardon; and to make it so, three things are required. It must be full, free, and everlasting. That is, it must extend to *all* sin; it must be vouchsafed without *any conditions* to be performed by the sinner; and it must be *absolutely irreversible.* But these things deserve a more particular consideration.

That forgiveness which is equal to the wants of a sinner, must be *full;* including all sins, be they ever so numerous; extending to all their aggravations, be they ever so enormous. Every sin being a transgression of Divine law, and every transgression subjecting the offender to a dreadful curse; if the guilt of every sin be not removed, if the penalty due to every sin be not remitted, the curse must fall upon us, and wrath must be our portion. Hence appears the necessity of a full pardon in order to happiness. And as it is essentially necessary, so it is granted. The Scriptures declare, that when our offended Sovereign pardons any of the human race, he forgives all

---

* Isaiah xliv. 22.

their sins. For, says the King, whose name is the LORD OF HOSTS : *I will cleanse them from* ALL *their iniquities whereby they have sinned against me: and I will pardon* ALL *their iniquities whereby they have sinned, and whereby they have transgressed against me.* Delightful declaration! To forgive sin is a Divine prerogative. None can dispense the unspeakable favour but God. This he declares he will do : and that he will not only forgive some sins, or a few, but all ; all entirely.

Let us hear another ambassador from the court of heaven. The prophet Micah, when speaking of the King Eternal, with an air of thanksgiving and of joy, declares, *He will turn again, He will have compassion upon us, He will subdue our iniquities ; and Thou wilt cast* ALL *their sins into the depths of the sea. He will turn again;* not as an incensed adversary, to execute vengeance ; but as a friend and a father to manifest his grace. Beholding with pity our miserable condition and helpless circumstances, *He will have compassion upon us;* he will relieve our distress, and richly supply our various wants. As disobedience is the cause of all our misery, and that abominable thing which he detests, *He will subdue our stubborn iniquities;* he will remove their guilt by atoning blood, and annul their dominion by victorious grace. *And* as a further expression of pardoning love, *Thou wilt cast*, not a few, or the greater part only, but ALL *their sins into the depths of the sea.* Their sins, as a burden too heavy for them to bear, as an object too hateful for thee to behold, thou wilt forever remove from them, forever cast out of thy sight. Here the fulness and the perpetuity of Divine forgiveness are expressed with all the force of language. Another infallible writer expresses the glorious truth, and celebrates the ineffable blessing, in language of exultation. To hear his words is delightful ; to partake in his joy is transporting. *Bless the Lord, O my soul, and all that is within me, bless his holy name—Who forgiveth* ALL *thine iniquities, who healeth* ALL *thy diseases.* Such is his language, and such the ground of his exuberant joy : and a solid foundation it is for incessant thanksgiving. For when, and to whomsoever, God pardoneth sin, he so forgives it, that, as to the eye of his vindictive justice, he *sees it no more;* there is *none to be found* that can be charged upon them.* Hence there is no condemnation to such persons.

This forgiveness is worthy of God, and suitable to the chief of sinners. Proceeding from sovereign grace, it reaches the foulest crimes and the most abominable transgressions. By this gracious pardon, scarlet and crimson sins are made *white as wool,* yea, *whiter than snow.* The bloody sins of Manasseh; the madness of rage in a persecuting Saul; the bitter taunts of the thief against the Son of God, when both were in their expiring moments; and the sin of crucifying the Lord of glory; these, all these, with their various and horrid aggravations, have been pardoned. These, though inconceivably heinous, and some of them such as were never committed, either before or since, have been forgiven by a gracious God. The blood of Christ is possessed of infinite energy, arising from the superlative dignity of Him who shed it, and is able to *cleanse from all sin.* From each sin, be it ever so heinous; from all sins, be they ever so numerous. Thus grace, like a mighty and compassionate monarch, passes an act of oblivion on millions and millions of the most aggravated offences and complicated crimes.

Did the most abandoned profligates know what forgiveness there is with God, they would no longer be held by the devil under that injurious persuasion and fatal snare, *There is no hope.* Nor would they form the rash conclusion, *We have loved strangers, and after them will we go.*†—JEHOVAH is the God of pardon. This is his name and this is his glory.‡ For thus saith the Lord, *I will pardon all their iniquities—and it shall be to me a* NAME OF JOY, A PRAISE, AND AN HONOUR, *before all the nations of the earth,* and all the angels in heaven, *which shall hear of all the* superlative *good that I do unto them.*§ Astonishing words! The Sovereign of all worlds

---

* Num. xxiii. 21. Jer. l. 20. Rom. viii. 33. † Jer. ii. 25.
‡ Exod. xxxiv. 6, 7. Neh. ix. 17. § Jer. xxxiii. 8, 9

seems to glory in pardoning mercy, as one of the brightest jewels in his own eternal crown. Well, therefore, might the church cry out in a transport of joy, *who is a God like unto thee? that pardoneth iniquity* of the most complicated and shocking kind ; *and passeth by*, with the utmost readiness, *the transgression of the remnant of his heritage? He retaineth not his anger forever;* and the glorious reason is, a reason which ought never to be forgotten, *because he* DELIGHTETH *in mercy.**

Come, then, poor trembling sinner! though conscious that the number and magnitude of your sins are inexpressibly great : come, let us reason together, and contemplate the riches of grace. What though you are by nature an apostate creature and a child of wrath; though you have, by innumerable transgressions, violated the law of God and incurred its everlasting curse; though you are grown hoary in rebellion against your divine Sovereign, and look upon yourself as a monster of iniquity; though your sins of heart, of lip, and life; sins of omission, and sins of commission ; sins of ignorance, and sins against knowledge; like an armed host in terrible array besiege you on every side, and call aloud for vengeance on your guilty head ; though, to heighten your misery, the enemy of mankind should come in like a flood, and load you with horrid accusations ; should tell you that, by your offences, you have dared God's vengeance to his face, and solemnly mocked him in your duties ; and so set a keener edge on all your sensations of guilt; and, to complete your distress, though your own conscience turn evidence against you, ratify the dreadful verdict, and pronounce the deserved sentence, so that you are ready to conclude you are almost a damned soul, and that *your* case is absolutely desperate ; yet still there is relief to be had. Notwithstanding all these deplorable circumstances, there is no reason to sink in despair. For, behold! there is full forgiveness with God ; and such is his mercy, *he waits to be gracious* in bestowing the invaluable blessing. As he never confers the favour on ac-

---

* Micah vii. 18.

count of any thing amiable in the object, so he never withholds it, on account of any peculiar aggravations in the sinner's conduct or character. To dispute this, is to deny that salvation is by grace. Divine mercy is not conditional, narrow, or limited; not like that which is exercised by men, backward to interpose, till something inviting appear in its object. No; it is divinely sovereign, and absolutely free.

Consider, O disconsolate soul! how many millions now inhabit the regions of immortal purity and exult in bliss, that were once loathsome with sin, and laden with guilt; pressed with fears, and ready to sink in despair; in a word, altogether as abominable and wretched as you can possibly be. Reflect a moment, and see whether you cannot find, among those *spirits of the just made perfect*, such as were by nature the same, and before mercy was showed, no better by practice than yourself. There you will find that adept in every kind of wickedness, the idolatrous and bloody Manasseh.* There you may see the perfidious Peter; the man who, contrary to the dictates of his conscience, to the warnings of his Master, and to his own most solemn protestations, denied, with oaths and curses,† his Lord and Saviour. There you may behold many of the profligate Corinthians; persons that were once a reproach to their country, and a scandal to human nature. While near to the Son of God, and seated on thrones of bliss, you cannot but behold many of those Jerusalem sinners, who imbrued their hands in the blood of our divine Lord. These make a distinguished figure among the shining hosts; the very thought of which must revive the heart of a drooping sinner. In a word, there you will see sinners of every sort and of every size. So that, be your sins like a debt of millions of talents; be they more in number than the stars in the firmament, and heavier than the sand of the sea; yet this *full* forgiveness superabounds. Let this be your rest and this your joy, that grace reigns in the pardon of all sin.

The next requisite in a complete pardon is, that it be

* 2 Kings xxi. 2 Chron. xxxiii. † Mark xiv. 71.

free; or, in other words, not vouchsafed on any conditions to be performed by the sinner. In regard to Christ, our surety, the pardon of any, even the least offence, was suspended on the performance of the most dreadful conditions and the hardest terms. The terms, the conditions were, his incarnation, his most perfect obedience to the divine law, and subjection to the most infamous death of the cross. As to Christ our substitute, blood was the rigorous condition; blood was the dreadful demand; even the pouring out of *his own blood* was the righteous requisition of Divine justice. For *without shedding of blood,* even the blood of the Prince of life and Lord of glory, *there is no remission* of any offences. The atonement of our glorious High-Priest is that which satisfies the claims of justice, which procures the pardon of sin, and pacifies the consciences of men when pained with a sense of guilt.

This forgiveness is, notwithstanding, absolutely free to the pardoned sinner. It is dispensed according to the riches of divine mercy, and is received in a way of grace. As it is written, *We have redemption through his blood, even the forgiveness of sins, according to the riches of his grace.* The death of Christ is the meritorious cause, and the glory of God is the ultimate end that Jehovah has in view when he bestows the blessing. *God for Christ's sake hath forgiven you—I, even I, am he, that blotteth out thy transgressions for my own sake.* The last passage is so remarkably apposite that I cannot forbear transcribing it more at large. *But thou hast not called upon me, O Jacob; but thou hast been weary of me, O Israel. Thou hast not brought me the small cattle of thy burnt-offerings, neither hast thou honoured me with thy sacrifices. I have not caused thee to serve with an offering, nor wearied thee with incense. Thou hast brought me no sweet cane with money, neither hast thou filled me with the fat of thy sacrifices: but thou hast made me to serve with thy sins, thou hast wearied me with thine iniquities.* After such a heavy charge; rather, after such a complication of charges exhibited against them, who could expect but the next words would flash vengeance, and denounce utter destruction ? But, lo !—rejoice, O ye heavens ! and shout for joy, O ye children of men !—every syllable is balm, every word teems with consolation. JEHOVAH speaks ; let the worst of sinners attend and hear ! *I, whom thou hast so notoriously offended, even I am he that blotteth out thy transgressions;* not because thou art humble, or any way qualified for mercy, but *for mine* OWN SAKE ; to demonstrate the riches of my grace, and to display the glory of all my perfections. *And* so fully and effectually shall this be done, that *I will not remember thy sins* any more.—Here we have the apostle's declaration finely exemplified ; *Where sin abounded, grace did much more abound.* In the instance before us, we behold a people, highly favoured of the Lord, neglecting his positive appointments, though easy to be performed ; we behold them *restraining prayer before God*, and quite weary of his worship. Yea, we hear their Sovereign complain that they have caused him to serve with their sins, and wearied him with their multiplied crimes ; and yet these impious wretches are pardoned. Amazing mercy ! Sin abounds like a flood, but grace abounds like an ocean. If pardon thus circumstanced be not absolutely free, in respect of the criminal, I think it would puzzle the most fruitful invention to contrive a form of words to express any such a thing.

The Spirit of inspiration, speaking by the same prophet in another place, declares, *For the iniquity of his covetousness was I wroth and smote him; I hid me and was wroth, and he went on frowardly in the way of his heart.* What expedient does the Lord try next? Since these milder methods did not reclaim the obstinate, rebellious, covetous wretch, it might naturally be expected that God would proceed immediately to lay on severer strokes, and to make him feel the vengeance of his lifted arm. But reigning grace does wonders, such wonders as will fill heaven with hallelujahs to all eternity. *I have seen his ways,* says the Lord. Surely, then, he will teach him not to offend any more, by inflicting an awful punishment, and by making him a signal example of avenging justice! Such would be the determination and conduct of men, in dealing with a stubborn, yet impotent adversary. But Jehovah's methods of reclaiming offenders, and of softening the hearts of his hardened enemies, are not like ours; they are in a peculiar manner his *own*, and highly becoming himself. He adds—(amazingly gracious indeed!)—he adds, *and will heal him* of these his inveterate maladies. *I will* pardon all his offences, and *lead him also* in the ways of obedience. *And*, having shown him the infinite evil of his former conduct, and possessed his heart of godly sorrow, I will *restore comforts unto him, and to* all *his mourners*. A gloriously free pardon indeed! Here grace takes the rebels in hand; and what is the consequence? Why, their spiritual diseases are healed; their crying sins are pardoned; the sons of Belial are reduced to obedience, and made partakers of heavenly joy.

Let us now consider some few of those eminent and everlasting monuments of grace as it reigns in the free pardon of sin, that stand recorded in the New Testament. Saul, afterward called Paul, was a barbarous persecutor of the children of God. The sacred historian informs us, that his rancorous heart *breathed out threatenings and slaughter* against the saints of the Most High. Had it been in his power, he would have dealt destruction among the Christians by every breath he drew. Would you see a further description of his malice and rage against the peaceful and holy disciples of Jesus? Would you behold this tiger in human form pursuing and devouring the innocent lambs of Christ, to the utmost extent of his power? then read the following words: *I punished them oft in every synagogue, and compelled them to blaspheme. And, being* EXCEEDINGLY MAD *against them, I persecuted them even unto strange cities*. Is it possible for words to express a more diabolical temper, or a more savage barbarity? What had the objects of his implacable fury done, that he became so highly incensed against them? The grand offence was, they loved our Lord, and owned him for the true Messiah. For this he stirred up all his rage, and would not suffer them to live. He might well acknowledge, when he came to his right mind, *I was a blasphemer, a persecutor, and injurious.* Yet this man, than whom none can be greate enemies to God, none more vile or unworthy, this butcher of the members of Christ, *obtained mercy.* On a sudden, when his thoughts were big with slaughter, and his heart thirsting for blood ; when he was aiming, if possible, to extirpate the Christian character, and cause the remembrance of a crucified Messiah to cease from the earth; even *that* was the time the persecuted Saviour chose to manifest his love to him. He was powerfully struck with conviction, called by grace, pardoned and justified, and became an heir of eternal salvation. Nor was he required to perform any condition, as in the least entitling to these blessings, or as qualifying for them. Is it recorded of him, that he was *exceedingly mad* against the Christians ? His own pen has informed us, that the grace of our Lord was *exceeding abundant* toward him. So that though *sin abounded, grace did much more abound.*

But some, perhaps, may be inclined to think, that the grace exercised toward Paul was as extraordinary as the means of his conversion were miraculous. Let the apostle himself determine the case. He says, *For this cause I obtained mercy, that*—what ? That I might appear as a singular instance of Divine mercy ? that I might enjoy a favour not vouchsafed to any of my fellow-sinners ? No ; but *that in me first, Jesus Christ might show forth all long-suffering,* FOR A PATTERN *to them who should hereafter believe on him to life everlasting.** Hence it is plain, that the long-suffering and grace, which were manifested in the pardon and salvation of Saul the persecutor, are to be considered, not as a particular instance of sovereign bounty, rarely, if ever, to be repeated, but as the very *exemplar* of what should be showed to millions and millions of transgressors in succeeding ages— even to all who should afterward believe on Christ to life eternal.†

* 1 Tim. i. 15. Eph. ii. 6, 7.

† That lively and evangelical writer, Hervey, when treating on the conversion of Paul, expresses himself in the following manner : " Ob

The case of Zaccheus the publican, of the Samaritan woman, and of the Philippian jailer, loudly attests the glorious truth for which I am pleading. Zaccheus was chief among the publicans, and, it is highly probable, was not the least among the extortioners. Among his neighbours, his employment was detestable, his character profligate, and his company scandalous. That his em-

serve this man. in his unconverted state. He *breathes out threatenings and slaughter* against the Christians. Can any thing denote a more iniquitous and savage temper? The roaring lion and the raging bear are gentle creatures, compared with this monster in human shape.— Still the description of this barbarity heightens. *I was exceedingly mad against them. I compelled them to blaspheme; and punished them in every synagogue.* The practice, not of a man, but of a fiend! 'Tis the very picture of an incarnate devil.—What has this infernal wretch that may recommend him to the Divine favour? If ever there was a sinner on earth, that had sinned beyond the reach of mercy, beyond the possibility of pardon, surely it must be this Saul of Tarsus.

"But the Divine mercy, disdaining all limits, is overflowing and unmeasurable. Where sin has abounded like a flood, Divine mercy abounds like an ocean. The favour of man is backward to interpose till something amiable and inviting appears in the object. But the grace of God is immensely rich and infinitely free. It prevents the most vile and hardened rebels. It brings every requisite and recommendation, in its own unspeakably beneficent nature. It accomplishes all its blessed ends, not by any towardly disposition in the sinner, but by that one glorious righteousness provided in the Saviour.—This overtook the persecutor on his journey to Damascus. Light and life were poured upon him, not from any dawn of reformation in himself, but from a very different quarter. By opening, as it were, a window in heaven, while he was sojourning even in the suburbs of hell. *He saw that* Just One. He received the inestimable gift. He was made partaker of the salvation which is in Jesus Christ.

"See, now, what an effect this faith has upon his conduct. It causes a total revolution in the sentiments of his mind. It gives a new bias to every faculty of his soul. It introduces an absolute change into the whole tenor of his behaviour. As great and marvellous a change, as if you should behold some mighty torrent, turned by the shock of an earthquake; and rolling those waters to the east, which, from the beginning of time, had flowed incessantly to the west. He adores that Jesus whom he lately blasphemed. He preaches that faith which he once destroyed. And he is ready to lay down his life for those believers whom, not long ago, he persecuted unto death." *Theron and Aspasio,* vol. iii. p. 233, 234. edit. 5th.

ployment was detestable, none can doubt. That his character was profligate, appears from hence. The office of *chief among the publicans*, was what no son of Abraham, who had not lost his reputation, or who was not of an abandoned, shameless character, would undertake. And that his company was esteemed scandalous, is evident from that keen reflection upon the conduct of Jesus, when he became a guest at his table. *They murmured, saying, that he was gone to be a guest with a man that is a sinner;* a worthless, infamous fellow. A complaint of the same kind with that of Simon the Pharisee: *This man, if he were a prophet, would have known who, and what manner of woman this is that toucheth him, for she is a sinner;* a person of ill-fame, one that is a reproach to her sex. But, notwithstanding the unworthy character or conduct of this Jewish publican, he is instantaneously converted. No course of duties, prior to his believing on Christ, is assigned him. No qualifications, as predisposing for pardon, mentioned. *This day*, without any previous preparation, *is salvation come to this house.* Nay, before our Lord expressed those gracious words, Zaccheus made haste, came down from the tree, and *received him joyfully.* Now, as things were then circumstanced in reference to the entertaining of Christ, it is not at all probable that he should have received him *joyfully*, without believing in him; nor could that have been, without receiving the remission of sins. This, therefore, is a noble instance of an absolutely free and unconditional pardon.

The conversion of the Samaritan woman is an instance much to our purpose. This woman lived in ignorance of God and his worship, and in the vile practice of adultery, till, by a remarkably gracious providence, she met with our Lord. He made himself known to her. She believed on him; confessed her faith in him; and, consequently, received that forgiveness which is by him. Nor can we suppose, without offering violence to reason and Scripture, that Christ considered her as having complied with any terms, or having performed any conditions, qualifying for that pardon and those blessings which were vouchsafed to her.

The conversion of the Philippian jailer is equally apposite, and equally strong in proof of our point. The jailer was a Gentile idolater, a barbarous persecutor, and, in purpose, a self-murderer. Yet, being awakened in his conscience, he was directed by an infallible guide to *believe on the Lord Jesus Christ* immediately; with the strongest assurance that in so doing he *should be saved.* Had Paul and Silas thought of any predisposing or qualifying conditions, to be attained in any way, or performed by any means; had they thought the performance of religious duties, a course of humiliation for sin, or the evidence of any degree of love to God, previously necessary to faith in Jesus for pardon and acceptance; no doubt but those ambassadors of Christ, who shunned not to declare the whole counsel of God, would have given some intimation of these things to the trembling querist. But as they directed him immediately to trust in the Saviour, as free for any, free for the vilest of sinners, without giving him any such intimation; we may conclude that they did not consider any thing necessary for that purpose. Now, as their judgment and conduct in these important affairs are acknowledged to have been according to the mind of God, we may venture to assert, that there is no good disposition, no holiness, nor any fruits of sanctification requisite, as the condition of pardon.

I might produce various other instances, from the volume of revelation, to the same purpose; but I shall content myself at this time with selecting one. It is that of the thief on the cross: and as his case is very remarkable, the reader will excuse me if I a little enlarge upon it. This man died the most ignominious death; a death which was not commonly executed on any offenders, but such as were the refuse of mankind, and guilty of atrocious crimes. To this death he was deservedly brought; his own conscience acknowledging the justice of the execution. A hardened villain we find he was, according to the testimony of two evangelists, even after he was fastened to the cross. Matthew informs us, *that the*

THIEVES *also, which were crucified with Christ,* took up the words of reproach and blasphemy, which were uttered by the chief priests, scribes, and elders, against Jesus the Son of God, then dying for the sins of men ; and *cast the same in his teeth.* And Mark says, THEY *that were crucified with him, reviled him.** Hence it appears, that they were both most obdurate wretches ; that they were both guilty of persecuting the dying Saviour, to the utmost of their power, and of blaspheming his offices and work. This vilest of miscreants, justly suffering for his own crimes, could not be ignorant that Jesus was nailed to the cross for claiming to be the Son of God, and for professing himself to be the Messiah ; nor could he be unacquainted with the meaning of those sarcastic reflections, that were cast upon him by malevolent rulers and an insolent rabble. Yet he joined the common cry ; he poured the bitterest reproaches on the most innocent and glorious Person that ever appeared in the world. This he did when Jesus was in his dying moments, and when his own body was extended on a cross, transfixed with nails in the most sensible parts, and racked with exquisite pain. Such a conduct, in such circumstances, evidently discovers the most astonishing degree of impenitence for his own crimes ; the greatest abhorrence of the bleeding Immanuel ; the highest insensibility of his own state toward God, and unconcernedness about the momentous affairs of an eternal world. He acted as if his tormenting others were a relaxation of his own pains. Whence could such a conduct proceed ? whence, indeed, but from the principles of atheism, or from the rage of a devil ?

Such was the state of this thief, till some time after he was crucified. Such were the qualifications which he possessed, predisposing for pardon. Yet he, though enormously vile, (let reigning grace have the glory!) was pardoned. Being convinced of the superlative dignity of Jesus Christ, as well as the injustice of his condemnation ; being informed of the design of his sufferings, and of the nature of that work he was then finishing ;

* Matt. xxvii. 44. Mark xv. 32.

when the other thief, his companion in wickedness, continued his opprobrious language, he rebuked him sharply, and addressed a prayer to the dying Jesus. In which prayer he acknowledged his deity; owned him as Lord of the unseen world; and as having authority to dispose of crowns and thrones in glory, to whomsoever he pleased. In doing which, he paid him the highest honour which mortals can pay to the true God. His petition is, *Lord, remember me when thou comest into thy kingdom!* Jesus answers him with that majesty and condescension which becomes none but the Supreme Possessor of heaven and earth. *Verily I say unto thee, To-day shalt thou be with me in paradise.** The petition of the dying criminal supposes faith in the illustrious sufferer, as the all-sufficient Saviour; and the gracious answer which Jesus returned, irrefragably proves it. His comprehensive petition being readily granted, we may infer that his offences were pardoned and his person accepted. Now, can it be supposed that the dying Redeemer, when he vouchsafed

---

* How amazing the methods of grace! How mortifying to human pride is the conduct of Christ! In the time of his public ministry he was addressed by a very decent, respectable, and apparently *devout young ruler*. A person who, to outward appearance, was very promising, and likely to be an honour to the Redeemer's rising interest. Yet, notwithstanding all his recommendations of worldly property and polished manners, of honourable character and devout address; he was sent away *exceedingly sorrowful*. But here we behold the holy Jesus returning the most gracious answer to the very first petition of an abandoned malefactor, a thief even just before he breathed his last. Consequently, he was so far from having any recommendations, either of person or of character, that every thing about him was quite the reverse. So true are those words, though spoken with an ill intent; *Behold a friend of publicans and sinners.—The whole have no need of a physician, but they that are sick*, appears to have been the maxim on which Messiah formed his conduct. And why should the righteous, or the self-sufficient, be offended at this? If they can do without the manifestation of such grace, others cannot. But if the elder brother will be displeased, because the prodigal is accepted, who can help it? Such, however, as feel their want, and look to the cross alone for relief, will entirely acquiesce in the conduct of Christ; being well persuaded, that it is for his eternal honour, and for their everlasting salvation. Luke xviii. 18—23.

pardon to him, considered him in any other light than that of a notorious offender, a most ungodly wretch? Is it possible to conceive, with any appearance of reason or of Scripture, that this thief performed any entitling or qualifying conditions, previous to the mercy and forgiveness that were granted and manifested to him?

Can we imagine that this thief, when he said *remember me*, could possibly consider himself as any other than the vilest miscreant?* Yet, with great boldness, and no less acceptably, he uttered the words. Nature teaches and pride suggests : " This is a kind of language becoming none but the dying lips of prophets, of apostles, or of martyrs; of such as have been eminent for good works and pious services all their days." Whence, then, could this infamous man derive such a degree of holy boldness, so acceptable to the bleeding Immanuel? With what confidence, or upon what ground could he say, *Remember* ME? It is impossible, I should think, for the invention of man to find any other reason; nor can all the hosts of angels find a better, than that grace which reigns. That grace—(let angels and the spirits of just men made perfect dwell on the charming sound! let the worst of sinners look at it and rejoice in it!)—that grace, which was the only basis of hope for the greatest apostles, and the most holy among the children of men, is an all-sufficient ground of dependence, even for blasphemers and persecutors, for thieves and murderers; or, as Paul says, for the *chief of sinners.*

Here we behold with wonder and contemplate with joy the conduct of the Lord Redeemer in making choice of one as his companion to glory, when he made his exit and left the world. Of one who had—not like Enoch, walked with God; not like Abraham, rejoiced to see the day of Christ, and longed for its commencement; nor like old Simeon, waited with ardent expectation for the

---

* "*Memento mei*, hominis flagitiosissimi sub peccatum venditi, bipedum pessimi, et peccatorum maximi; *quando veneris in regnum tuum*, ut et ego gratiam inveniam apud te, et firmam ac securam sub alis æternæ tuæ majestatis stationem." MERCKEN, *Observ. Crit. in Passion. D. N. I. C.* p. 789.

consolation of Israel; but of one who, for aught appears to the contrary, had devoted all his time and all his talents to the service of Satan; of one, whom the sword of civil justice permitted not to live; and who, in the eye of the public, was less worthy of mercy than Barabbas himself, who was guilty of *sedition and murder;* was a vile incendiary and a bloody ruffian. Astonishing procedure of Jesus, the Judge of the world! When such a wretch is saved, who can despair? At that ever-memorable and amazing period, when the Son of the Highest was in the pangs of dissolution, Jehovah was determined to show, by an incontestable fact, that the salvation which was then finishing, originated in sovereign mercy, flowed in atoning blood, was equal to the wants of the most abominably wicked, and terminated in his own eternal glory, as its ultimate design. This, this is grace, indeed! Grace,

> "Not to be thought on, but with tides of joy,
> Not to be mention'd, but with shouts of praise."

Can we cease to admire the power of his divine grace in the salvation of this thief? What an amazing difference takes place in a few hours, as to his character and state! When first extended on the cross, we view him one of the most hardened wretches whose character is recorded in any history. Then we hear him pray, and behold him a sincere penitent. And lo! before the day is elapsed, even while his body—a deformed spectacle!—still hangs on the gibbet and declares to all the world that he was not fit to live; his immortal spirit enters the portals of paradise, and is blessed with the beatific vision. Surprising transition! As a nuisance to society and a pest to the public, he is brought to the cross, and from thence is translated to a throne of glory. Here, also, we behold, in a striking light, the sovereignty of grace. For the other thief, though not more unworthy, dies unrelenting, and is lost forever. Here the Almighty shows that he *will have mercy on whom he will have mercy; for, one is taken and the other left.*

I cannot conclude my remarks on this very extraordinary fact, without observing, That as the death of the

Son of God was the most wonderful event that ever did, or ever will take place on the theatre of the world; and as it was intended to be a foundation of hope for sinners, in the most desperate cases; so the circumstances attending it were wisely adapted to answer that gracious design in its utmost latitude. The Prince of life was *numbered among transgressors;* was crucified between two thieves. He died, not only the most abhorred of deaths, but in the worst of company. Nor was this a casual thing: it was determined by Jehovah, and the subject of ancient prophecy. This was graciously ordered, in the purpose and providence of God, to afford relief to the most flagrant offenders. Had any the least regard been paid to moral character and human excellence, in that most amazing of all transactions, unbelief and pride would soon have concluded that it was principally intended for the more respectable part of mankind, for those who want but little assistance, and would be able to do tolerably well without it. On such a supposition, what must have become of notorious criminals, and of those who consider themselves as awfully guilty and wretched? What, but absolute despair would have awaited the entirely worthless? though these are the persons in whose salvation mercy delights, and for whom the great atonement was provided. Had the companions of Christ on the cross been persons of a shining character for humanity and piety; nay, had they been of equal repute with Ezekiel's worthies, Noah, Daniel, and Job; though mankind by common consent might have agreed to pronounce their execution an outrageous violation of justice, and have execrated the Judge who condemned them; yet the dying Jesus would still have been *numbered with transgressors.* But this would have afforded small encouragement to those, who are not only condemned by divine law, and stand guilty in their own consciences, but have also, by a criminal conduct, incurred the public odium. Such would have been ready to infer, that their case was entirely hopeless; and, therefore, as despair of the future was the most rational thing, so present pleasures, however sinful, would have been still more eagerly pursued by them. But reigning grace was by no means willing that the most abhorred of men should be reduced to such a dreadful situation. In order, therefore, to prevent this, the Holy One of Israel was not only *crucified*, to show that he died under a charge of the highest guilt, and was made a curse, but he was crucified between *two convicts* that were thieves and ruffians. He made his exit, and was numbered with such as all the world agree to pronounce *transgressors;* with such as have ever been esteemed by all nations as unworthy to live But why was this, if not to show, that as the best of men have no solid foundation of hope, except the blood of the cross; so the very worst and the vilest that ever deserved a gibbet, have no reason to sink in despair while they behold the Lord of life expire in such company; and especially when they remember that he took one of those villains with him to glory?

My reader, perhaps, would be ready to think it a gross affront to his character, were I to assert that he stands on the *very same terms* with this thief, in regard to acceptance with God; and that the most upright of men have nothing more to plead before their Maker than he had. Yet this is a certain truth. For salvation is entirely by grace; and grace is unconditional favour. Grace, therefore, has no regard to any real or supposed difference among men. All whom it relieves are considered as on the same level; the most moral, and the most profligate, being equally without help and hope in themselves. We may therefore conclude, that whoever looks for salvation by any other grace than that which saved this thief, will meet with a dreadful disappointment.

In the several foregoing instances, grace, in the free pardon of sin, does not only appear, but appears with majesty; it not only shows itself, but demonstrates its power to be infinitely great and supremely glorious. These remarkable cases stand engrossed by the pen of inspiration, as so many *acts* and *precedents* of the court of heaven; and were recorded for our—yes, reader, for *our* observation, instruction, and comfort. They were ordered to be transmitted to posterity by the King eternal.

that in the ages to come he might show the exceeding riches of his grace, through Christ Jesus.

The blessed effects produced on the minds and morals of all these enormous offenders, by the manifestation of grace and a grant of pardon, deserve our consideration; as they are a standing testimony to the truth of that saying, *There is forgiveness with Thee, that thou mayest be feared.* When Paul came to experience the power, and to taste the sweetness of pardoning grace, no labours were too great for him to undertake; no sufferings were too severe for him to undergo, on the behalf of his Divine Master. He counted not his very life dear, so that he might propagate the glorious truth, and promote his Redeemer's honour. Zaccheus was instantly changed in his dispositions and conduct: for the extortioner made restitution, and put on bowels of mercy. The woman of Samaria immediately drew numbers to hear that gracious voice which quickened her own soul; and to receive him, as the Christ, by whom she was instructed, pardoned, and comforted. The jailer manifested a ready obedience to the commands of our Saviour, as King in Zion, by submitting to the ordinance of baptism. He evinced his love to the saving truth, by washing the stripes of his two illustrious prisoners, and by treating them at his hospitable board with a cordial welcome. And the thief, the few moments he had to live, after he enjoyed the blessings of grace, confessed his offences, justified God in the punishment he then suffered, and, in love to the soul of his partner in villany and infamy, reproved him for his blasphemy, and warned him of his danger—the dreadful danger of suffering eternal wrath.

I am persuaded that the testimonies and facts, already produced and pleaded, in order to prove that pardon is *free;* detached from all works, dependent on no conditions, to be performed by the sinner, are quite sufficient. Otherwise, I might easily add to their number, by producing other examples and more declarations from the sacred volume. But these I omit, and shall only remind my reader of that remarkable and truly evangelical text,

When we were enemies, we were reconciled to God by the death of his Son. Now, as none can deny that pardon of sin is essential to a state of reconciliation with God, so it is impossible the reconciliation and forgiveness of those who are *enemies* to him, should ever take place on account of any thing amiable which they possess, or of any thing good which they have done. Such a supposition, if any were absurd enough to make it, would confound the two absolutely contradictory ideas of enmity and friendship.

Here let us pause a moment and indulge reflection. Is there no forgiveness of any offender, or of the least offence, but by *shedding of blood*—the infinitely precious blood of Jesus, our incarnate God? How awfully evil, how inconceivably great the malignity of sin! The dignity of the Person who suffered for it; the superlative interest he had in his Father's love; and the more than mountainous weight of Divine wrath which he bore in his complicated sufferings; much more strongly express the exceeding sinfulness of sin, and the infinite purity of God, than the everlasting punishment of the damned. Here we behold in the clearest light, that our Sovereign is absolutely just, as well as divinely merciful, in granting a free pardon to the worthless and guilty. Here we behold the righteous Judge, and the suffering Saviour, inflexible justice, and triumphant grace, in the same point of light. The curse is executed in all its rigour, and mercy is manifested in all its riches. Here the great Lord of all appears, dispensing innumerable and free pardons; but in such a way as preserves the honours of his law inviolate, and maintains the rights of his Divine government—in such a way, as is the surprise of angels and the wonder of heaven. To contrive it, was the work of infinite wisdom; to manifest it, a display of boundless grace. In such a method of dispensing forgiveness, how safely may the alarmed conscience rest! For while it is most happily adapted to impress the mind with an awful sense of the infinite evil of sin, the purity of the divine nature, and the extensive demands of the holy law; it encourages the most unreserved confidence in mercy thus revealed, and cherishes the liveliest hope in grace thus reigning.

Is there a full and free forgiveness; a forgiveness vouchsafed without any terms or conditions to be performed by the enfeebled and corrupted creature? How shamefully then do those persons injure the grace of God, and veil its most shining excellencies, who teach, or imagine, that pardon of sin is not to be expected, nor can be received, till the sinner is prepared for it by a course of humiliation, of self-denial, or of holy conversation? This pardon, far from being suspended on conditions to be performed by us, flows from sovereign grace, is according to the infinite riches of grace, and is intended by Jehovah to aggrandize his grace, in the view of all the redeemed, and before the angels of light, both here and hereafter. That *forgiveness which is with God*, is such as becomes the Majesty of heaven; such as is suited to his infinite excellencies. When the Lord of the world pardons offenders, in so doing he demonstrates his DEITY; or, that he is infinitely superior to all his creatures in acts of forgiveness, as well as in every perfection of his nature. For thus it is written: *I will not execute the fierceness of mine anger; I will not return to destroy Ephraim.* What is the reason of this forbearance? It follows—FOR I AM GOD, *and not man.* In reference to the pardon of sin, Jehovah again declares, *For my thoughts are not your thoughts, neither are your ways my ways, saith the Lord. For as the heavens are higher than the earth, so are my ways higher than your ways, and my thoughts than your thoughts.* He freely forgives our *ten thousand talents*, whereas we can scarcely forgive those who are indebted to us *an hundred pence.* Thus the Lord, in bestowing a full and free pardon on guilty, perishing creatures, exceeds—the utmost of human deserts? the highest instances of human compassion?—rather, all our expectations and all our thoughts. May a lively sense of this free forgiveness rest on the mind, comfort the heart, and elevate the affections of my reader! Then shall his conduct declare, that, as it is a blessing immensely great, and comes to sinners through atoning.

blood, so it is connected with true holiness—that it is a strong incentive to *fear the Lord ;* to love, adore, and obey him. Then shall he *be filled with the fruits of righteousness, which are, by Jesus Christ, to the glory and praise of God.*

This forgiveness is *everlasting* and irreversible, which is the last and crowning requisite of complete pardon. Various passages in sacred writ evince this glorious truth. Among many others, that charming clause in the new covenant is not the least remarkable. *I will be merciful to their unrighteousness, and their sins and their iniquities* WILL I REMEMBER NO MORE. This declaration, and the blessing signified by it, enter into the very essence of the new, the better, the unchangeable covenant. If the Lord, whose royal prerogative it is to punish, or to pardon the criminal, declare that he will *remember his iniquities no more,* we may rest assured, that it is an everlasting pardon, a forgiveness never to be reversed. This declaration is not simply a *promise ;* though a mere promise, from the God of truth, is irrevocable; but it is a promise in a federal form—an absolute promise, which faithfulness itself is engaged to fulfil. The continuance of a pardoned state, not depending on conditions to be performed by the sinner, but on the perpetual efficacy of our Lord's atonement, and on the inviolable faithfulness of the eternal God, there is all possible security that a full and free pardon, once granted, shall ever abide in its full force, and in all its glory.

The same comfortable truth is taught and confirmed by David. *As far as the east is from the west, so far hath he removed our transgressions from us.* Hence we infer, that the sins of those who are forgiven shall never come against them to their condemnation, unless those two opposite points, the east and the west, should ever meet, and so cease to be what they are. Nor can that blessedness which the Psalmist, in another place, ascribes to the pardoned sinner, be accounted for on any other supposition. *Blessed is he, whose transgression is forgiven.* For if *all* his offences were not forgiven, and that *forever,* what peace for his conscience here, what hope of glory hereafter, could he enjoy? If the continuance of his pardoned state depended on his own obedience; if, by a relapse into sin, he should again be liable to condemnation and wrath, all his present enjoyments and future hopes would not deserve the name of *blessedness*, the tenure by which they are held being so precarious. *Precarious!* I retract the expression. There would be all the certainty on the opposite side that could be had; not the least probability in his favour, or the least ground to suppose that he would ever obtain eternal happiness. The conscience being awake, present peace will always keep pace with a hope of future felicity.

Another inspired penman thus expresses the joyful truth. *Thou wilt cast all their sins into the depth of the sea.* The transgressions of the pardoned sinner are here compared to a stone, or to some other ponderous thing; which, when cast into the fathomless deep, is absolutely irrecoverable by all the art and power of man. The loftiest towers, the most enormous mountains, with all their cumbrous load of rocks and forests, if cast into the ocean, would all entirely disappear and be lost forever. By this expressive and striking image does the Holy Ghost represent the perpetuity of that forgiveness which is with God, and is vouchsafed to the believer. Conformably to which, the Lord says, *The iniquity of Israel shall be sought for, and there shall be none; and the sins of Judah, and they shall not be found.* The reason of this assertion is contained in the following words: *For I will pardon them whom I reserve.* A convincing proof, that those who are pardoned by the God of grace, have all their sins forgiven, and that forever. Isaiah, the evangelist of the Jewish church, has a passage much to our purpose. He represents the Redeemer, the Holy One of Israel, addressing his people in the following manner. *As I have sworn that the waters of Noah should no more go over the earth; so have I sworn that I would not be wroth with thee nor rebuke thee. For the mountains shall depart, and the hills be removed; but my kindness shall not depart from thee, neither shall the covenant of my peace be removed, saith the Lord, that hath mercy on thee.* Here we have, not only the word, but the oath of Jehovah, in attestation to the glorious truth: and if these fail,

> "The pillar'd firmament is rottenness,
> And earth's foundation stubble."

The apostle of the Gentiles having this glorious truth full in his view, is bold to challenge every enemy, and to defy every danger. What less can be the import of that heroic language—*Who shall lay any thing to the charge of God's elect? Who shall condemn?* If the blessing of pardon were ever to be reversed; if a sinner, having been once acquitted from condemnation, should again fall under the curse and be liable to perish, there would be no foundation for these bold expressions.

Such is the nature and such the properties of Divine forgiveness; even of that forgiveness, which is the purchase of Immanuel's pains, and the price of redeeming blood. The doctrine of pardon is an essential branch and a capital article of that truth, which is by way of eminence called THE GOSPEL. For the cheering language of that heavenly message is—*Be it known unto you, men and brethren, that through this* illustrious Jesus *is preached unto you the forgiveness of sins.* Such is the import of the evangelical testimony; and the glorious blessing is received by faith in the dying Redeemer. As it is written; *To him give all the prophets witness, that, through his name, whosoever believeth in Him shall receive remission of sins.* Believing the infallible record which God has given of his Son, we receive the atonement. The propitiating blood of Christ is sprinkled on our hearts, pardon is applied to our consciences, and peace enjoyed in our souls.

It is no real objection to the truth advanced, that the Lord lays his chastising hand on the objects of this forgiveness. For though he corrects them, and frequently with some degree of severity, on account of their backslidings, yet those chastisements are instances and evidences of his paternal affection, and of his constant care over them. They have the strongest assurances that he *will never take from* them *his loving kindness, nor suffer his faithfulness to fail.*

Nor is it any way inconsistent with the doctrine maintained, that believers are expressly commanded to pray for the pardon of sin, and that this command has been frequently acknowledged in the conduct of eminent saints, whose characters are recorded in the holy Scriptures. For, to use the words of a learned author, " Very frequently when the saints pray, either for the forgiveness of their own or others' sins, their meaning is, that God would, in a providential way, deliver them out of present distress; remove his afflicting hand, which lies heavy upon them ; or avert such judgments which seem to hang over their heads, and very much threaten them, which, when he does, is an indication of his having pardoned them. We are to understand many petitions of Moses, Job, Solomon, and others in this sense.* Besides, when believers now pray for the pardon of sin, their meaning is, that they might have the sense, the manifestation, and application of pardoning grace to their souls. We are not to imagine, that as often as the saints sin, repent, confess their sins, and pray for the forgiveness of them, that God makes and passes new acts of pardon ; but, whereas they daily sin against God, grieve his Spirit, and wound their own consciences; they have need of the fresh sprinklings of the blood of Jesus, and of renewed manifestations of pardon to their souls : and it is both their duty and their interest to attend the throne of grace on this account."

How glorious, then, is that *forgiveness which is with God,* that pardon I have been describing ! It has every requisite to make it complete in itself, and suitable to the indigent, miserable sinner. It has not one discouraging circumstance to forbid the most guilty, or the most unworthy, applying to the ever-merciful Jehovah for it. It is full, free, and everlasting, every way complete and worthy of God. It was absolutely necessary to the peace of our consciences, and to the salvation of our souls, that

---

* Exod. xxxii. 32. Num. xiv. 19, 20. Job vii. 21. 1 Kings viii 30. 34. 36. 39. 50.

it should be of such unlimited extent, of such unmerited freeness, and of such everlasting efficacy. Less than this would not have supplied our wants, or have served our purpose. If it had not been *full*, taking in every kind and every degree of sin, we must have suffered the punishment due to some part of it ourselves, and then we had been lost forever. If it had not been entirely *free*, we could never have enjoyed the inestimable blessing, for we have nothing, nor can we do any thing to purchase it, or to qualify for it. And if it had not been *everlasting*, never to be reversed, we should have been under continual anxiety and painful apprehensions, lest God should, on account of our present unworthiness or future failings, recall the blessing when once bestowed. But, being possessed of these properties, the vilest sinner has no reason despondingly to say, " My sins, alas ! are too many and great for me to expect pardon." None have any cause to complain, " I long for the blessing ; it is dearer to me than all worlds ; but my strong corruptions, and utter unworthiness, render me incapable of ever enjoying it." Nor have any occasion to fear lest, after the comfortable enjoyment of the superlative privilege, they should forfeit it, and again come under condemnation and wrath.

What shall we then say to these things? Shall we continue in sin that grace may abound in a perfect pardon ? God forbid ! So to act, would, if possible, be worse than devilish, and more damnable. Rather let the pardoned criminal say, yes, he will say, with the warmest gratitude, *Bless the Lord, O my soul; and all that is within me, bless his holy name. Who forgiveth all thine iniquities; who healeth all thy diseases ; who redeemeth thy life from destruction ; who crowneth thee with loving kindness and tender mercies.*

Before I conclude this momentous part of my subject, I will transcribe a few lines from a celebrated author of the last century ; celebrated, not more for his very superior learning, than for his great penetration in spiritual things, and his experience in the Christian life. Treating of Divine forgiveness, he says, " The *forgiveness that is* *with* God, is such as becomes him, such as is suitable to his greatness, goodness, and all the other excellencies of his nature; such as that therein he will be *known to be* God. What he says concerning some of the works of his providence, *be still, and know that I am* God, may be much more said concerning this great effect of his grace, *Still yourselves, and know that he is* God. It is not like that narrow, difficult, halving, and manacled forgiveness, that is found amongst men; but it is full, free, bottomless, boundless, absolute—such as becomes his nature and excellencies. It is, in a word, *forgiveness that is with* God, and by the exercise of which he will be known so to be. If there be any pardon with God, it is such as becomes him to give. When he pardons, he will *abundantly pardon.* Go, with your half forgiveness, conditional pardons, with reserves and limitations, unto the sons of men. It may be, it may become them; it is like themselves. That of God is absolute and perfect; before which, our sins are as a cloud before the east wind and the rising sun. Hence he is said to do this work *with his whole heart and his whole soul;* freely, bountifully, largely to indulge and forgive unto us our sins, and to *cast them into the bottom of the sea.* Remember this, poor souls, when you are to deal with God in this matter. If we let go the free pardon of sin, without respect unto any thing in those that receive it, we renounce the gospel. Pardon of sin is not merited by antecedent duties, but is the strongest obligation unto future duties. He that will not receive pardon, unless he can one way or other deserve it, or make himself meet for it, or pretends to have received it, and finds not himself obliged to universal obedience by it, neither is nor shall be partaker of it."*

* Dr. Owen, *On the hundred and thirtieth Psalm,* p. 202. 227, and on *Heb.* viii. 12. This eminent writer loudly proclaims the charming truth. He no more feared this doctrine leading to licentiousness, than he valued the applause of the self-sufficient moralist. He treats of a full, free, and final forgiveness, like one who knows its real value, experiences its unutterable sweetness, and glories in it as his own privilege. He labours his noble subject, and repeats the joyful truth. Whereas, many of our modern preachers, who

Now, reader, what think you of this glorious pardon? Is it suitable to your wants? Is it worthy of your acceptance? You are, perhaps, one of those careless mortals that are at ease in their sins, and eagerly pursuing the tantalizing pleasures of this uncertain life. But can you be contented to live and die in utter ignorance of this forgiveness? Is pardon a blessing of small importance, or have you no occasion for it? Sinned you have, condemned you are, and, without forgiveness, you die to eternity. Start, O start from your stupor! Your state is dreadful, though not desperate. Your sins are upon you, the law of God curses you, and you are in extreme danger of eternal damnation. You are tottering, as it were, on the brink of a dreadful precipice, and nodding on the verge of the burning lake. Can you sleep in your sins, can you rest in an unpardoned state, when it is all uncertainty whether the next hour may not transmit you into an eternal world; place you at the bar of God, and put you beyond the possibility of relief? May Divine grace forbid your continuing another moment in such an awful situation! For, another moment, and your life may be gone; another moment, and your soul may be lost; and then your loss will be irreparable, inconceivable, and eternal.

Is my reader sensible of his want, and longing for the matchless blessing? Then look to the dying Jesus. Your iniquities, it is true, abound; but pardoning mercy, through his atonement, superabounds. Be of good cheer: take encouragement: for the favour you so earnestly desire is a free gift. Blessed be God for the amazing mercy! Such are the methods of grace, and such is the nature of this forgiveness, that as your eternal salvation is bound up in the enjoyment of it, so the everlasting honour of Jehovah is unspeakably advanced by freely bestowing it. There is no reason, therefore, that you should stand at a

pretend to reverence the doctor's memory, admire his profound learning, and, in a general way, applaud his judgment; when handling the same subject, either directly contradict him, or whisper the grand truth in faint accents, as if they questioned the certainty of what they would seem to affirm, or were apprehensive of some pernicious consequences attending it.

trembling distance, as if there were no such favour for you; but with boldness you may look for it; in a way of grace through the blood of Christ, and truth itself has most solemnly declared that you shall not be disappointed.

Are you comfortably acquainted with the pardoning goodness of God? having much forgiven, you should love much. The remembrance of a blessing so immensely rich, the sense of a favour so extremely high, should enlarge your heart with all holy affections toward the Lord Redeemer; should animate all your devotional services; should cause you to compassionate your offending brother, in forgiving him his *hundred pence*, considering that God has forgiven you *ten thousand talents*, and make you zealous of every good work. This forgiveness, far from being an incentive to vice, will bias your affections on the side of virtue; will cause you to love God as infinitely holy, and to abhor sin, as a direct opposition to his immaculate purity and revealed will. Yes, a sense of pardon, when warm on your mind, will work in you godly sorrow for all sin, for the latent corruptions of your heart, no less than the open transgressions of your life, and will cause you to confess them before God with shame and grief. Such are the genuine effects of Divine forgiveness. These fruits will necessarily appear, in some degree; and he who professes to know the pardon of his transgressions, but does not forgive his offending brother, and lives under the dominion of sin, *is a liar, and the truth is not in him.*

CHAPTER VI.

OF GRACE, AS IT REIGNS IN OUR JUSTIFICATION.

THE doctrine of justification makes a very distinguished figure in that religion which is from above, and is a capital article of that *faith which was once delivered to the saints.* Far from being a merely speculative point, it spreads its influence through the whole body of divinity, runs through all Christian experience, and operates in every part of practical godliness. Such is its grand importance, that a mistake about it has a malignant efficacy, and is attended with a long train of dangerous consequences. Nor can this appear strange, when it is considered, that this doctrine of justification is no other than the way of *a sinner's acceptance with God*. Being of such peculiar moment, it is inseparably connected with many other evangelical truths, the harmony and beauty of which we cannot behold, while this is misunderstood. Till this appears in its glory, they will be involved in darkness. It is, if any thing may be so called, a *fundamental* article; and certainly requires our most serious consideration.*

How shall sinful *man be just with God?* is a question of the most interesting nature to every child of Adam.

---

* Let it be carefully observed by the reader, that though I here treat upon justification as distinct from pardon, yet I am fully persuaded that they are blessings which cannot be separated. For he who is pardoned is justified, and he who is justified is also pardoned. It is readily allowed that there is, in various respects, a great resemblance between the two blessings. They are both gifts of grace; both vouchsafed to the same person, at the same time; and both are communicated through the mediation of Christ. Notwithstanding which agreement, the *signification* of the terms, and the *nature* of the blessings intended by them, are so far different as to lay a sufficient foundation for distinguishing between the one and the other. I would just hint at a few things in confirmation of this. When a person is pardoned, he is considered as a *transgressor;* but when he is justified, he is considered as *righteous*. A criminal when pardoned, is freed from an *obligation to suffer death* for his crimes; but he that is justified is declared *worthy of life*, as an innocent person. *Wisdom* is said to be justified; *Christ* is said to be justified; nay, *God* himself is said to be justified. Matt. xi. 19. 1 Tim. iii. 16. Luke vii. 29. Rom. iii. 4. But neither God, nor Christ, nor Wisdom, is ever said to be pardoned; nor indeed is it possible, in any sense, that they should be forgiven. Though we may, therefore, with the Scripture affirm that they are *justified*, we cannot without absurdity, or blasphemy, say they are *pardoned*. This one consideration, I humbly conceive, is an irrefragable proof, that there is a real, an important difference between justification and pardon. To which I may add, Paul treats upon them as distinct blessings, in Acts xiii. 38, 39.

A question which, notwithstanding its infinite importance, could never have been resolved by all the reason of men, nor by all the penetration of angels, if the Lord of heaven and earth had not exercised and manifested reigning grace, toward his disobedient and rebellious creatures. But, with the Bible in his hand, and the gospel in view, the mere infant in religious knowledge and in Christian experience is at no loss for an answer; for *the wayfaring man, though a fool, shall not err therein.* Nay, such is the pleasure of God, that he frequently reveals this truth in its glory, to those who are esteemed fools by the haughty sons of science, that no flesh might have the least ground of boasting.

Justification is a forensic term, and signifies *the declaring*, or *the pronouncing a person righteous according to law.* Justification is not the *making* a person righteous, by a real, inherent change from sin to holiness, in which the nature of sanctification consists; but it is the act of a judge, *pronouncing the party acquitted, from all judicial charges.* That the blessing of which we speak does not consist in a real change from sin to holiness, will further appear from considering, that *justification* is diametrically opposite to *condemnation.* Now the sentence of condemnation is never supposed to make the person criminal on whom it is pronounced. There is no infusion of evil qualities into the culprit's mind; nor is he made guilty, either in the eye of the public, or in his own estimation. But being arraigned as a criminal, and proved guilty of a capital offence, according to the tenor of that law by which he is tried, he is esteemed worthy of death, and condemned accordingly. So, in justification; the subject of it is pronounced righteous in the eye of the law, is deemed worthy to live, and his right to life is declared. Hence that justification of which the Scripture speaks, and is now the subject of our inquiry, is called the *justification of life.** That the words *justify, justified,* and *justification* are used by the sacred writers in a forensic sense, and as opposed to the words

---

* Rom. v. 18.

condemn, *condemned*, and *condemnation*, is manifest to every attentive reader.*

Justification, in a theological sense, is either *legal* or *evangelical*. If any person could be found that has never broken the divine law, he might be justified by it, in a manner strictly legal. But in this way none of the human race can be justified, or stand acquitted before God For *all have sinned; there is none righteous, no, not one*. The whole world, having transgressed, are guilty before the eternal Judge, and under the sentence of death by his righteous law. On this ground, every offender is excluded from all hope, and abandoned to utter destruction. For as an obedience absolutely perfect is the only righteousness which the law can accept, so punishment inconceivable, or death eternal, is the least penalty it will inflict, on those that fall under its curse. That justification, therefore, about which the Scriptures principally treat, and which reaches the case of a sinner, is not by a personal, but an imputed righteousness; a *righteousness without the law*,† provided by grace and revealed in the gospel: for which reason, that obedience by which a sinner is justified, and his justification itself, are called *evangelical*. In this affair, there is the most wonderful display of Divine justice, and of boundless grace. *Of Divine justice*, if we regard the meritorious cause and ground on which the justifier proceeds, in absolving the condemned sinner, and in pronouncing him righteous. *Of boundless grace*, if we consider the state and character of those persons to whom the blessing is granted.

Justification may be further distinguished, as being either at the bar of God, and in the court of conscience, or in the sight of the world, and before our fellow-creatures. The former is by mere grace, through faith, and the latter is by works. It is the former of these I shall now consider, which may be thus defined; *Justification*

---

* To this purpose the following texts, instead of many more, may be consulted. Exod. xxiii. 7. Deut. xxv. 2. 1 Kings viii. 31, 32. Job xiii. 18; and xxvii. 5. Prov. xvii. 15. Matt. xi. 19, and xii. 37. Luke vii. 29. Rom. ii. 13; and iii. 4; and viii. 30. 33, 34.

† Rom. iii. 21.

is a judicial, but gracious act of God, by which a sinner is absolved from the guilt of sin, is freed from condemnation, and has a right to eternal life adjudged, merely for the sake of our Lord's obedience, which is imputed to him, and received by faith.

To justify, is evidently a divine prerogative. *It is God that justifieth.* That Sovereign Being against whom we have so greatly offended, whose law we have broken by ten thousand acts of rebellion against him, has, in the way of his own appointment, the sole right of acquitting the guilty, and of pronouncing them righteous. Jehovah, whose judgment is always according to truth, is the Justifier of all that believe in Jesus. Here grace reigns. For the infinitely wise God appoints the way; the righteous and merciful God provides the means, and (let the sacred name be repeatedly mentioned with profound reverence) the God of all grace imputes the righteousness and pronounces the sinner acquitted, in perfect agreement with the demands of his violated law, and the rights of his offended justice.

What is here, as well as in several passages of Scripture, affirmed concerning God, considered essentially, is, in some places of the infallible word, more particularly appropriated personally to the Father. It is manifest, however, that all the three divine Persons are concerned in this grand affair, and each performs a distinct part in this particular, as also in the whole economy of salvation. The eternal Father is represented as appointing the way, and as giving his own Son to perform the conditions of our acceptance before him. The Divine Son, as engaging to sustain the curse, and make the atonement, to fulfil the terms, and provide the righteousness by which we are justified. And the Holy Spirit, as revealing to sinners the perfection, suitableness, and freeness of the Saviour's work; enabling them to receive it, as exhibited in the gospel of sovereign grace, and testifying to their consciences complete justification by it in the court of heaven. Thus the triune God justifies. And may we not ask, in the triumphant language of Paul, *Who shall condemn?* If Jehovah pronounce the sinner acquitted, who, in earth or hell, shall reverse the sentence? If the Most High entirely justify, who shall bring in a second charge? There is no higher court to which any appeal can be made. There is no superior tribunal at which a complaint can be lodged, against any of those happy souls whose invaluable privilege it is to be justified by the eternal God. When he acquits in judgment, he absolves from all guilt, he accepts as completely righteous; otherwise, a person, immediately after he is justified, must be supposed to stand in need of a further justification, which is highly absurd. This divine sentence shall never be made void, by any unworthiness of him on whom it is passed, nor by the accusations of Satan: but shall stand, firmer than the everlasting hills; unshaken as the throne of God. This sentence—(let my reader dwell on the ravishing truth, let his very soul feast on the precious doctrine)—this sentence, being *the justification of life*, is pregnant with all the blessings of the everlasting covenant; with all the felicity of the world of glory.

Superlatively great, glorious, and divine, is the blessing of justification. Most ardently to be sought, most thankfully to be enjoyed. Can any one, conscious of possessing it, cease to exult in God his Justifier, who, by being so, is also the God of his praise? Or, who that is convinced of his guilty, condemned condition, can cease to pray and most earnestly to long for it? O, sinner! are you insensible to the worth of this blessing, and supinely negligent about it? be assured, then, that you are in your sins, and under condemnation. The justification of which we treat is far from you. And what, if you should never be justified? What, if your affronted Sovereign should swear in his wrath, that he will never forgive, never accept you; but that you shall die under the curse already passed upon you? In such a case, though awful beyond conception, what could you have to object? You have trampled his authority under your feet, and cherished a spirit of the most malignant enmity against him. Your conscience testifies, that you have neither obeyed his law, nor loved his gospel; that you have had little concern whether he was pleased or offended, so that you could but gratify your impetuous lusts, and obtain your sordid purposes. You have, it may be, never considered the death of the Son of God as worthy of your serious notice; though it is the greatest and most wonderful event that ever took place in the universe, and the only thing that can save you from final condemnation. Remember, thoughtless reader! that you have a cause to be tried at the bar of God, and before Jehovah your Judge, which involves your all. An eternal hell to be suffered, or an eternal heaven to be enjoyed, will be the awful or the glorious consequence of being cast or acquitted in judgment. Can you rest, then, can you take any comfort, while entirely ignorant whether the Judge immortal will absolve or condemn you? Consider the ground on which you stand, and the reason of that hope which is in you. A mistake about the way of acceptance with God will be attended with the utmost danger; such danger that, where it is final, inevitable and eternal ruin must be the consequence. May the God of grace and the Father of lights awaken the sleepy consciences of the inconsiderate, into an earnest solicitude about it! and may he direct the steps of such as are anxiously inquiring, *How shall a man be just with God?*

The persons to whom the wonderful favour is granted, are *sinners* and *ungodly*. For thus runs the Divine declaration, *To him that worketh is the reward* of justification, and of eternal life as connected with it, *not reckoned of grace, but of debt. But to him that worketh not, but believeth on him that justifieth*—whom? the righteous? the holy? the eminently pious? Nay, verily, but the UNGODLY; *his faith*, or that in which he believes, *is counted unto him for righteousness.* From this remarkable text we learn, that the subjects of justification, considered in themselves, are not only destitute of a perfect righteousness, but have performed no good works at all. Nor are they only described as having performed no good works, but also as being entirely destitute of every heavenly quality and righteous disposition. They are denominated and considered as ungodly when the blessing is bestowed upon them. The mere sinner, the ungodly person, he *that worketh not*, is the subject on whom grace is magnified; toward whom grace reigns in justification. Thus it is written in those sacred canons of our faith and practice which are unalterable.

Before I dismiss this important passage, I will present my reader with the thoughts of Dr. Owen upon it. " To say, he who *worketh not*, is justified through believing, is to say, that his works, whatever they be, have no influence in his justification; nor hath God, in justifying him, any respect unto them. Wherefore he *alone* who worketh not, is the subject of justification, the person to be justified. That is, God considereth no man's works, no man's duties of obedience, in his justification; seeing we are justified *freely, by his grace.* And when God affirmeth expressly, that he justifieth him *who worketh not*, and that *freely, by his grace*, I cannot understand what place our works, or duties of obedience, can have in our justification. For why should we trouble ourselves to invent of what consideration they may be, in our justification before God, when he himself affirms that they are of none at all? Neither are the words capable of any evading interpretation. He that worketh not, *is* he that worketh not, let men say what they please and distinguish as long as they will. And it is a boldness not to be justified, for any to rise up in opposition to such express divine testimonies; however they may be harnessed with philosophical notions and arguings, which are but the thorns and briers which the word of God will pass through and consume. But the apostle further adds, in the description of the subject of justification, that God *justifieth the ungodly.* This is that expression which hath stirred up so much wrath among many, and on the account whereof some seem to be much displeased with the apostle himself. If any other person dare but say, that God *justifieth the ungodly*, he is presently reflected on as one that, by his doctrine, would overthrow the necessity of godliness, holiness, obedience, or good works. For what need can there be of any of them, if God justifieth the *ungodly?* Howbeit this is a periphrasis of God, that he is he *who justifieth the ungodly.* This is his prerogative and property: as such he will be believed and worshipped, which adds weight and emphasis unto the expression. And we must not forego this testimony of the Holy Ghost, let men be as angry as they please. "But the difference is about the meaning of the words. If so, it may be allowed without mutual offence, though we should mistake their proper sense. Only it must be granted, that God *justifieth the ungodly.* That is, say some, those who *formerly were* ungodly; not such who *continue* ungodly when they are justified. And this is most true. All that are justified, were before ungodly; and all that are justified, are at the same instant made godly. But the question is, whether they are godly or ungodly, *antecedently*, in any moment of time, unto their justification? If they are considered as godly, and are so indeed, then the apostle's words are not true, that God justifieth the ungodly; for the contradictory proposition is true, God justifieth none but the godly. Wherefore, although in and with the justification of a sinner he is made godly; (for he is endowed with that faith which purifieth the heart, and is a vital principle of all obedience, and the conscience is purged from dead works by the blood of Christ,) yet antecedently unto his justification, he is ungodly and considered as ungodly; as one that *worketh not;* as one whose duties and obedience contribute nothing to his justification. As he worketh not, all works are excluded from being the cause; and, as he is ungodly, from being the condition of his justification?"*

That the mere sinner is the subject of justification, appears from hence. The Spirit of God speaking in the Scripture repeatedly declares, that we are justified by *grace.* But grace, as already observed, stands in direct opposition to works; all works and worthiness of every kind and of every degree. Whoever therefore is justified by grace, is considered as absolutely unworthy, in that very instant when the glorious blessing is vouchsafed to him. This momentous truth is yet more strongly

---

* On Justification, chap. xviii.

expressed in the following emphatical words: *Being justified freely by his grace.** *Freely by grace.* If these words do not prove that justification is entirely free, without the least regard to any supposed holy qualities in the sinner, or any good works performed by him, antecedent to his being possessed of the unspeakable favour; I think it is impossible to express any such thing. The most fruitful invention would be at a loss to contrive a form of words better adapted to express the communication of any benefit in a way of mere favour. This text informs us that, in regard to God, justification is an act of pure, unmixed grace; exclusive of all good works, and absolutely independent on any such thing as human worthiness: and, in respect of us, that it is entirely *without cause;* for so the adverb in the original signifies.† The word *freely*, does not so immediately respect, either the blessing itself, or the giver, as it does the state and character of the persons to whom the inestimable blessing is granted. It denotes that there is no cause in them, why they should be thus treated by a righteous God. In this sense the original word is used and translated in the following passage: *They hated me without a cause.*‡ Was the holy Jesus hated, by the malevolent Jews, without the least cause in himself? certainly: to assert the contrary would be a contradiction of the sacred text, and blasphemy against the Son of God. The person, therefore, that is justified freely by grace, is accepted *without any cause* in himself. Nothing in him, or about him, is considered by the sovereign Dispenser of every favour, when he bestows the blessing, as preparing or qualifying for it.

Hence it appears, that if we regarded the persons who are justified, and their state, prior to the enjoyment of this immensely glorious privilege; Divine grace appears and reigns in all its glory: there being no conditions, or prerequisites, no terms to be fulfilled, or good qualities to be obtained, either with or without the Divine assistance, in

---

* Rom. iii. 24. † Δωρεαν.
‡ John xv. 25. Ps. xxxv. 19. lxix. 4. Septuag.

order to a full discharge before the eternal Judge. Justification is a blessing of pure grace, as well as transcendently excellent. So the true believer esteems it, and as such rejoices in it. In this, as in every other part of his salvation, he is willing to be nothing, less than nothing; that grace may reign, that grace may be all in all.

The various facts and testimonies produced from sacred writ, when treating about the freeness of pardon, equally prove the point under consideration: and might, with many others, be adduced and pleaded on this occasion. For he that is pardoned is justified; and he that is justified is pardoned, as before observed. Consequently, if our pardon be free, our justification cannot be conditional. But, to avoid prolixity, I shall not further enlarge in proof of the glorious truth; only would just observe, that so great a blessing, yet absolutely free; so Divine a favour, yet not suspended on any condition to be performed by the sinner, discovers astonishing grace. This must silence the fears and raise the hopes of the guilty, the accursed, the self-condemned. And may their hopes be raised by such a consideration; and also by beholding the glory of that infinite Being, whose honour and sovereign prerogative it is, to be inviolably just, yet the *Justifier of the ungodly.*

Having considered the antecedent state of the person whom God justifies, and the freeness with which the important blessing is bestowed upon him; the way appointed in the eternal counsels and revealed in the everlasting gospel, in which the condemned criminal may be honourably acquitted before the Divine tribunal, and accepted as righteous, now demands our attentive regard. Here we behold immaculate holiness and strict justice harmonizing with tenderest mercy and freest favour. Nor can it be otherwise. The Judge of all the earth must do right He can acquit none without a complete righteousness. For to justify a person, and judicially to pronounce him righteous, are the same thing. Justification is evidently a forensic term, and the thing intended by it a judicial act So that were a person to be justified without a righteousness, the judgment would not be according to truth; it would be a false and unrighteous sentence.

That righteousness by which we are justified must be perfect; must be equal to the demands of that law, according to which the sovereign Judge proceeds in our justification. Every judge, it is evident, must have some rule by which to proceed in his judicial capacity. This rule is the law. To talk of passing judgment, without having any regard to law, is absurd, and involves a contradiction. For, to judge, is nothing else but to determine whether the object of judgment be according to rule. A judge first considers what is fact, and then, comparing the fact with the rule of action, he pronounces it right or wrong, and approves or condemns the performer of it. An imperfect obedience, therefore, before a judge, is not righteousness: For, in this case, righteousness is no other than a complete conformity to that law which is the rule of our conduct. To accept of any obedience short of the rule, instead of that which perfectly answers it, is to act, not in the capacity of a righteous judge, but under the character of an absolute sovereign. So Jehovah himself declares, that he *will by no means clear the guilty* in judgment; that he *will not at all acquit the wicked;* and, consequently, that he will justify none without a perfect righteousness. That obedience, therefore, which is available for this grandest of all purposes, must answer the demands of Divine law. It must be such as will vindicate the honour of eternal justice, and of inviolable truth, in declaring the subject of justification completely righteous. Yes, reader, it must be such as you may venture to plead, without the least imputation of arrogance, at the throne of grace and the bar of judgment; such to which you may warrantably ascribe your happiness in the heavenly world, and in which you may glory to all eternity.

Many persons talk of, I know not what, *conditions* of justification; some supposing one thing, and some another, to be the condition of it. But hence it appears, that the only condition of our acceptance with God, is a *perfect righteousness.* This the law requires; nor does the gospel substitute another. For as the Divine law can have no more, so it will admit of no less. Those persons, therefore, who think of any thing short of complete obedience being sufficient, let them call the supposed condition by what name they please, may do well to consider, how they can free themselves from the charge of Antinomianism. For the gospel does not, in any degree, make void the law. So far from it, that the voice of the gospel and the death of Christ demonstrate Jehovah to be absolutely inflexible, as to all that his holy law requires or forbids. The way in which sinners are justified, does not in the least infringe on its rights. For, considered as moral, it is unalterable and eternal. Perfect obedience was demanded by it of man, while in a state of innocence, as the condition of life. Perfect obedience it still requires of man, though in a state of apostasy. And perfect obedience it must have, either at our own, or a surety's hand, or we must fall eternally under its curse.

Where then shall we find, or how shall we obtain a justifying righteousness? Shall we flee to the law for relief? Shall we apply, with diligence and zeal, to the performance of duty, in order to attain the desired end? Such a procedure, though it might flatter our pride, would betray our ignorance, disappoint our hopes, and issue in eternal ruin. The apostle of the Gentiles, when professedly handling the doctrine of justification, positively affirms and strongly proves, that there is no acceptance with God *by the works of the law.* Now, the works of the law, are those duties of piety and of humanity which the law requires. Nor can any acceptable obedience be performed, which is not required by that law which demands perfect love to God, and perfect love to man. So that when the infallible teacher excludes the works of the law from having any concern in our justification, he entirely rejects all our works, all our duties of every kind. But let us hear his words and consider their import.

By the deeds of the law, by our own obedience to it, however sincere, *shall no flesh be justified,* accepted of God, and pronounced righteous *in his sight.* The reason is evident; *for by the law is the knowledge of sin,* as an opposition to the Divine revealed will, and as deserving an everlasting curse.* But if so, it is absolutely impossible that we should be justified by it; for a law which proves us guilty, is far from pronouncing us righteous in the eye of the lawgiver. *The law entered,* was promulgated at Sinai, *that the offence might abound,* that the abundance of our iniquities might be manifested, and their exceeding sinfulness appear.† *The law worketh wrath.* It reveals the wrath of God against all ungodliness and unrighteousness of men. It fastens a charge of guilt on the criminal, and works a sense of deserved wrath in his conscience. Far from justifying any offender, it denounces utter destruction against him, and unsheaths the sword of vengeance.‡ *As many as are of the works of the law;* who do their best endeavours to keep it, and are looking for justification by it; *are*—what? In a promising way to obtain acceptance with God, and to be rewarded with life eternal? quite the reverse. They are *under a* dreadful *curse. For it is written* by the pen of infallibility, and is awfully expressive of Jehovah's unchangeable purpose: CURSED IS EVERY ONE, without any respect of persons, without any regard to please, THAT CONTINUETH NOT IN ALL THINGS *which are written in the book of the law to do them.*§ From this alarming text we learn that there never was, nor can be any acceptance with God, without a perfect obedience—an obedience, perfect in its principle, complete in all its parts, and without the least interruption in thought, word and deed. For he who *fails in one point,* breaks the law, is guilty before God, and exposed to ruin.‖

The apostle argues in proof of his point, from the opposition there is between living *by faith,* and living *by the works of the law.* These are his words; *That no man,* however excellent his moral character, however righteous in his own esteem, *is justified by* his own obedience to *the law in the sight of God, it is evident: For the just,* the truly righteous and justified person, *shall*

* Rom. iii. 20.   Gal. ii. 16.   † Rom. v. 20.
‡ Rom. iv. 15.   ‖ Gal. iii. 10.   § James ii. 10.

live by faith. *And,* that he does not obtain the character, or enjoy the blessedness connected with it, in virtue of his own obedience, appears from hence; *the law is not of faith;* it makes no mention of a Redeemer, or of believing in him. *But,* its uniform language is, *the man that doeth them;* that punctually performs the duties enjoined, and entirely avoids the things prohibited; he, and he only, *shall live in them;* shall find acceptance and enjoy peace.*

The inspired penman, ever jealous of his Master's honour, ever concerned for the glory of Divine grace, argues from an absurdity; an absurdity, obvious to the meanest capacity, and shocking to every mind that has the least esteem for the Lord Redeemer. *If righteousness come by the law;* if men either were or could be justified by their own duties and endeavours, *then* it would inevitably follow that *Christ is dead in vain;* all his obedience and all his sufferings were useless things; there was no occasion for them.† Again; *If they which are of the law be heirs;* if they who rely on their own legal performances be accepted of God, and entitled to the heavenly inheritance; *faith* in a dying Redeemer *is made* entirely *void, and the promise* of life by him is *made of none effect.*‡

Nor are the works of the law, which Paul so expressly and repeatedly excludes from having any concern in our justification, to be understood only of an obedience to those *positive* institutions of Jehovah, which, being of a temporary kind, were abrogated by the death of Christ. His design was to set aside all our obedience to every law; all our works and duties of every kind. That this was his intention, appears from the following considerations. The apostle excludes *all works* in general. *God imputeth righteousness without works—By grace ye are saved—not of works—If by grace, then it is no more of works. Not by works of righteousness which we have done—Who hath saved us—not according to our works.* He does not only say, that we are not justified by

* Gal. iii. 11, 12.   † Gal. ii. 21.   ‡ Rom. iv. 14.

the works of *the law;* but also, that we are not justified by *works,* performances, duties, obedience, in general, what rule soever may be their object, or however they may be denominated. He does not give the least hint, as if he meant only to exclude the works of some particular law, or duties of some particular kind, in contradiction to others. And when the Spirit of God declares, without limiting the phrase to any particular kind of duties, that we are not justified *by works;* what authority have we to restrain the sense to this or that sort of works, to the exclusion of others? For as all duties performed in obedience to a law are *works,* whether the law be considered as moral or ceremonial, old or new; so all works, whatever they be, are here excluded without any exception.

That law which the apostle designs, stands in direct opposition to the grace of the gospel, and the promise of life; to faith in Christ, and the righteousness of faith. *The* promise *that he should be the heir of the world, was not to Abraham, or to his seed through the* law, *but through the* righteousness of faith. *For if they which are of the* law *be heirs,* faith *is made void, and the* promise *made of none effect. Because the* law *worketh wrath; for where there is no* law, *there is no transgression. Therefore it is of* faith, *that it might be by grace, that the* promise *might be sure to all the seed.** Now it is the moral, and not the ceremonial law, that stands opposed to grace, and the promise; to faith, and the righteousness of faith. For the ceremonial law, exhibiting in various ways the grace of God, the promised Messiah, and life by him, as the great objects of faith and hope under the ancient Jewish economy; cannot be stated and considered in this contrasted view, without a manifest impropriety. But the moral law is *not of faith;* it contains no revelation of grace: it exhibits no foundation of trust, no object of hope for sinners; nor does it make the least promise to them, but all the reverse. Besides, the law here intended, *worketh wrath.* By a transgression of it, wrath is incurred; and by a conviction of the evil of such diso-

---

* Rom. iv. 13—16.

bedience, a sense of deserved wrath possesses the conscience. Which, though perfectly applicable to the moral law, and to mankind in general as breakers of it; yet cannot be affirmed of the ceremonial institutions, neither in regard to Jews nor Gentiles. Because, as to the former, those rites were long since abrogated; and, as to the latter, they never were under any obligation to observe them.

The important reasons assigned by the sacred disputant, why we cannot be justified by the works of the law, but by faith in Jesus, make it evident, that he intended to exclude, not only all ceremonial performances, but also all our moral obedience. Having asserted, that there is no justification by the deeds of the law, he adds, *For by the law is the knowledge of sin.** Now the apostle informs us from his own experience, that the knowledge of sin comes by that law which forbids all irregular desires, and every unsanctified affection. *I had not known sin but by the law; for I had not known lust, except the law had said, Thou shalt not covet.*† Hence it is plain to a demonstration, that all the duties of that law by which is the knowledge of sin, are entirely excluded from all concern in our justification: and, that the law which convinces of sin, is spiritual; reaches the thoughts and intents of the heart, saying, *Thou shalt not covet.* Whether it be the moral, or the ceremonial law, that is here intended, the reader, I presume, will be at no loss to determine. Another reason assigned, is, *Lest any man should boast.* For thus it is written; *By grace ye are saved—not of works, lest any man should boast—To declare at this time his righteousness, that he might be just and the justifier of him that believeth in Jesus. Where is boasting, then? it is excluded. By what law? of works? Nay: but by the law of faith* Whence the apostle infers the following conclusion: *Therefore we conclude, that a man is justified by faith without the deeds of the law.*‡ Now, of what are men

---
* Rom. iii. 20. † Rom. vii. 7.
‡ Eph. ii. 8, 9. Rom. iii. 26—28.

ready to boast, in a religious view, but of their supposed moral goodness? Of what, except the integrity of their hearts, and the regularity of their lives; their sincere intentions, and their pious performances? These, therefore, we may justly infer, are entirely excluded. For if no works be excepted but those of a ceremonial kind, and if our moral obedience be any way concerned in procuring acceptance with God, how is boasting excluded? Does not the performance of moral precepts afford as fair a ground for boasting, as a submission to ceremonial rites? and were not the ancient Pharisees guilty in both respects?*

Nor is *faith* itself our righteousness, or that for the sake of which we are justified. For though believers are said to be justified *by* faith, yet not *for* faith. That faith is not our righteousness, is evident from the following considerations. No man's faith is perfect; and if it were, it would not be equal to the demands of the Divine law. It could not, therefore, without an error in judgment, be accounted a complete righteousness. But the judgment of God, as before proved, is according to truth, and according to the rights of his law. That obedience by which a sinner is justified, is called *the righteousness* OF *faith; righteousness* BY *faith;* and is represented as *revealed* TO *faith* :† consequently, it cannot be faith itself. Faith, in the business of justification, stands opposed to all works. *To him that worketh not*, BUT *believeth*. Now, if it were our justifying righteousness, to consider it in such a light would be highly improper. For, in such a connexion, it falls under the consideration of a *work*, a *condition*, on the performance of which our acceptance with God is manifestly suspended. If faith itself be that on account of which we are accepted, then some believers are justified by a more, and some by a less perfect righteousness, in exact proportion to the strength or weakness of their faith. *He was strong in faith—O ye of little faith.* Consequently, either more of justice

Luke xviii. 11.   † Rom. iii. 22.   Phil. iii. 9.   Rom. i. 17.

and less of grace must appear in the justification of some, than in that of others; or else it must be concluded, that some are more fully justified than others; each of which is absurd. That which is *the end of the law*, is our righteousness; which, certainly, is not faith, but the obedience of our exalted Substitute. *Christ is the end of the law,* FOR RIGHTEOUSNESS, *to every one that believeth.* That righteousness by which many are justified, is the obedience of *One.* The believer, therefore, is not justified for the sake of his own faith; for then there must be as many distinct righteousnesses, as there are justified persons. Were faith itself our justifying righteousness, we might, without either pride or folly, depend upon it, plead it before God, and rejoice in it. For whatever the Most High is pleased to accept as our justifying righteousness, may be pleaded before him as such. Whatever may be so pleaded, must be esteemed a proper ground of our confidence—may be used as an argument in prayer at the throne of grace, and as the foundation of our expecting final happiness: and whatever is the ground of our confidence, must be the source of our spiritual joy. So that, according to this hypothesis, not Christ, but faith, is the capital thing; the object to which we must look. The glorious Redeemer and his undertaking are only considered as auxiliaries in the affair of justification; while faith is the grand requisite, as it renders Immanuel's work effectual, and crowns the whole. To understand those words, *Faith was imputed to him for righteousness,* in the Arminian sense, is to contradict the whole scope and design of the apostle's argumentation, when treating about the justification of sinners. For his main design is to prove, that the eternal Sovereign justifies *freely; without any cause* in the creature. But, according to this hypothesis, *faith* is the condition; is the cause; is that on account of which we are accepted as righteous. For it is considered under the formal notion of righteousness. Hence it appears, that it is not faith itself, but its glorious *Object,* which Paul intends, when he speaks of faith being imputed for righteousness

But is not that law, which man was originally under, which requires an absolutely perfect obedience, and denounces a curse on the least offender, abrogated by the mediation of Jesus Christ? And is not a new, remedial, milder law, introduced in its place; one that is more happily adapted to the infirmities of a fallen creature, requiring only a *sincere* obedience, as the condition of acceptance before the sovereign Judge? No: for, not to take notice that such a scheme represents the gospel as *making void the law;* not to mention many other things which might be urged; the sentiment supposes that the old, the eternal law of God, was either too strict in its precepts, or too severe in its penal sanction; and that its requisitions never were, nor ever will be performed, either by ourselves or by our Surety. An imagination this, which deserves the utmost abhorrence; as, in one view, it denies perfection to that law which is *holy, and just, and good;* and as, in another, it highly reflects on the wisdom, or equity, or goodness of the supreme Legislator for enacting a law, the repeal of which was so necessary in order to accomplish the designs of his grace. Besides, the scheme is absurd. For it supposes that the law which man is now under requires only an *imperfect* obedience. But an imperfect righteousness cannot answer its demands, whether it be denominated old or new. For every law requires perfect obedience to its own precepts and prohibitions. Under whatever law we are, it must be the standard of duty and the rule of our obedience; and every rule requires, and cannot but require, a complete conformity to itself. That law which forbids every irregularity in our tempers and conduct, whatever name it may bear, is the rule of our duty, the law which is now in force; otherwise, such irregularity would not be sin; such a deviation from perfect rectitude would be no fault. That which is not prohibited, that which is the breach of no law, cannot be sin; *for sin is a transgression of the law.* If then we are forbidden to commit sin, it must be by a law that is now in force; and if every sin be a breach of it, nothing short of perfect obedience can be required by it. Consequently, nothing can be accepted as righteousness by our eternal Judge, but an obedience in all respects complete; a perfect obedience, either performed by us or imputed to us.*

* To obviate objections and to enforce my argument, I will introduce a paragraph or two from a late excellent writer; who, when touching upon this subject, observes: "They," the Arminians, "strenuously maintain, that it would be unjust in God to require any thing of us beyond our present power and ability to perform; and also hold, that we are now unable to perform perfect obedience, and that Christ died to satisfy for the imperfections of our obedience, and has made way that our imperfect obedience might be accepted instead of perfect; wherein they seem insensibly to run themselves into the grossest inconsistency. For they hold, 'That God in mercy to mankind, has abolished that rigorous constitution, or law, that they were under originally; and, instead of it, has introduced a more mild constitution, and put us under a new law, which requires no more than imperfect, sincere obedience, in compliance with our poor, infirm, impotent circumstances since the fall.' Now, how can these things be made consistent? I would ask, What *law* these imperfections of our obedience are a breach of? If they are a breach of no law that we were ever under, then they are not sins. And if they be not sins, what need of Christ's dying to satisfy for them? But if they are sins, and the breach of some law, what law is it? They cannot be a breach of their *new* law; for (according to their principles) that requires no other than imperfect obedience, or obedience with imperfections: and, therefore, to have obedience attended with imperfections is no breach of it; for it is as much as it requires. And they cannot be a breach of their *old* law; for that, they say, is entirely abolished, and we never were under it. They say, it would not be just in God to require of us perfect obedience, because it would not be just to require more than we can perform, or to punish us for failing of it. And, therefore, by their own scheme, the imperfections of our obedience do not deserve to be punished. What need, therefore, of Christ's dying to satisfy for them? What need of his suffering, to satisfy for that which is no fault, and, in its own nature, deserves no suffering? What need of Christ's dying to purchase that our imperfect obedience should be accepted, when, according to their scheme, it would be unjust in itself that any other obedience than *imperfect* should be required? What need of Christ's dying to make way for God's accepting such an obedience, as it would be unjust in him not to accept? Is there any need of Christ's dying to prevail with God not to do unrighteously?— If it be said, *That Christ died to satisfy that old law for us, that so we might not be under it, but that there might be room for our being under a milder law:* Still I would inquire, What need of Christ's dying that we might not be under a law, which, by their principles, it would be in itself unjust that we should be under, whether Christ

Nor are we accepted of God on account of any holiness wrought in us by the Holy Spirit; or of any good works performed by us through the assistance of Divine grace after regeneration. For, however attained or performed, if it be ours by way of inherency, it comes under the denomination *of our own righteousness*. But all our own righteousness is extremely imperfect, and is therefore entirely excluded. This appears from hence. All righteousness consists, either in habit, or in act; either in principle, or in practice. Now if our external obedience to the commands of God be not *our own righteousness*, there is no such thing; and so the phrase, as used in the sacred writings, must be entirely destitute of all propriety. As to the principle of all obedience, what is it but the love of God? This is purity of heart, this is true holiness. And though this heavenly affection be not natural to man, but a fruit of the Spirit, yet it is included under the general idea of *our own righteousness;* for there is no such thing as righteousness, or moral goodness, where God is

had died or no; because, in our present state, we are not able to keep it?

"So the Arminians are inconsistent with themselves, not only in what they say of the need of Christ's *satisfaction*, to atone for those imperfections which we cannot avoid; but also in what they say of the *grace* of God granted to enable men to perform the sincere obedience of the new law. They grant, *that by reason of original sin, we are utterly disabled for the performance of the condition without new grace from God.* But they affirm, *that he gives such grace to all, by which the performance of the condition is truly possible: and that upon this ground he may and doth most justly require it*. If they intend to speak properly, by *grace* they must mean that *assistance* which is of grace, or of free favour and kindness. But yet they speak of it, as very *unreasonable, unjust*, and *cruel*, for God to require *that*, as the condition of pardon, that is become impossible by original sin. If it be so, what *grace* is there in giving assistance and ability to perform the condition of pardon : Or why is that called by the name of *grace*, that is an absolute *debt*, which God is bound to bestow, and which it would be unjust and cruel in him to withhold; seeing he re quires that, as the condition of pardon, which we cannot perform without it?"—See that masterly work entitled, " A careful and strict Inquiry into the modern prevailing Notions of that Freedom of Will, which is supposed to be essential to Moral Agency," part iii. sect. iii. by Mr. JONATHAN EDWARDS.

not the object of supreme affection; where our Maker is not sincerely loved. A rational creature who does not love the infinitely amiable Jehovah, far from having any thing that may be called *righteousness,* is actuated by the temper, and bears the very image of Satan: For where Divine love has no place in the heart, the dispositions of the mind are entirely sinful, and the whole conduct a direct opposition to the revealed will of God. Consequently, if nothing be worthy the name of righteousness, where the love of God has no influence; and if all our own obedience be excluded, in the article of justification; all that holiness, and all those duties which follow regeneration, and are performed by the assistance of the Holy Spirit, must be totally set aside, as to that important affair. According to those words: *By grace ye are saved—not of works.* What works? those to which they *were created in Christ Jesus,* and *in which God ordained that they should walk.** Hence the apostle very evidently distinguishes between that righteousness by which he was justified, in which also he desired to be *found,* and all his own righteous deeds. *And be found in Him not having mine own righteousness, which is of the law; but that which is through the faith of Christ, the righteousness which is of God by faith.*† Nor can any man, with the least shadow of reason, suppose, that the apostle ever imagined himself to have attained that holiness, or to have performed those good works included under the general phrase, *his own righteousness,* without the Divine assistance.

To assert that our own righteousness is the condition of justification, is to confound the two opposite covenants of works and grace. What was the covenant of works? Was it not a constitution which required personal obedience, as the condition of life, and promised acceptance with God on the performance of that condition? This was the tenor of it, and in this its distinguishing nature consisted. Whatever covenant therefore proceeds on the same terms, whether expressed or implied, is, however it

* Eph. ii. 8—10. † Phil. iii. 9.

may be varied in other respects, a covenant of works. As in the renewal of the first promise concerning the Messiah, in which the essence of the covenant of grace was contained; though the Sovereign Dispenser of all good was pleased to vary his language, and to exhibit his mercy in different views, under the Patriarchal, Mosaic, and Christian dispensation; yet, in substance, it was always the same: so, whatever variations we may suppose to have taken place, respecting the covenant of works, while its grand characteristic, Do THIS AND LIVE, is retained, it is nevertheless the same covenant.

To set the point in a clearer light, be it observed; that our first parents before the fall were under the covenant of works: and, supposing the condition of it had been performed, they would have had a right to life, and would have enjoyed the promised blessing. Now, though the enjoyment of life was suspended on the performance of perfect obedience, yet that was easier to them in their primitive state, than the least supposed condition would be to us in our fallen, corrupted state. And, how great soever the disparity was, between the obedience prescribed and the blessing promised; yet, had the condition been performed, and life enjoyed in consequence of it, the happy state would have been possessed, not as a gift of grace, but as a *reward of* pactional *debt*.* Nor would it have been of grace at all, in that sense in which the sacred writers use the term, when treating about the justification of sinners.

But supposing the condition of that covenant had been performed by our first father, and that life had been enjoyed by him as the reward of his own obedience; how, or by what means, could he have performed it? By that power and rectitude with which his nature was endued. But who gave him that power and rectitude? Who endued him with holy qualities, and fitted him for such obedience? Who maintained those moral abilities, and preserved him in existence itself? The answer is obvious. It is plain, however, that his being furnished with suffi

---

* Rom. iv. 4.

cient capacities, and having them preserved by the Lord his Maker, would not have prevented the reward from being by works. Life would still have been by the legal covenant; and entirely opposite, therefore, to that way of justification which is revealed in the gospel.

Yet further to evince the truth and confirm the argument, it may be observed, that the covenant of works itself did not require, even from innocent Adam, the performance of its condition by a power independent on Divine assistance. Nor could it, consistent with the nature of a dependent being, as man in his best estate, and every mere creature, must necessarily be. For conservation is as much owing to a Divine power, as creation itself. Those holy qualities, therefore, with which man was at first endued, could no otherwise be maintained, than by a continual divine influence from his Creator and Preserver. For if Divine agency be necessary to a continuance in mere existence, it must certainly be allowed necessary to a holy and happy existence; such as our original parents would undoubtedly have enjoyed, had they continued in a state of innocence. If then we talk of terms and conditions respecting the covenant of grace, the question is not whether they be great or small, hard or easy? but wnether, properly speaking, there be any condition at all, to be performed by the sinner, in order to obtain acceptance with God? and whether a supposition of any such thing does not annihilate the radical difference between the covenant of works, and the covenant of grace?*

* If the covenant of grace be duly considered, it will appear, that the execution of it, and the final happiness of the covenantees, do not depend on the proper exercise of the human will, or on any condition to be performed by man: that covenant having all its virtue and benign efficacy from the authority, love, and faithfulness of God himself. This glorious constitution consists of *absolute promises.* Eph. ii. 12. Jer. xxxi. 31—34. Heb. viii. 10—12. Nor is there any thing like a *condition*, which is not contained in the promises themselves. Those persons, therefore, must act a very injudicious part, who endeavour to explain the nature of this divine covenant, by considering the properties of those compacts which are common among men. For in so doing they entirely obscure the glory of sovereign grace, and

If then the subject of justification be, in himself, ungodly; if the Supreme Governor of the world neither will nor can justify any without a perfect righteousness; and if such a righteousness cannot possibly be found in our own performances, nor in faith itself, nor in any of the graces or fruits of the Holy Spirit; it is absolutely necessary that righteousness, wrought out by a substitute, should be imputed to us, or placed to our account. Where then, where, but in *the finished work of* Jesus Christ, shall we find this vicarious righteousness? Yes, the spotless obedience, the bitter sufferings, and the accursed death of our heavenly Surety, constitute that very righteousness by which sinners are justified before God. That amazing work which the incarnate Son completed when he expired on the cross, is the grand requisite for our justification before the heavenly tribunal. To this, and to this only, the eternal Sovereign has respect, when he pronounces the sinner just, and acquits him in judgment. Hence we are said to be *made righteous by the obedience* of Christ, and to be *justified by his blood.* This blood being shed, and that obedience being performed by our Divine Substitute, on the sinner's behalf and in his nature, are placed to his account as fully and as much to his advantage, as if he had in his own person underwent the sufferings and performed the obedience. The sufferings of the Holy Jesus, those dreadful sufferings of the Son of God and the Lord of glory, considered in connexion with this consummate obedience to the preceptive part of the law, which, for the superexcellency of it, is called THE RIGHTEOUSNESS OF GOD—these, including all that the righteous but broken law requires, being accepted by the Judge and imputed to sinners, are the united cause and the only ground of their full discharge. This—let me indulge the pleasing idea, and repeat the precious truth—this, without any addition, of any sort whatever, is that work for the sake of which the wretched sinner is pro-

leave the awakened sinner destitute of all hope. See Dr. Owen's *Theologoumena,* l. iii. c. i. Witsii *Œcon. Fœd.* l. iii. c. i. § 8—13. *Acta Synod. Dordrech.* part. iii. p. 312. Hoornbeekii *Summa Controvers.* l. x. p. 805.

nounced just and adjudged to life, by Him who is *of purer eyes than to behold iniquity.* By this obedience the law is honoured, and eternal justice completely satisfied. Jehovah declares himself well pleased with it, and treats as his children all those that are found in it.

That we are not justified by a personal, but by an imputed righteousness, appears from the Scripture with superior evidence. There the doctrine is taught in the plainest terms; there the important truth is set in the strongest light. It was in this way that Jehovah justified the Father of the faithful; to the consideration of which notable example of Divine grace and free acceptance Paul referred his Jewish brethren for their conviction, and for the instruction of all who should at any time inquire after the methods of grace. Abraham was the renowned progenitor of the Israelitish nation; and he was honoured with that exalted character, THE FRIEND OF GOD. His resignation and faith, his obedience and piety, stand on everlasting record. Few, among all the saints, ever manifested so cheerful a submission to the Divine will, or so unreserved a confidence in the Divine promise. No sooner did the true God signify his will to Abraham, that he should leave his native country and his father's house, than he *obeyed; and went out, not knowing whither he went.** No sooner did the Great Possessor of heaven and earth intimate his sovereign pleasure, that he should sacrifice his only son, his Isaac, whom he loved, than he readily submitted; though the heavenly mandate was quite unprecedented, and the thought of performing it enough, one would think, to astonish and confound him. Yet these acts of obedience, though highly pleasing to God, and such as will be had in everlasting remembrance, were neither the cause, nor the condition, of his justification. They, indeed, afforded the noblest testimony that his faith was genuine, and his piety real; and, in that sense, he was *justified,* or declared righteous, *by his works.*† But they were far from being placed to his account in the article of Divine acceptance. *For if Abra-*

---

* Gen. xii. 1. Heb. xi. 8. † James ii. 21—25.

ham *was justified by* his own *works*, though amazingly great, and in one instance quite unparalleled ; *he hath whereof to glory*, in comparison with others, who come far short of that elevated pitch of obedience to which he arrived. *But* though he might, on that supposition, have gloried before his fellow-creatures, yet *not before God. For what saith the Scripture? Abraham believed* the promise of *God*, concerning the Messiah and the work to be accomplished by him, *and it was counted unto him for righteousness*. Nor was the method of Divine proceeding, in the justification of this illustrious patriarch, any way singular. In this respect he had no exclusive privilege. For it is added, *Now it was not written*, in the ancient Scriptures, *for his sake alone, that it*, the work of a dying and rising Redeemer, *was imputed to him; but for us also*, whether Jews or Gentiles, *to whom it shall be imputed, if we believe on Him that raised up Jesus our Lord from the dead.* For *they which be of faith, are blessed with faithful Abraham.** Now if a person of such victorious faith, exalted piety, and amazing obedience as he was, did not obtain acceptance with God on account of his own duties, but by an imputed righteousness ; who shall pretend to an interest in the heavenly blessing, in virtue of his own sincere endeavours, or pious performances?—performances not fit to be named, in comparison with those that adorned the conduct and character of JEHOVAH'S FRIEND.

The apostle having shown in what way the Father of the chosen tribes was justified before the King immortal; and having intimated, that the patriarch was considered as an *ungodly* person, as one who had *no good works*, when the Lord imputed righteousness to him, in order to his final acceptance; to illustrate and confirm the momentous truth, he presents his reader with a description that David gives of the truly blessed man. And how does the royal psalmist describe him? To what does he attribute his acceptance with God? To an inherent, or to an imputed righteousness? Does he represent him as attaining

---

* Rom. iv. 2, 3. 22—24. Gal. iii. 6—9

the happy state, and as enjoying the precious privilege, in consequence of performing sincere obedience, and of keeping the law to the best of his power? No such thing. His words are, *Blessed are they whose iniquities are forgiven, and whose sins are covered. Blessed is the man to whom the Lord will not impute sin.* The blessed man is here described as one who is, in himself, a polluted creature, and a guilty criminal. As one who, before grace made the difference, was on a level with the rest of mankind; equally unworthy, and equally wretched: and the sacred penman informs us, that all his blessedness arises from an imputed righteousness. For what else can be intended by those remarkable words, with which he introduces the evangelical declaration? *Even as David describeth the blessedness of the man*—what man? Why, *he to whom the Lord imputeth righteousness without works.** The righteousness here intended, cannot be understood of a person's own obedience; because it is expressly said to be *without works.* His own virtues and duties, however excellent, contribute nothing toward it. No; it is perfect in itself, and entirely detached from every thing which he either has done, or can do. The phraseology of the inspired writer is very remarkable. He does not only speak of blessedness, as the result of an imputed righteousness; but he describes the obedience which is thus applied to the sinner, as being *without works.* This he does, more strongly to assert the truth he defends, and more effectually to secure the honour of grace. *Righteousness imputed: righteousness without the law: righteousness without works.* Such was the language of Paul; such was the doctrine that he preached; and such was the faith of the primitive church. Now, alas, the phrases are cashiered as obsolete, and are become offensive; so offensive that their frequent use is considered by the generality of those who call themselves Christians, as a certain indication of an enthusiastic turn of mind. And as the language is disapproved by multitudes in the present age; so the sentiment expressed by

---

* Rom. iv. 5—8.

it is discarded with contempt, as offering an insult to common sense. But, however much the doctrine of imputed righteousness may be despised as absurd, or abhorred as licentious, by any of our modern professors, it is evident that the great apostle considered it as intimately connected with the happiness of mankind, and esteemed the blessing as the only solid basis of all our hope, and of all our comfort.

Having seen what Paul says concerning the justification of Abraham, and the application he makes of that description which David gives of the blessed man; let us now consider what was the foundation of his own hope of eternal felicity, and on what righteousness he relied. Of these particulars the infallible teacher informs us in the following passage: *Yea, doubtless, and I count all things but loss, for the excellency of the knowledge of Christ Jesus my Lord. For whom I have suffered the loss of all things, and do count them but dung that I may win Christ, and be found in Him; not having mine own righteousness, which is of the law, but that which is through the faith of Christ, the righteousness which is of God by faith.* In this context the apostle relates his own experience. In these words he declares what was the frame of his mind, and what were his views with regard to the doctrine of justification. Here he presents himself as a guide and a pattern to all that inquire the way to happiness.

Let us attend to his words, and a little more particularly consider their import. *Yea, doubtless;* I affirm it with the utmost confidence, *and* am determined to abide by it; that I *count all things;* my birth-privileges, and pharisaical zeal; my submission to ceremonial rites, and performance of moral duties; these, all these I esteem *but loss.* Nor do I only reject all my duties before conversion; but also whatever I now have, and all that I now perform, I count of no worth in the grand article of Divine acceptance. These, though highly ornamental, useful, and excellent, when standing in their proper places and referred to suitable ends, are little, are nothing, are *loss* itself, compared with *the excellency of the knowledge of Christ Jesus my Lord.* Yea, such is the love that I have for my Saviour, and such the dependence I place on his righteousness, that for his sake *I have* cheerfully *suffered the loss of all things* which once I so highly valued. *And I do* with the greatest deliberation again declare, in the presence of Him who searches the heart, that *I count them* vile as the offals which are thrown to the dogs, and loathsome as *dung* which is cast out of sight. Such is the worth of my own performances, and such my estimate of them, if set in competition with the work of Jesus, or presuming to stand in the place of his righteousness. Now, therefore, it is my chief desire and supreme concern *that I may win Christ,* who is able to supply every want, and to render me completely happy. That when the Judge ascends the throne, at the last tremendous audit, when all nations shall appear before Him, and when none but the perfectly righteous are able to stand, I may be *found in Him* the Beloved, as the Lord my righteousness Then impartial justice must entirely acquit, and immaculate holiness completely approve. Would you know more particularly what I mean by being *found in Him?* It is, my *not having,* not depending upon, or so much as once mentioning *mine own righteousness, which is of the law;* the holy qualities I now possess, and the righteous deeds I have performed in obedience to the law, as a rule of conduct, and by the influence of grace, as the principle of spiritual life;—*But,* being adorned with, and relying upon *that* righteousness *which is through the faith of Christ;* which was finished by him, is revealed in the gospel, and received by faith—Even that obedience which, being performed by the incarnate Son, is dignified with every excellence, and bears that exalted character, *The righteousness of God by faith.*

On this instructive and very important passage I would further observe, that the manifest design of the sacred penman is to show, what that is in which a sinner may safely confide, and what is a warrantable ground of rejoicing. He intimates, that there can be no confidence toward God, no acceptance with him, and consequently no cause of spiritual joy, without a righteousness: for condemnation and wrath must be our portion, if we appear in our sins before the righteous Judge. He further suggests, that there is a twofold righteousness. The one he calls *our own;* and informs us it *is of the law.* The other, he describes as *through the faith of Christ;* and this he characterizes, *the righteousness of God.* These, he signifies, are entirely distinct, and far from having a united influence in procuring our justification: so far from it, that they are opposite and absolutely inconsistent, as to any such purpose. In reference therefore to acceptance with the Most High, he who embraces the one, must reject the other; and on the one or the other all mankind depend. He also informs us, with all the fervour of holy zeal, and in the most emphatical manner, which of these obtained his regard and supported his hope; was the ground of his confidence and the source of his joy. How much soever the Judaizing teachers, of whom he speaks in the beginning of the chapter, might *confide in the flesh,* or depend on their own duties, he was determined to adopt a very different method, and to seek for acceptance in a contrary way. Having warned them of their danger, and guarded the Philippians against their destructive mistakes, he declares that the righteousness which he esteemed sufficient was not *his own;* was not *of the law;* but a gift of grace, and *through the faith of Christ.* Even that obedience which our Lord performed in the capacity of a surety; which is *without works,* and *without the law;* was the object of his dependence, and in that only he glorified. But as to all that is included under the phrase, *his own righteousness,* when he considered the purity of the Divine law, the majesty of the eternal Judge, and that he must soon stand before him, he accounted it of no avail. Under such a consideration, he rejected it with disdain, and poured the utmost contempt upon it, calling it *loss* and *dung.* Such was the experience, and such was the hope of that wonderful man, whose apostolic gifts and Christian graces, whose ministerial usefulness and exemplary conduct, rendered him an eminent blessing to the world, and an honour to the great Redeemer's cause.

Many are the arguments which might be adduced from the unerring word, in proof of this capital doctrine and comfortable truth; but I shall only present my reader with the few that follow. It has been before proved, that the subject of justification is an *ungodly* person. His pardon and acceptance, therefore, cannot be the result of his own obedience: and it is equally clear, that *as* ungodly he cannot be justified. He must stand right in the eye of the law, and unreprovable before his Judge, before he can be acquitted in judgment. It must, consequently, be by the righteousness of another. But, what, or whose, righteousness can it be? Not the obedience of our fellow-mortals who are already justified; that would be to adopt the exploded doctrine of supererogation. Not the sanctity of angels; because they never became responsible for us. Not the essential rectitude of the Divine nature; for that is absolutely incommunicable. It must therefore be the righteousness of *Christ;* or his complete conformity to the holy law, as a voluntary substitute for the ungodly. Now, in what way can his obedience be applied to us, except by *imputation?* This argument, I am persuaded, will remain conclusive till it be proved, either that the subject of justification is not in himself ungodly; or that the Judge of all the earth can justify without a righteousness. The former is expressly contrary to the Divine testimony, and the latter involves a palpable contradiction.

Paul, when treating about our awful ruin by sin, and our wonderful recovery by grace, and when professedly handling this capital doctrine, informs us, that Adam was *a type of Him that was to come,* even of the Lord Messiah. He forms a striking comparison between the first and the second Adam; between the disobedience of the one, and the obedience of the other, together with the effects of each. He represents Adam as a public person, as constituted the federal head of all his posterity; and Christ, as the representative of all the chosen seed. The first offence of the former, he signifies, was imputed to all his natural offspring; the complete obedience of the latter, is imputed to all his spiritual seed. By the imputation of that offence, all mankind were *made sinners;* came under a charge of guilt, and the awful sentence of condemnation to eternal death: by the imputation of this obedience, all that believe are *made righteous;* are acquitted from every legal charge, and adjudged to eternal life. And as it was *one offence,* of *one man,* that brought death and misery on all the human race: so it is by *one righteousness,* of *one man,* even of the Lord from heaven and Jehovah's Fellow, that spiritual life and eternal happiness are introduced. According to that saying, *As by one offence, judgment came upon all men to condemnation: even so, by one righteousness,** *the free gift came upon all men to justification of life. For as by one man's disobedience many were made sinners: so by the obedience of One shall many be made righteous.*† That the *one offence,* and the *disobedience of one,* are to be understood of Adam's actual transgression of the Divine law, none can dispute. By his first iniquitous act and bold offence many were *made sinners,* before they were guilty of actual transgression; so made sinners as to be, on principles of justice, liable to condemnation and death. Nor is it conceivable how this could be, except by imputation; for which imputation, their natural relation to Adam, and his federal relation to them, were a sufficient foundation. It is equally evident, that the *one righteousness* and the *obedience of One,* are the complete performance of Divine precepts by our Lord Jesus Christ, his actual conformity to the holy law. This the antithesis in the text requires; this the scope of the apostle's reasoning demands. By this consummate obedience *many are made righteous.* By this *one* most excellent *righteousness,* all that believe are justified and entitled to immortal glory, without any good works of their own, and before they have performed any acceptable duty. Now, in whatever way the first offence of our original parent was made ours to condemnation; in the same way is the righteousness of his glorious Antitype made ours to justification. If that was by imputation, so is this.

The momentous truth for which I am pleading, is em

---

* Δι' ἑνὸς δικαιώματος. † Rom. v. 18, 19.

phatically taught in the following nervous passage. *He hath made Him to be sin for us, who knew no sin, that we might be made the righteousness of God in Him.* Hence it is plain, that as Christ the surety was made sin, so are we made righteousness; in the very same way that our sins were made his, does his obedience become ours. How, then, and in what sense, was the Holy One of God made sin? By being *punished* for it? No; for He was made that sin which he *knew not ;* but he knew by painful experience what it was to be punished. Besides, he could not have been punished for sin, if he had not stood guilty in the eye of the law; for punishment always supposes *guilt*, either personal or imputed. A person may suffer, but he cannot be *punished* without a previous charge of guilt; without being considered as the breaker of some law; for punishment is no other than the evil of suffering, inflicted for the evil of sinning. Was he made sin by becoming a *sacrifice* for it? That he was an expiatory sacrifice, is readily granted, is the Christian's glory: but that this is the sense of the phrase may be justly questioned. For, to omit other considerations, it is plain from the text, that he was made that *sin* which stands opposed to *righteousness ;* which cannot be affirmed of an expiatory sacrifice. Nor could he have been offered as an atoning victim, without having sin transferred to him prior to his being offered. So that He was in some way or other made sin before he shed his blood and made expiation. Was he then made sin by *inhesion*, or by *transfusion?* Was it communicated to him, so as to *reside* in him? The idea is absurd, the fact was impossible, and the very thought is blasphemy. It remains, therefore, that if he was made sin, that sin which is opposed to righteousness, it must be by *imputation.** This was the way in which our adorable Sponsor came under a charge of guilt. Hence it follows, by necessary consequence, according to the rule of opposition, except we would entirely destroy the apostle's beautiful antithesis, and the whole force of his argument, that those who are

---

* Non per tropum est explicandum, sed ῥητῶς sumendum est, prout oppositio monstrat. WALTH. Vide CALOVIUM *in loc.*

truly righteous, are made so by *imputation*, and by imputation only. For as it is impossible that any person, perfectly innocent, should be made sin, but by having the sins of others placed to his account, or charged upon him in a judicial way; so those that are in themselves guilty, cannot be made righteous in another, and by his obedience, without having it imputed to them. And as the blessed Jesus is said to be made sin, so we are said to be made righteousness. Strongly implying, that it was not by any criminal conduct of His that he became sin; so it is not by any pious activity of ours that we become righteous. As it was not on account of any evil qualities infused, that he was treated by Divine justice as an offender; so it is not in virtue of any holiness wrought in us, that we are accepted and treated as righteous. And as that sin, for which the condescending Jesus was condemned and punished, was not found in him, but charged upon him; so that righteousness by which we are justified and entitled to happiness, is not inherent in us, but imputed to us.

The objections also with which the apostle meets, and the way in which he refutes them, when handling the doctrine of justification, strongly imply that his design was entirely to exclude all the works of every law, and all duties of every kind: consequently, that our acceptance with God is a blessing of pure grace, and only by an imputed righteousness. The objections plainly suppose, that the method of justification, as clearly stated and fully explained by Paul, is not only injurious to the interests of holiness, but subversive of all morality. His doctrine was charged with *making void the Divine commands*—with encouraging those by whom it was adopted, to *continue in sin, because they were not under the law*—to multiply transgressions *that grace might abound*—and to do all manner of evil, *that good might come*.* Now if Paul had taught, or given the least intimation that righteous deeds, or holy dispositions, were any way necessary to a sinner's justification; if, in reference to that affair,

---

* Rom. iii. 8. 31, and vi. 1. 15.

he had not in the fullest sense renounced all human obedience, and directed sinners to place their whole dependence on the work and worthiness of Christ alone; it is highly improbable that the apostolic gospel would have been charged with such horrid consequences. For on that supposition, the enemies of sacred truth would not have had the least plausible pretence for traducing his doctrine as licentious.

But supposing any, through stupid ignorance or violent prejudice, to have so far mistaken his meaning as to imagine, that he entirely rejected all holy desires and pious endeavours without exception, as constituting no part of that righteousness for the sake of which a sinner is justified; when at the same time he only excluded a *spurious* kind of holiness, and works of a particular sort: we may reasonably conclude that, in his replies to those reproachful charges against his ministerial character, and against that gospel which was dearer to him than his very life, he would not have failed to point out the egregious mistake on which the objector proceeded, by distinguishing the works he did admit, from those which he renounced.

Had he rejected only the works of the ceremonial law, or such duties as are performed prior to regeneration, and without the aids of grace, while he maintained the necessity of evangelical obedience; it would have been easy, natural, and necessary for him, when refuting the blasphemous accusations, to have drawn the line of distinction, in order to prevent future mistakes. But not the least vestige of any such distinction appears, in his answers to the several hateful charges. He does not so much as hint that the objector was under a mistake in supposing, that he entirely excluded all the duties and works of men without any difference.

When he puts the objection, *What shall we say then? shall we continue in sin that grace may abound?* he answers by a strong negation, expressing the utmost abhorrence of any such thought; *God forbid!* Then he argues from an absurdity; *How shall we that are dead to sin, live any longer therein?* By which he signifies, that those who are the subjects of grace and believe in Jesus

Christ, being dead to sin, cannot walk in the ways of ungodliness. For, so to do, would be absolutely inconsistent with their new state, and with that principle of spiritual life which they have received. But he gives not the least intimation of the necessity of holiness, or of obedience in order to gain the favour of God, or to procure acceptance before him. If my reader should suppose that his views of justification are the same which Paul had, and yet is persuaded that some holiness, or moral goodness of his own, is necessary to obtain pardon, or to procure acceptance, I would advise him to consider, whether, if his sentiments were charged with being licentious, he would not immediately think of a different reply—one better adapted to answer his purpose, than any of those which the apostle made in a similar case. And whether he would not be ready to vindicate his creed by observing, That as he had no expectation of being accepted before the eternal Sovereign without a *personal* obedience, to charge him with *making void the law*, or with saying, *let us do evil that good may come*, could proceed from nothing less than the most palpable mistake, or the greatest malevolence. Such persons, however, as maintain the necessity of good works, in order to justification before God, are in little danger of being charged by ignorant people with holding licentious principles; which is a strong presumptive argument, that the doctrines which they espouse are not the same that Paul preached, and which the primitive saints professed. For, that their character and sentiments were so aspersed, is clear beyond a doubt: nor does it appear that natural men are any more capable of discerning spiritual things, or any more friendly toward the genuine gospel now, than they were in the apostolic times.

That righteousness by which we are justified is a *free gift*, as appears by the following words, *The gift of righteousness;* conformably to which, the apostle represents believers, not as performing, but as *receiving* it.*
The gospel of sovereign grace, proclaiming the sufficiency, suitableness, and freeness of it, is thence denominated *the*

* Rom. v. 17.

word of righteousness—the ministration of righteousness;* and one of the glorious characters which our Divine Sponsor bears, is, THE LORD OUR RIGHTEOUSNESS. In perfect correspondence with which, He is said to be *made unto us righteousness;* and it is affirmed of believers, that they are *made the righteousness of God in Him.*† Hence it is that they are declared, by the Spirit of infallibility, to be *justified in Him—accepted in Him —complete in Him—and saved in Him.*‡ Such is the divinely appointed method of justification; and such the provision which grace has made, for the final acceptance of guilty, ungodly, and wretched creatures.

The grand design of the gospel is to *reveal this righteousness of God,* and to display the riches of that grace which provided and freely bestows the wonderful gift. The gospel informs us that, in regard to justification, what is required of the transgressor, both as to doing and suffering, was performed by our adorable Substitute. This perfect obedience, therefore, being revealed in the word of truth for the justification of sinners, it is the business of true faith, not to come in as a condition, not to assert its own importance, and to share the glory with our Saviour's righteousness, but to *receive* it as absolutely sufficient to justify the most ungodly sinner, and as entirely free for his use. For what is evangelical faith, but *the receiving of Christ and his righteousness?*§ Or, in other words, *a dependence on Jesus only for eternal salvation?* A dependence upon Him, is all-sufficient to save the most guilty; as every way suitable to supply the wants of the most needy, and as absolutely free for the vilest of sinners. The Divine Redeemer, and his finished work being the object of faith,‖ and the report of the gospel its warrant and ground, *to believe,* is to trust

---

* Heb. v. 13.   2 Cor. iii. 9.   † 1 Cor. i. 30.   2 Cor. v. 21.
‡ Isa. xlv. 25.   Eph. i. 6.   Col. ii. 10.   Isa. xlv. 17.
§ Isa. xlv. 22.   John i. 12.   Col. ii. 16.   Rom. i. 17, and v. 17.
‖ Agreeable to those remarkable and instructive words, 2 Pet. i. 1. Τοις ισοτιμον ημιν λαχουσι πιστιν εν δικαιοσυνη του Θεου ημων και σωτηρος Ἰησου Χριστου. "To them that have obtained by lot equally precious faith with us, IN THE RIGHTEOUSNESS OF OUR GOD AND SAVIOUR JESUS CHRIST."

entirely and without reserve, on the faithful word which God has spoken, and on the perfect work which Christ has wrought. Such is the faith of God's elect: and the comfortable evidences of its truth and reality, are the love of God, and holy obedience; peace of conscience, and hope of glory. These, to a greater or less degree, are its proper effects and genuine fruits.

Happy, thrice happy they that are interested in this Divine righteousness, and have received the atonement! All such are pronounced righteous by the eternal Judge. There is nothing to be laid to their charge. They are acquitted with honour to all the perfections of Deity, and everlastingly free from condemnation. Their sins, though ever so numerous or ever so hateful, being purged away by atoning blood, and their souls being vested with that most excellent robe, the Redeemer's righteousness, they are *without spot, or wrinkle, or any such thing*. They are *presented*, by their great Representative, *in the body of his flesh, through death, holy, unblameable, and unreprovable* in the sight of Omniscience. They are fair as the purest wool; whiter than the virgin snow. Yes— let believers exult in the thought!—the work and worthiness of the Lord Redeemer give them acceptance with infinite Majesty, and dignity before the angels of light. These afford consolation on earth, and procure estimation in heaven. Through these they shall stand with courage at the bar of judgment, and make their appearance with honour among the inhabitants of glory. Let the legalist boast of his good works, his devout services, and strict holiness; the man that is taught of God esteems them all, if set in competition with Christ, or presuming to stand in the place of his righteousness, sordid as dross, and vile as the dung, lighter than vanity, and worse than nothing. Were he endued with all the shining virtues that ever adorned the lives and characters of the most excellent saints; did he possess the exemplary meekness of Moses, and the amazing patience of Job, the everactive zeal of Paul, and that love which glowed in the bosom of John, he would not, he durst not, advance the least claim to justification and eternal life on that footing.

No, blessed Jesus! it is in thy righteousness only that he dares to confide; it is only in thy obedience he presumes to glory. This obedience is an immovable basis for the anxious mind to rest upon by faith. This is a sure foundation to support the believer's hope of glory, even when he views the righteous law in its full extent and unabated purity. This foundation of confidence will support the soul in the view of death, and when on the confines of an eternal world. Nor will it fail (such is its high perfection and sovereign efficacy) in the near prospect of the awful judgment. Here then grace reigns, in freely bestowing this righteousness, and in our complete justification by it.

As it is the imputed righteousness of Christ, and that only, by which any of the children of men can be justified, let us look to it, rely on it, and glory in it. For it is dignified with every honourable character, and free for our use. Cheering thought! This way of justification is completely fitted to pull down the pride of the self-righteous professor, who considers himself as standing on more respectable terms with his Maker, than his ungodly neighbour. Nor is it less happily adapted to raise the drooping spirits of the trembling sinner; of him who has nothing to plead why sentence of condemnation, already pronounced upon him, should not be executed in all its rigour. If, indeed, we were not allowed to look to this unequalled obedience, till conscious of having some righteousness of our own, we might then be discouraged; despair would be rational, and damnation certain. But, thanks be to God for the unparalleled favour! this righteousness, and justification by it, are free, perfectly free for the worst of sinners. For the works of every law, in every sense, as performed by man, are entirely excluded from having any concern in our acceptance with God.* Since, therefore, it is in Christ alone, as our head,

---

* Dr. Owen, having quoted Rom. iii. 28, and iv. 5, and xi. 6. Gal. ii. 16. Eph. ii. 8, 9, and Tit. iii. 5, adds, "I am persuaded that no unprejudiced person, whose mind is not prepossessed with notions and distinctions, whereof not the least tittle is offered unto them from the texts mentioned, nor elsewhere, can but judge, that the law

representative, and surety, that we are or can be justified,
he alone should have the glory. He is infinitely worthy
to have the unrivalled honour. Let the sinner, then, the
ungodly wretch, trust in the obedience of the dying
Jesus, as being absolutely sufficient to justify him, without any good works or duties, without any good habits or
qualities, however performed or acquired; and eternal
Truth has declared for his encouragement, that he shall
not be disappointed.

Here, sinner, self-ruined and self-condemned; even
you that are tempted to execrate the day of your birth,
on account of your multiplied provocations and utter unworthiness; here is a complete righteousness revealed for
your full relief and immediate comfort. In this righteousness you may read the Divine character; JUST, YET THE
JUSTIFIER OF THE UNGODLY. True it is, if nothing but
equity had appeared in Jehovah's name, nothing but
misery could have been expected by the guilty. But
when we behold the idea of a compassionate Saviour,
connected with that of a righteous Judge; such a character, though supremely venerable, is greatly inviting.
For it speaks deliverance, and administers consolation.
Yes, disconsolate soul, though you have no righteousness,
nor any recommendation, yet the wisdom of God has
appointed a way, and the infinite riches of sovereign grace
have provided effectual means for your full discharge before the great tribunal, and for attaining that honour and
joy, which are commensurate to your utmost wishes,
which exceed your highest conceptions, and shall render
you happy to all eternity. Is my reader oppressed with
guilt, and harassed with tumultuous fears of deserved
ruin? wearied with *going about to establish his own
righteousness*, and sensible that he is possessed of no
worth, nor any thing that might be a probable mean of

in every sense of it, and all sorts of works whatever, that at any time,
or by any means, sinners or unbelievers do or can perform are, not in
this or that sense, but every way and in all senses excluded from our
justification before God. And if it be so, it is the righteousness of
Christ alone which we must betake ourselves unto, or this matter
must cease forever." *Doct. of Justification,* chap. xiv.

recommending him to the Redeemer? Remember, distressed fellow mortal, that no such recommendation is needful. Nothing is required at your hand for any such purpose. " Come, and take *freely*," is the language of Jesus. He has all that you want, however impoverished; and he gives all with the most liberal hand. *Grace reigns;* and let that be your encouragement when thinking about acceptance with Christ, and of your justification in him before the Almighty.

If my reader, notwithstanding all that has been said, should yet think it prudent and safe to depend on his own obedience, let me remind him before I dismiss the subject, of the absolute purity and infinite holiness, the transcendent majesty and awful glories of that GOD with whom he has to do, and before whom he must soon appear. Consider, presumptuous mortal! that with your supreme Judge is terrible majesty. That *He is of purer eyes than to look upon evil, and cannot behold iniquity, will by no means clear the guilty,* and *is a consuming fire.* His righteous judgment is, *that those who commit sin are worthy of death;* and, therefore, his law denounces an awful curse on every offender. Remember that he, whose divine prerogative it is to justify, is a *jealous God;* jealous of his honour, as a righteous governor, and determined to support the rights of his throne. So terrible his indignation, that, when once his wrath is kindled, it will consume every refuge of lies, *and burn to the lowest hell.* So awfully majestic is Jehovah, that before him the everlasting *mountains quake, the pillars of heaven tremble, and are astonished at his reproof.* As his condescending smile irradiates the countenances of angels, and crowns them with unutterable bliss; so his righteous frown is nothing less than absolute destruction. So flaming his purity, and so dazzling his glory, that he *looketh to the moon and it shineth not, and the stars are not pure in his sight.* In his presence the seraphim, those most exalted of mere creatures, *veil their faces and cover their feet,* in token of profound humiliation; while they cry in loud responsive strains, HOLY! HOLY! HOLY! is the LORD OF HOSTS! *How, then*, to use the language of Bildad in Job, how, then, *can man be justified with God? or how can he be clean*, before his Maker, *that is born of woman?* When he whose eyes are as a flame of fire, whose peculiar province it is to search the human heart, and to explore its latent evils; when he shall sift your conduct, and mark your offences, *laying judgment to the line and righteousness to the plummet*, you will not be able to *answer him one of a thousand:* and to what refuge will you then flee? Trusting in your own duties, you slight the great atonement, you despise the revealed righteousness, and Christ shall profit you nothing. You may talk in lofty strains about man's moral excellence, and the dignity of human nature, the worth of personal obedience, and the efficacy of penitential tears: you may declaim upon the necessity of good works, and reject with disdain the doctrine of imputed righteousness, while your conscience is unimpressed with a sight of the Divine purity, and with a sense of the Divine presence: but when you come to consider yourself as before the MOST HIGH, and that the important question is, *How shall I be just before the* MOST HOLY?—when you form your ideas of the God of heaven, not from the character you have drawn of him in your own imagination, but agreeably to that which is given in the inspired volume; then your pretensions to personal worthiness must subside, and your mouth must be stopped. Or, if not entirely silent, you must exclaim with the men of Bethshemesh, when Jehovah's hand was heavy upon them; *Who is able to stand before this Holy Lord God?* Then, if the atonement be not presented for your immediate relief, you will be ready to add, *Who shall dwell with devouring fire? who shall dwell with everlasting burnings?*

The Holy Spirit, speaking in the Scripture, directs us to conceive of justification as *before* God and in *his sight*. Intimating, that when final acceptance is the subject of our inquiry, we should look upon ourselves as in the immediate presence of Him who will soon ascend the *great white throne*, to pass the irreversible sentence; that we should consider on what ground we shall be able to stand, when *heaven and earth shall flee away from the face of our Eternal Judge, and no place shall be found for them.* Yes, reader, if you would not deceive yourself in a matter of the last importance; if you would come to a satisfactory persuasion, in what righteousness you may venture to trust, you should consider yourself as at the bar of God, and as having a cause depending which is pregnant with your everlasting fate; a cause which must inevitably issue, either in your eternal happiness, or infinite misery. You should anticipate, in your own meditations, that great decisive day, and then ask your own conscience, " On what shall I then depend? or what shall I dare to plead when my astonished eyes behold my Judge?" Because it would be superlative folly for you to rely on any obedience now, or to dispute for it as necessary to justification, of which your own conscience cannot approve as a plea that will then be admitted as valid.

Consider the ingenuous acknowledgments and deep confessions, which the greatest saints and holiest men that ever lived have made of their impurity and sinfulness, when their acceptance with that sublime Being, who is *glorious in holiness*, came under consideration. Job was an eminent saint: he had not his equal on earth, according to the testimony of God himself. Conscious of his integrity, he avowed it before men, and vindicated his exemplary conduct against the accusations of censorious friends. But when the Almighty addressed him, and when he considers himself as standing before the Divine tribunal, he says not a word about his inherent rectitude, or his pious performances. Then, in language of the deepest self-abasement, he exclaims, *Behold, I am vile! I abhor myself, and repent in dust and ashes.* Yea, he declares, *If I justify myself, my own mouth shall condemn me. If I say I am perfect, it shall also prove me perverse. Though I were perfect,* in my own apprehensions, *yet,* before Him that is infinitely holy, I would be so far from pleading my own extraordinary attainments, that *I would not know my soul;* nay, *I would despise my life,* with all its most shining accomplishments. For *if I wash myself with snow-water, and make my hands never so clean, yet shalt Thou*, O righteous and eternal Judge, *plunge me in the ditch;* manifest me, notwithstanding all my endeavours to obtain purity and find acceptance, to be a polluted creature and a guilty criminal. So abominably filthy and highly criminal, that *my own clothes*, were they sensible of my pollution and guilt, *would abhor me.* For He, to whom I am accountable, *is not a man as I am*, but a being of such discernment, that the minutest faults cannot escape his notice; and so perfectly holy, that the least spot of defilement is infinitely abhorrent in his sight. It is therefore absolutely impossible *that I should answer him*, plead my cause and gain acceptance, on the foundation of my own obedience; *or that we should*, on any such footing, *come together in judgment*, without inevitable ruin to my person and all my immortal interests.* David, the man after God's own heart, made it his earnest request that God would *not enter into judgment with him* according to the tenor of his own obedience: being well aware that neither he nor any man living could be justified in that way. To rebuke the pride of self-righteous confidence, with emotions of holy reverence and sacred awe, he asks, *If thou, Lord, shouldst mark iniquities; O Lord, who shall stand*, who can be acquitted?† Isaiah also, though an eminent prophet, and a distinguished servant of God, when he beheld Jehovah's glory, and heard the seraphim proclaim his holiness, loudly exclaimed, *Wo is me! for I am undone! because I am a man of unclean lips.* Nor was his consternation removed, or his conscience relieved, till pardon through the atonement was applied to him.‡

Now, is it prudent, or can it be safe, to trust in your own imperfect duties, when persons of such eminent character and exalted piety made these acknowledgments, and had such views of themselves and of their own attainments? If *their* personal obedience would not bear the Divine scrutiny, what a wretched figure must *yours* make before the heart-searching God? If Jehovah *charge*

---

* Job xl. 5; xlii. 6; ix. 20, 21, 30—32.
† Ps. cxliii. 2; cxxx. 3.   ‡ Isa. vi. 2—7.

his angels with folly, and if *the heavens be not pure in his sight; what then is man, who drinketh iniquity like water, that he should* presume to *be clean?* or *the son of man, that he should* pretend *to be righteous?* For, between human obedience and angelic holiness, there is no more comparison than between a clod of the field and a star in the firmament. *Vain man would be wise, though he is born like a wild ass's colt:* proud man would be righteous, though loathsome with sin and obnoxious to ruin. But, however highly the self-sufficient may think of their own obedience, the sinner, whose conscience is pressed with a sense of guilt, and every real Christian will deprecate appearing in their own righteousness, before the final judge. Yea, the man who is taught of God will ardently cry, " Fall upon me, ye rocks! cover me, ye mountains! yea, rather let me lose my existence than appear before the Most Holy in the filthy rags of my own duties ; or in any righteousness but that which is perfect, in any obedience but that which is divine."

CHAPTER VII.

OF GRACE, AS IT REIGNS IN OUR ADOPTION.

Those whom God has justified, and admitted into a state of reconciliation with himself, he has also adopted for his children. Hence their interest in all the blessings of grace, and in the unknown riches of glory, depends not merely on the favour of friendship, though that be of the noblest kind ; but also upon an indisputable right of inheritance, which right they have in virtue of adoption.

The word *Adoption*, signifies that act *by which a person takes the child of another, not related to him, into the place, and entitles him to the privileges of his own son.* In the Grecian and Roman states, it was customary for a man of wealth, in default of issue from his own body, to make choice of some person upon whom he put his name; requiring him to relinquish his own family never to return to it again, and publicly proclaimed him his heir. The person thus adopted was legally entitled to the inheritance, upon the decease of his adopter; and though previously void of all claim to such a benefit, or any expectation of it, was invested with the same privileges, as if he had been born an heir to his benefactor.*

That spiritual and divine adoption about which we treat, is, *God's gracious admission of strangers and aliens into the state, relation, and enjoyment of all the privileges of children, through Jesus Christ:* according to that glorious promise of the new covenant, *I will be a Father unto you, and ye shall be my sons and daughters, saith the Lord Almighty.* Reconciliation, justification, and adoption, may be thus distinguished. In *reconciliation*, God is considered as the injured party, and the sinner as an enemy to him. In *justification*, our Maker sustains the character of supreme Judge, and man is considered as a criminal standing before his tribunal. In *adoption*, Jehovah appears as the fountain of honour, and the apostate sons of Adam as aliens from him, as belonging to the family of Satan, and as denominated *children of wrath*. In reconciliation, we are made *friends;* in justification, we are pronounced *righteous;* and in adoption, we are constituted *heirs* of the eternal inheritance.

That believers are the children of God, the Scriptures expressly declare. They may be so called, as they are begotten and born from above; as they stand in a conjugal relation to Christ; and as they are adopted into the heavenly family. These different ways in which the Scripture speaks of their filial relation to God, are intended to aid our feeble conceptions when we think upon the grand, ineffable blessing; one mode of expresssion, supplying, in some degree, the ideas that are wanting in another. To express the original of spiritual life, and the restoration of the Divine image, we are said to be *born of God*. To set forth, in the liveliest manner, our most intimate union with the Son of the Highest, we are said

---

* Mr. Venn's *Complete Duty of Man*, p. 470, 471. edit. 2d

to be *married* to Christ. And, that we might not forget our natural state of alienation from God, and to intimate our title to the heavenly patrimony, we are said to be adopted by Him. The condition therefore of all believers is most noble and excellent. Their heavenly birth, their Divine Husband, and their everlasting inheritance, loudly proclaim it. The beloved apostle, amazed at the love of God manifested in the privilege of adoption, could not forbear exclaiming with astonishment and rapture, *Behold what manner of love the Father hath bestowed upon us, that we should be called* THE SONS OF GOD! Here grace reigns. The vessels of mercy were predestinated to the enjoyment of this honour and happiness before the world began. The great Lord of all chose them for himself, chose them for his children, that they might be *heirs of God, and joint heirs of Christ.* This he did, not because of any worthiness in them, but of his own sovereign will. As it is written, *Having predestinated us unto the adoption of children by Jesus Christ to himself, according to the good pleasure of his will, to the praise of his glorious grace.* According to *the good pleasure of his will;* this is the eternal source of the heavenly blessing. By *Jesus Christ;* this is the way of its communication to sinners. *To the praise of his glorious grace;* this is the end of bestowing it.

The persons adopted are sinners of Adam's race; who, considered in their natural state, are estranged from God, and guilty before him, under sentence of death, and obnoxious to ruin. Their translation therefore out of this deplorable condition, into a state and relation so glorious, is an instance of reigning grace. That the children of wrath should become the inheritors of glory, and the slaves of Satan be acknowledged as the sons of Jehovah; that the enemies of God should be adopted into his family, and have an indefeasible right to all the privileges of his children, are astonishing to the last degree. Our character and state, by nature, are the most indigent, wretched, and abominable; such as render us fit for nothing, after this life, but to dwell with damned spirits and accursed fiends, in the abodes of darkness and of despair. But, by the privilege of adoption, we are invested with such a character, and are brought into such a state, as render us fit to associate with saints in light, with angels in glory. What but omnipotent, reigning grace, could be sufficient to effect so noble, so astonishing, so divine a change?

If we take a cursory view of those invaluable privileges which, in virtue of adoption, the saints possess, and of which they are heirs, our ideas of the superlative blessing will be still heightened. They have the most honourable *character;* for they are called, not merely the servants, or the friends, but the *sons* of God. This dignified character is unalterable; for the Lord himself declares, that it is *an everlasting name that shall not be cut off.** If David so highly esteemed the character of son-in-law to an earthly king;† how much more should believers esteem that sublime title, *the sons of God;* of Him who is King of kings, and Lord of lords! They are also called *kings* and *priests;* besides which august and venerable titles, they are distinguished from the world by a rich variety of others, that are obvious to every intelligent reader of the sacred writings. The dignity of their *relation* is immensely great. For, being the children of God, Jehovah himself is their father, and Christ acknowledges them for his brethren. Nor do they stand in relation to Jesus merely as brethren; they are also his bride. Than their conjugal relation to him, nothing can be conceived more honourable, or more beneficial. For *he is the chief among ten thousand, and altogether lovely.* When David, though not yet in possession of the crown, sent his men to Abigail to take her to wife, that discreet widow *bowed herself to the earth,* and said, *Behold, let thine handmaid be a servant to wash the feet of the servants of my Lord.* Now, may not the believer, for infinitely greater reasons, with gratitude and astonishment adore that beneficent hand which broke off his yoke of basest vassalage, and joined him to David's Antitype, the heavenly Bridegroom: joined him in a marriage-covenant that shall never be broken, in a union that shall never be dissolved?

---

* Isa. lxii. 2; and lvi. 5.   † 1 Sam. xviii. 23.

Believers, being the children of God, are the objects of his paternal affection and unremitting care. As a father, he guides them by his counsel and guards them by his power. Their disobedience he visits with a rod of correction; and in their distresses he feels for them with bowels of paternal compassion. In the whole of his dealings with them he manifests his love, and causes all things to work together for their good. Yes, they are the darlings of Providence, and the charge of angels. Those ministering spirits, who are active as flame, and swift as thought, encamp around them; and, in ways unknown to mortals, subserve the designs of grace in promoting their best interests.

Nothing can exceed the riches and excellency of that *inheritance* to which they have a right, in virtue of their adoption; that eternal inheritance which is bequeathed to them by an inviolable testament. This testament, recorded in the sacred writings, was confirmed by the death of Christ. Their inheritance includes all the blessings of grace here, and the full fruition of glory hereafter. Though, as to temporal things, they be frequently indigent, and much afflicted; yet the blessings of common providence are dispensed to them in such measures as paternal wisdom sees best for their spiritual welfare, and the glory of God. For *godliness hath the promise of the life that now is*, as well as *of that which is to come;* and *their heavenly Father knoweth that they have need* of his providential favours, while they continue in the present state. So that whether they be things temporal, spiritual, or eternal; whether they be things present or things to come, all are theirs. According to that admirable text, *All things are yours, whether Paul, or Apollos, or Cephas, or the world, or life, or death, or things present, or things to come;* ALL *are yours*. But, which is yet more emphatical, and the highest that words can express, the utmost our ideas can reach; the Divine Spirit declares that they are HEIRS OF GOD, and JOINT-HEIRS OF CHRIST.* Each, therefore, has a right to say, "Jeho-

* Rom. viii. 17. So it is literally; and so MONTANUS, BEZA, CASTALIO, and many others, render the passage.

vah himself is my reward, my portion, and my inheritance." Yea, such is the mutual property which God and his people have in each other, that the inheritance is reciprocal between them. *For the portion of Jacob is the Former of all things, and Israel is the rod of his inheritance; the Lord of hosts is his name.* All the awful, the amiable, the adorable attributes of Deity, will appear glorious in the children of God, and be enjoyed by them to their everlasting honour and unutterable bliss. What can the heart of man desire more? Or, what good thing will God withhold from them for whom he gave his Son, to whom he gives himself?

In testimony to this their sublime relation, and as an earnest of their future inheritance, they receive the *Spirit of adoption;* by whom they cry, with appropriation and confidence, *Abba, Father.* The spirit of adoption, as opposed to the spirit of bondage, is the spirit of light and of liberty, of consolation and of joy. He glorifies Christ in the believer's view, and sheds Divine love abroad in his heart. He brings the promises to his remembrance, and enables him to plead them at the throne of grace. He elevates the affections to heavenly things, and seals him, as an heir of the kingdom, to the day of redemption. Such are the privileges of God's adopted sons, in the vouchsafement of which grace reigns.

What a mercy might we esteem it, not to be confounded before the God of heaven! What a favour to obtain the least indulgent regard from the King eternal! What an honour to be admitted into his family, to occupy the place and to bear the character of his meanest servant! But, to be his adopted children, who is the Fountain of all bliss; and his espoused bride, who is the Sovereign of all worlds; to have him for our everlasting Father, who is the former of all things; and him for our Husband, who is the object of angelic worship; are blessings divinely rich indeed! That sinful mortals, who may justly say to corruption, *Thou art our father;* and to the worm, *Thou art our sister*, should be permitted to say to the infinite God, "Thou art our portion: All that thou hast and all that thou art are ours, to render us completely happy and eternally blessed; is an astonishing, delightful, transporting thought! These are blessings, than which none greater can be conceived; none more glorious can be enjoyed.

Let the grandees of the earth, and the sons of the mighty, boast of their high birth and large revenues; their pompous titles and splendid retinues; their delicate fare and costly array; still the poorest peasant that believes in Christ is incomparably superior to them all. What though they shine in silk and embroidery, or glitter in gold and jewels; though their names be adorned with the highest epithets that men can bestow, while a profusion of worldly riches is poured into their lap; yet they must soon *lie down in the dust*, on a level with the meanest of mortals. The *worms shall* quickly *cover them*, and their *memory shall rot*. But your name, O weakest of Christians! your new name is everlasting. However neglected or despised among men, it shall stand forever fair in the book of life. Though you are not distinguished as a person of eminence, while you proceed on your pilgrimage, and receive not the acclamations of the people, but walk in the vale of life; yet you are high in the estimation of Heaven, nor destitute of the sublimest honours. Your praise is not of men, but of God. He knows the way that you take, and commands the angels to consider you as the object of their regard. Though you cannot boast of illustrious ancestors, or of noble blood; yet, being born from above, the blood-royal of heaven runs in your veins. Though not a favourite of your temporal sovereign; yet, like a prince, you have power with the God of Israel. Though ever so poor as to this world, the unsearchable riches of Christ are all your own. Though you have not a numerous train of attendants, and though your mansion be a cobwebbed cottage; yet the holy angels are your guard and minister to your good; while the God of glory not only condescends to come under your lowly roof, but even to dwell with you. Yours is the honourable character; yours is the happy state. This is felicity which all the wealth of the Indies cannot procure. This is honour, which all the

crowned heads in the world cannot confer. The Lord
of hosts hath purposed to stain the pride of all other
glory, but this honour shall never be laid in the dust.*
What a shade it casts on every secular distinction, when
forced to feel how very fleeting it is! How encouraging to reflect on the durable and exalted happiness of
the sons of God! Christianity! it is thine to ennoble
the human mind and to make it really great. Grace! it
is thine to raise the poor from the dunghill, and the needy
out of the dust. Thine it is, to number them among the
princes of heaven, and to seat them on thrones of glory.

And now, reader, what is your character? You, very
probably, call yourself a Christian. If so in reality, you
are a child of God, and an adopted heir of immortal glory.

Do you know then by experience, what are the privileges attendant on such a state, and connected with such
a character? If not, you bear the name in vain. So far
from being a Christian, you are—how shall I speak it?
will you believe it? can pride forgive it?—you are an enemy to God and a child of the devil. For these two characters, *the children of God*, and *the seed of the serpent*,
include all mankind. Consider, then, where to class
yourself, and what is your proper name.

Are you a believer? a child of God by adoption, and
an heir of eternal riches? Be careful to act agreeably
to your high character and exalted privileges. Let the
children of this world satisfy their little minds, and be
captivated by the low enjoyments and perishing vanities
of the present state; but you should disdain to act upon
their principles, or to be governed by their maxims.
The riches of the world, which engross the cares of the
covetous; its honours, that are so earnestly pursued by
the ambitious; and its various pleasures, in which the
sensualist delights, you should be far from desiring. Why
should you be discontented at the want of that which,
though enjoyed in all its fulness, could not make you
happy? equally far should you be from performing religious duties on the same principles and with the same

---

* M‘Ewen's *Essays*, vol. ii. p. 309—312.

views, as the legal moralist and selfish Pharisee; which generally are, either the applause of men, or their own acceptance with God. *That* is the most abominable hypocrisy in the sight of Him who searches the heart, and stands abhorred by every generous mind; *this* is a criminal usurpation of the office of Christ, and the highest dishonour to his undertaking. For it proceeds on a supposition, that the work of the Lord is either not perfect in itself, or not free for the sinner. The former basely reflects on his power, or faithfulness, and the latter on his grace: both which are equally far from honouring the adored Redeemer under his cheering and sacred character, Jesus. The children of light should act from the most generous motives and for the sublimest end. Love to their heavenly Father, and gratitude to the bleeding Saviour, should ever be the fruitful source of their obedience; and the glory of God, the exalted end.

Are you an heir of the kingdom? You should be careful to preserve a steady conduct in the church of God, and in the world. Not only to be zealous for your Father's honour, as we vulgarly say, by fits and starts; but maintain an uniform behaviour through the whole of your conduct. Endeavour to make it appear that you are a diligent servant, as well as a dignified son of God. Your practice should be, as much as possible, agreeable to your holy profession, and your glorious hope. Remember, that as your gracious Father and loving Husband, your glorious relatives and bright inheritance, are all in heaven; there also should be your heart, and your conversation. For though you are an heir of a kingdom, it is not *of this world:* and though you are *in,* you are not *of* the world. Nor will you have any reason to be surprised, or ashamed, if the world should hate you. *Whatsoever things are true; whatsoever things are honest,* grave, or venerable; *whatsoever things are pure; whatsoever things are lovely; whatsoever things are of good report; if there be any virtue, and if there be any praise,* the children of God undoubtedly ought, above all others, to *think on these things.* For no man can free himself from the odious charge of being a dishonour to Christ, and a reproach to his Christian profession, if he live under the dominion of sin, and be a servant of Satan Such a person, whatever speculative knowledge he may have of the doctrine of grace, or whatever his professions of love to it may be, is destitute of the faith of the gospel, and an enemy to the cross of Christ; is a stumbling block in the way of young converts; and, leaving the world in this condition, will feel a severer vengeance, will fall under double damnation to all eternity.

CHAPTER VIII.

OF GRACE, AS IT REIGNS IN OUR SANCTIFICATION.

Having treated upon that relative change, which takes place in the state of God's people in justification and adoption, I now proceed to consider, that real change which is begun in sanctification and made perfect in glory. This real change is absolutely requisite. For though Christ is proclaimed in the gospel, as entirely free for the sinner; and though we are considered as ungodly, when the obedience of the righteous Jesus is imputed to us for our justification before God; yet, before we can enter the mansions of immortal purity, we must be sanctified. Christ, indeed, finds his people entirely destitute of holiness, and of every desire after it; but he does not leave them in that state. He produces in them a sincere love to God, and a real pleasure in his ways. Hence they are called *an holy nation*. As holiness is the health of the soul, and the beauty of a rational nature; as it is the brightest ornament of the church of God, and essential to true blessedness; so, in a treatise on reigning grace, it must by no means be overlooked; for we may assure ourselves that grace reigns in it.

The vast importance of sanctification, and the rank it holds in the dispensation of grace, appear from hence. It is the end of our eternal election—a capital promise and a distinguished blessing, of the covenant of grace; a precious fruit of redemption by the blood of Jesus; the design of God in regeneration; the primary intention of justification; the scope of adoption, and absolutely necessary to glorification. So that in the sanctification of a sinner, the great design of all the divine operations, respecting that most glorious of all works, REDEMPTION, are united.

Sanctification, therefore, may be justly denominated a capital part of our salvation, and is much more properly so termed, than a *condition* of it. For, to be delivered from that bondage to sin and Satan, under which we all naturally lie, and to be renewed after the image of God, must certainly be esteemed a great deliverance and a valuable blessing. Now, in the enjoyment of that deliverance, and in the participation of this blessing, consist the very essence of sanctification. Hence the word is used to signify, *That word of Divine grace by which those that are called and justified are renewed after the image of God.* The effect of this glorious work is true holiness: or a conformity to the moral perfections of the Deity. In other words, love to God, and delight in him as the chief Good. *The end of the commandment is love, out of a pure heart.* So to love the Supreme Being, is directly contrary to the bias of corrupt nature. For as natural depravity consists in our aversion to God, which manifests itself in ten thousand various ways; so the essence of true holiness consists in love to God. This heavenly affection is the fruitful source of all obedience to Him, and of all delight in Him, both here and hereafter. Nor is it only the true source of all our obedience; for it is also the sum and perfection of holiness. Because all acceptable duties naturally flow from love to God; nor are they any thing else but the *necessary expressions* of that divine principle.

Though justification and sanctification are both of them blessings of grace, and though they are absolutely inseparable; yet they are so manifestly distinct, that there is in various respects a wide difference between them. This distinction may be thus expressed. Justification respects the person in a legal sense, is a single act of grace, and terminates in a relative change; that is, a freedom from punishment, and a right to life. Sanctification regards him in a physical sense, is a continued work of grace, and terminates in a real change, as to the quality both of habits and actions. The former is by a righteousness without us; the latter is by holiness wrought in us. That precedes, as a cause; this follows, as an effect. Justification is by Christ as a priest, and has regard to the guilt of sin; sanctification is by him as a king, and refers to its dominion. The former annuls its damning power; the latter its reigning power. Justification is instantaneous and complete, in all its real subjects; but sanctification is progressive, and perfecting by degrees.

The persons on whom the blessing of sanctification is bestowed, are those that are justified, and in a state of acceptance with God. For concerning them it is written, and it is the language of reigning grace; *I will put my laws into their mind, and write them in their hearts.* The blessing here designed, and the favour here promised, are, that love to God, and that delight in his law and ways, which are implanted in the hearts of all the regenerate; constantly inclining them to obey the whole revealed will of God, so far as they are acquainted with it. Sanctification is a new covenant blessing; and in that gracious constitution it is promised as a choice privilege, not required as an entitling condition.

Those happy souls who possess the invaluable blessing, and are delivered from the dominion of sin, *are not under the law;* neither seeking justification by it, nor obnoxious to its curse; *but under grace;* are completely justified by the free favour of God, and live under its powerful influence. This text strongly implies, that all who are under the law, as a covenant, or are seeking acceptance with the eternal Judge by their own duties, are under the dominion of sin; whatever their character may be among men, or however high their pretences may be to holiness. And as those that are under the law have no holiness, they can perform no acceptable obedience. For *they that are in the flesh,* in their carnal, unregene rate state *cannot please God.* Every one that is under the law, is condemned by it; and while his person is accursed, his duties cannot be accepted. A man's person must be accepted with God, before his works can be pleasing to him.

To set the subject in a clearer light, it may be of use to consider, that to constitute a work truly good, it must be done from a right principle, performed by a right rule, and intended for a right end. It must be done from a right *principle.* This is the love of God. The great command of the unchangeable law is, *Thou shalt love the Lord thy God.* Whatever work is done from any other principle, however it may be applauded by men, it is not acceptable in the sight of Him who searches the heart. For *by Him* principles, as well as *actions, are weighed.* It must be performed by a right *rule.* This is the revealed will of God. His will is the rule of righteousness. The moral law, in particular, is the rule of our obedience.* It is a complete system of duty; and considered as moral, is immutably the rule of our conduct. However chargeable therefore any work may be to him that performs it; or however diligent he may be in its performance; yet, if it be nowhere commanded by the authority of Heaven, it stands condemned by that Divine query; *Who hath required this at your hands?* And though it be pretended that the love of God is the principle, and the glory of God the end, as the dupes of superstition, both ancient and modern, have generally done; yet being nowhere enjoined in our only rule of faith and practice, it is no better than *reprobate silver,* and will certainly be rejected of God. So that, however highly the performer may please himself, or gratify his own pride by the deed, he cannot be commended for his obedience. For where there is no command, explicit or implied, there can be no obedience; consequently no good work. It must be intended for a right *end.* That is, the glory of the Supreme Being. *Whatsoever ye do, do all*

* See my *Death of Legal Hope, the Life of Evangelical Obedience,* sect. vii. where this subject is professedly discussed, in opposition to the Antinomians.

to the glory of God, is the peremptory command of the Most High. And as this is the end for which Jehovah himself acts, in all his works, both of providence and grace, so it is the highest end at which we can possibly aim. No man, however, can act for so sublime an end, but he that is taught of God, and fully persuaded that justification is entirely by grace; in such a sense by grace, as to be detached from all works dependent on no conditions to be performed by him. For till then he cannot but refer his supposed good actions principally to self, and his own acceptance with God. This is the highest end for which such a person can possibly act, though other and baser ends are often proposed by him. But those works that are truly good, and which the Holy Spirit calls the *fruits of righteousness, are,* in the design of their performer, as well as in the issue, *to the glory and praise of God.* Now, though an unregenerate man may do those things which are materially good, and by a right rule; yet none that are ignorant of the gospel of Divine grace can act from that generous principle and for that exalted end, which are absolutely necessary to constitute a good work.

To confirm the argument, and to illustrate the point, I would observe, that man is a fallen creature; entirely destitute of the holy image and love of God. So far from loving his Maker, or delighting in his ways, he is an enemy to him. The language of an unregenerate man's heart and conduct, is that of those profane wretches in the book of Job, who say to God, *Depart from us; for we desire not the knowledge of thy ways. What is the Almighty, that we should serve him? And what profit should we have, if we pray unto him?** Neither the

---

* Job xxi. 14, 15. I humbly conceive that the unregenerate man's habitual forgetfulness of God, the uneasiness he feels when the thoughts of his Maker and Judge dart into his mind, and his endeavours to exclude them as unwelcome intruders—his passion for sinful pleasures, and his love to present enjoyments—the enmity he has to the people of God—and his aversion to serious, religious, heavenly conversation—and, finally, the treatment with which the gospel meets in his breast, even the GOSPEL of saving grace, that brightest mirror of the Divine perfections; are evidences of this humbling truth, and fully prove the

commands of the Divine law, though the strictest and purest imaginable, nor all the vengeance threatened against disobedience to those commands, can work in our hearts the least degree of love to God, the lawgiver: nor, considering ourselves as apostate creatures and under the curse, is it in the nature of things possible. For the more pure its precepts are, so much the more contrary to the bias of corrupted nature: and it is evident, that its awful sanctio cannot be approved by a person obnoxious to its condemning power. Consequently, the Divine Lawgiver can have no share in our affections, while we continue in this deplorable condition.

Fallen man therefore cannot love God, but as he is revealed in a Mediator. He must behold his Maker's glory in the face of Jesus Christ, before he can love him, or have the least desire to promote his glory. Now, as there is no revelation of the glory of God in Christ, but by the gospel, and as we cannot behold it but by faith, it necessarily follows, that no man can unfeignedly love God, or sincerely desire to glorify him, while ignorant of the truth. But as there is the brightest display of all the Divine perfections in Jesus Christ, and as the gospel reveals him in his glory and beauty; so, through the sacred influence of the Holy Spirit, sinners behold the infinite amiableness and transcendent glory of God, in the person and work of Immanuel. The gospel being a declaration of that perfect forgiveness which is with God, and of that wonderful salvation which is by Christ, which are full, free and everlasting; by whomsoever the gospel is believed, peace of conscience and the love of God are in some degree enjoyed. While in proportion to the believer's views of the Divine glory revealed in Jesus, and his experience of Divine love shed abroad in the heart, will be his returns of affection and gratitude to God as an infinitely amiable Being, considered in himself; as inconceivably gracious, to needy, guilty, unworthy creatures. His

---

opprobrious charge. Is not this a striking proof, that a Divine power, and invincible agency, is necessary to regenerate the soul and convert the heart?

language will be, *What shall I render to the Lord for all his benefits? Bless the Lord, O my soul! and all that is within me, bless his holy name!* Being born from above, he *delights in the law of God, after the inward man;* and is habitually desirous of being more and more conformed to it, as it is a transcript of the Divine purity, and a revelation of the Divine will. Now he is furnished with that generous principle of action, love to God. The obedience he now performs, and that which God accepts, is—not the service of a mere mercenary, in order to gain a title to life, as a reward for his work; much less of a slave, that is driven to it by the goad of terror—but the obedience of a child, or of a spouse; of one who regards the divine commands as coming from a father, or from an husband. Being *dead to the law,* he *lives to God.*

I said, being *dead to the law.* This is the case of none but those that are poor in spirit, and have received the atonement in the blood of Christ; those who rely on his work alone, as completely sufficient to procure their acceptance with God, and as perfectly satisfying an awakened conscience, respecting that important affair. So the apostle; *Ye are become dead to the law by the body of Christ—We are delivered from the law, that being dead wherein we were held.* In these remarkable words, the believer is described as being dead to the law, and the law as dead to him. By which are signified, that the law has no more power over a believer to exact obedience, as the condition of life, or to threaten vengeance against him, in case of disobedience, than a deceased husband has to demand obedience from a living wife; or, on account of disobedience, to threaten her with punishment—That the real Christian, being dead to the law, has no more expectation of justification by his own obedience to it, than a living wife has of assistance from a dead husband—And that, as she can have no expectation of receiving any benefit from him, he being dead; so she cannot rationally have any fears of suffering evil at his hand.

But though the law, as a covenant, ceases to have any demands on *them that are in Christ Jesus;* yet, as a rule of conduct, and as in the hand of Christ, it is of great utility to believers, and to the most advanced saint. Nor, thus considered, is it possible that it should be deprived of its authority, or lose its use. For it is no other than the rule of that obedience which the nature of God and man, and the relation subsisting between them, render necessary. To imagine the law vacated, in this respect, is to suppose that relation to cease, which has ever subsisted, and cannot but subsist, between the great Sovereign and his dependent creatures, who are the subjects of his moral government. Nor, thus considered, are its commands burdensome, or its yoke galling to the real Christian. He approves of it; he *delights in it, after the inward man.* For, as a friend and a guide, it points out the way in which he is to manifest his thankfulness to God for all his favours; and the new disposition he received in regeneration, from his Law-fulfiller, inclines him to pay it the most sincere and uninterrupted regards. The obedience he now performs is in *newness of spirit, and not in the oldness of the letter.*

Should any pretenders to holiness, the genuine offspring of the ancient Pharisees, object, that *by faith we make void the law,* our answer is ready: God forbid! Yea, rather, *we establish the law,* both by the doctrine and the principle of faith. By the *doctrine* of faith. Because we teach, that there is no salvation for any of the children of men, without a perfect fulfilment of all its righteous demands. This, though impossible to a fallen, enfeebled creature, was punctually performed by Messiah, the surety; which, being placed to the account of a believing sinner, renders him completely righteous. Thus the law, so far from being made void, is honoured—is magnified, and that to the highest degree. The obedience performed to the perceptive part of the law, by a Divine Redeemer, and the sufferings of an incarnate God on the cross, in conformity to its penal sanction, more highly honour it than all the obedience which an absolutely innocent race of creatures could ever have yielded; than all the sufferings, which the many millions of the damned can endure to eternity. By the *principle* of faith. For as it purifies the heart from an evil conscience, through the application of atoning blood; so it works by love—love to God, his people, and his cause, in some degree conformable to the law, as the rule of righteousness. Hence it is that those who believe, are said to be *sanctified by that faith which is in Jesus.* If any one therefore, pretend to believe in Christ, to love his name, and to enjoy communion with him, who does not pay an habitual regard to his commands; he *is a liar, and the truth is not in him.* For our Lord says, *If a man love me, he will keep my words.* He informs us also, that the reason why any one does not *keep his sayings,* is because he *does not love Him,* whatever he may profess to the contrary. That is no love, which is not productive of obedience; nor is that worthy the name of obedience, which springs not from love. Pretensions to love, without obedience, are glaring hypocrisy; and obedience, without love, is mere slavery.

The great and heavenly blessing of sanctification is the fruit of our union with Christ. In virtue of that union which subsists between Christ as the head, and the church as his mystical body, the chosen of God become subjects of regenerating grace, and are possessed of the Holy Spirit. According to those emphatical and instructive words: *Without me,* without vital union with me, similar to that of a living branch to a flourishing vine, *ye can do nothing* that is truly good and acceptable in the sight of God. It is by the Spirit of truth and the word of grace, that any sinner is, or can be sanctified. As it is written, *Ye have purified your souls in obeying the truth, through the Spirit.* Hence we read, of the *sanctification of the Spirit;* of the *holiness of truth;* and, of being *sanctified by the truth.** By comparing these passages together, it is evident that the Divine Spirit employs evangelical truth as the appointed instrument, in producing that holiness in the heart and life of a Christian, which is included in the blessing, and signified by the term, sanctification. For this reason it is that our great intercessor prays, *Sanctify them through thy truth; thy*

---

* 1 Pet. i. 2. 2 Thess. ii. 13. Eph. iv. 24. John xvii. 19.

word is truth: and asserts, *Ye are clean through the word which I have spoken unto you.**
The truth of the gospel is that mirror in which we behold the gracious designs of God respecting us; the all-sufficiency of Christ, and his finished work wrought out for the guilty. *Beholding, as in a glass, the glory of the Lord; we are changed into the same image, from glory to glory, even as by the Spirit of the Lord.* As the countenance of Moses, after his familiar converse with Jehovah, shone with such dazzling radiance that the chosen tribes could not steadily behold it; so the believer, viewing the King of glory in his matchless beauty, derives a likeness to the glorious object of his views and his love. For the more frequently he beholds Him, the more fully he knows his perfections, of which his holiness is the ornament. The more he knows them, the more ardently he loves them. The more he loves them, the more he desires a conformity to them; for love aspires after a likeness to the beloved. The more he loves the transcendently amiable God, the more frequently, attentively, and delightfully will he behold him. Thus he obtains, by every fresh view, a new feature of Jehovah's glorious image.† Hence it appears, that our advances in true holiness will always keep pace with our views of the glory of God in the face of Jesus Christ. Or, in other words, that a life of holiness to the honour of Christ, as our King and our God, will always bear an exact proportion to a life of faith upon him, as our Surety and our Saviour.

As the word of grace is the proper warrant and ground of faith, the more clear our conceptions are concerning its truth and certainty, the more firmly shall we confide in it: consequently, the fruits of holiness will more abundantly adorn our conversation. For the gospel *brings forth fruit in all them that know it in truth:* and it is by the *exceeding great and precious promises* contained in it, that we are made *partakers of a divine nature.* Hence the gospel is compared, by an infallible author, to a *mould*

---

* John xvii. 17, and xv. 3.
† Witsii Œcon. Fœd. l. iii. c. xii. § 111.

into which melted metals are cast; from which they receive their form and take their impression. *God be thanked that ye were the servants of sin; but ye have obeyed from the heart that type of doctrine, into which ye were delivered.** As the gospel of peace is the doctrine here designed, and as it is according to godliness; so those that receive impressions from it, must, in proportion to its heavenly influence, have their tempers and conduct conformed to the law of God as the rule of righteousness. Thus the truth becomes effectual, through the agency of the Holy Spirit, to produce that purity of heart which is the health of the soul; and those good works which are the only ornament of a Christian profession.

As all the ordinances of grace are calculated to increase our knowledge and love of Christ; so they are adapted to promote the work of sanctification. Whether, therefore, they be those of the closet or of the family; whether public or private; they ought, by all means, to be conscientiously observed, by all who profess themselves the disciples of the Holy Jesus. All that attend upon them in faith, shall certainly find them the happy means of promoting their knowledge of the true God, their growth in grace, and their advancement in real holiness.

We may now consider the principal motives, that are used in the book of God, to stir up the minds of believers to seek a larger enjoyment of sanctification, and to abound in every good work. These motives are various, yet all evangelical. Believers are exhorted to obedience, from the consideration of their distinguishing characters, as *the elect of God* and *a peculiar people*.† The *purchase* which Christ has made of his chosen, and the unequalled *price* which he paid for their deliverance, afford a charming, a constraining motive, to be holy in all manner of conversation. The price with which they were bought, being nothing less than the infinitely precious blood of Jesus, our incarnate God; a remembrance of it should kindle in their hearts the most fervent glow of heavenly gratitude,

---

* Rom. vi. 17. So the original reads.
† Col. iii. 12—14. 1 Pet. ii. 9.

and elevate them to a pitch of seraphic devotion; and this more especially, when they reflect on that abject slavery and miserable state, in which they were viewed by the Lord Redeemer, when he undertook their cause, and gave his very life a ransom for them. In the sufferings of Christ on the cross we behold his tenderest compassion to perishing souls, his intense regard to the rights of his Father's violated law, and the concern he had for the honour of his Divine government. Considerations these, most happily calculated to mortify our lusts and quicken our graces; to make us loathe sin and love the law, as being *holy, just, and good.*

Here we see the tenderest compassion to our perishing souls, expressed in a way superior to all the power of language; superior to all finite conception. This he expressed—be astonished, ye inhabitants of the heavenly world! while all the redeemed of the Lord are transported with holy wonder, and filled with adoring gratitude!— This he expressed in tears and cries, in groans and blood. Consider Him, O believer, loaded with reproaches by his enemies, deserted by his friends, and forsaken even by his God. Consider him in these circumstances of unparalleled wo, and see whether it will not fire your heart with holy zeal, and arm your hands with an heavenly resolution, to crucify every lust, to mortify every vile affection. Did HANNIBAL, by the command of his father, swear at the altar, to maintain an irreconcilable enmity against the Romans? So should the Christian, when standing as it were at the foot of the cross, and beholding the sufferings of his dying Saviour, swear to maintain a perpetual opposition against every lust and every sin. Here he will form his firmest resolves, to enter into no alliance, to admit of no truce, with those enemies of his soul and murderers of his Lord. Such a consideration, set home by the blessed Spirit, will be instead of a thousand arguments to persuade, instead of a thousand incentives to prompt to cheerful obedience. So struck was Paul with a view of this astonishing love, and the righteous claim which Jesus has to every heart, that he accounted a want of love to him the highest pitch of ingratitude and wickedness; and boldly pronounced the state of such to be accursed to the last degree.*

Here we behold the Redeemer's love to his Father's law, and the superlative regard that he had to the honour of his Divine government. For though he was determined that the rebels should be saved from deserved destruction; yet, rather than the least reflection should ever be cast on the violated law, as though its precepts were unreasonable, or its penalty cruel, he himself would obey, he himself would bleed. By which procedure he declared, in the most emphatical manner, that the law, in its precepts, is entirely holy and good; and, in its penal sanction, perfectly just. And at the same time he demonstrated, how justly those who die under its curse are punished with everlasting destruction. Reflect upon this, believer, and see whether it will not prove a noble incentive to labour, and strive after a more perfect conformity to its holy precepts, in all your tempers, words, and actions; in all that you are, and in all that you do. Then you will see, that as the Lord, out of love to your soul and in honour to the law, refused not to die the most infamous death for your salvation; you are laid under the strongest obligations to love his name, and reverence the law; to confide in his atonement, and imitate his example.

When the Christian considers that his whole person is the object of redeeming love, and the purchase of Immanuel's blood; when he reflects that the end intended by this purchase is, that he *should serve the Lord without fear, in holiness and righteousness all the days of his life;* and that he *should live to Him who died for him and rose again:* beholding such a deliverance, by such stupendous means, and for such a glorious end, he will exclaim with Ezra, on an infinitely less important occasion; *Seeing that thou, our God, hast given us such deliverance as this, should we again break thy commandments?* The heart that is not moved, by such considerations as these, to love the Redeemer and to

---

* 1 Cor. xvi. 22.

glorify his name, is harder than stone, and colder than ice; is entirely destitute of every grateful feeling. Were believers more fully acquainted with the love of a dying Saviour, and the infinite efficacy of his atoning blood; their dependence on him would be more steady, and their love to him would be more fervent. And, were this the case, how patient would they be under all their afflictions; how thankful in all their enjoyments: how ardent in all their devotions; how holy in all their conversation; how useful in all their behaviour! Yea, how peaceful, how joyful, in the prospect of death and a future world! Then would their lives be happy indeed. The purchase made by the holy One of God is therefore a noble, a constraining motive to holiness of life.

Their *calling* is another consideration used to the same purpose. *As he who hath called you is holy, so be ye holy in all manner of conversation.* The Christian should often meditate on the nature and excellence of his high, holy, heavenly calling. Being called by grace, he is translated *out of darkness into marvellous light;* and from under the *power of darkness, into the kingdom of God's dear Son.* Out of a state of wrath, and of alienation from God, he is brought into a state of peace, and of communion with him. Now, the very end of his calling is, that he might be holy; that he might show forth the praises of his infinite Benefactor here below, and finally attain his glory in the upper world. How great the blessing itself! How gracious, how glorious the design of God in bestowing it! The remembrance of this must necessarily have a tendency to holiness, in every heart that is in the least acquainted with it.

The *mercies* of God in general, and more particularly that special mercy manifested in the free pardon of all their sins, and the everlasting justification of their persons, constitute the noblest attractive of the heart:* An attractive of sovereign efficacy, to draw forth all the powers of their souls, in a way of cheerful obedience to the ever-merciful God. That *forgiveness which is with* our

---

* Rom. xii. 1.

Sovereign, and the manifestation of it; far from being an incentive to vice, causes them to fear and reverence, to love and adore him. The state of believers, as not being *under the law*, is considered and improved to the same excellent purpose. *Sin shall not have dominion over you.* On what is this positive assertion grounded? Is it because they are bound to obedience, on pain of incurring the curse of a righteous law? Or, on the dreadful peril of suffering eternal ruin? Far from it. The reason assigned, which ought ever to be remembered, is, *For ye are not under the law, but under grace.** Here grace is described as having dominion. Here grace reigns. This consideration the apostle applies, as a powerful motive to holy obedience.

The *filial* relation in which believers stand to God, and their hope of life eternal, constitute another motive to answer the same important end.† The inspired writers frequently take notice of that sublime relation, to remind them of the dignity and privileges attending it, and to promote a suitable conduct. And, surely, the children of God should act from nobler principles, and have more elevated views, than the slaves of sensuality and the servants of sin. A consideration of their heavenly birth, their honourable character, and infinite inheritance, must animate them to walk as becomes the citizens of the New Jerusalem, and the expectants of an eternal crown. The *indwelling* of the Holy Spirit, together with the safety and comfort of believers, which in various respects arise from it; are considered and urged for their advancement in holiness.‡ For the absolute necessity of his abiding presence with the people of God, is no small inducement not to grieve the sacred inhabitant, by a loose and careless conversation.

The *promises*, which *are all yea and amen in Christ Jesus*, those *exceeding great and precious promises*, which relate both to this world and that which is to come, are improved as a further motive, to induce the children

---

* Rom. vi. 14.   † Eph. v. 1.   Phil. ii. 15.
‡ 1 Cor. iii. 16, 17.   Eph. iv. 30.

of God to press forward after all holiness of heart and life.* The apostle Peter, as before observed, considering their tendency and design, scruples not to affirm, that it is *by them*, by their influence on the soul, that we are *made partakers of a divine nature.*† These glorious promises are great as the heart of man can conceive; great as Jehovah himself can make.

The consideration of those chastisements with which the Lord, as a father, corrects his children, when remiss in their duty and negligent in the practice of good works, is another motive to stir them up to follow after holiness, and to make them watchful against the incursions of temptation.‡ I said, with which the Lord as a father *chastises ;* not punishes. For it is the property and business of a tender father to correct his children, when disobedient; but of a Judge and of an executioner, to pronounce a person worthy of punishment and to inflict it, which, in the proper sense of *punishment*, makes no part of the Divine conduct toward the heirs of glory. When their heavenly Father chastises them, it is not merely to demonstrate his own sovereignty, but to correct for faults committed; and that not in wrath, but in love. Yea, he does it because he loves them, in order to *make them partakers of his holiness*, and that *they may not be condemned with the world.*§ This being the design of God in chastising his people, and the severest chastisements being a fruit of his paternal care ; though the means be grievous, yet they are salutary, and the end is glorious. Correct them he will, but not disinherit them. He will make them smart for their folly, but he will not abandon them to ruin. According to that declaration ; *If his children forsake my law, and walk not in my judgments ; if they break my statutes, and keep not my commandments ; then will I visit their transgressions with a rod, and their iniquities with stripes. Nevertheless, my loving kindness will I not utterly take from him, nor suffer my faithfulness to fail.*‖ As the Lord corrects his

---

* 2 Pet. i. 4. 2 Cor. vii. 1. † 2 Pet. i. 4.
‡ Psalm lxxxix. 30—32. § Heb. xii. 5—11. 1 Cor. xi. 32.
‖ Psalm lxxxix. 30—33.

children when disobedient; so he reveals more of his love to them when they walk steadily in the paths of duty. Such as maintain the closest communion with him, and most punctually obey his commands, have reason to expect richer manifestations of his love; to live more under the smiles of his countenance; and, consequently, to be more joyful in their pilgrimage here on earth, having larger foretastes of future glory. While those of his people that backslide more frequently, and are not so careful to perform his will, come oftener under his correcting hand, and their comfortable communion with him is more interrupted.

This motive, it must be confessed, is of a less generous kind than those before mentioned. Notwithstanding, in the present imperfect state, it has its use. Nor is it destitute of holy love. For though the redeemed of the Lord fear the frowns of their Father's face, and the lashes of his correcting rod; yet they do not live under the slavish apprehensions of eternal wrath, nor are they kept in the way of duty by the tormenting fears of that awful punishment. Though they may justly expect more copious manifestations of their Father's love, when they walk in obedience to him; yet they do not obey to obtain life, or to gain a right of inheritance. No, they are already heirs. They are not only servants, but sons; and are possessed of a filial affection for him who has begotten them to a lively hope. Though the motive therefore be not so free, and pure, and noble as those before mentioned, which are taken from blessings already conferred; yet it savours of love to God, and has a regard to his glory. The obedience performed under its influence, is of a different kind from all the duties of the most zealous moralist, that is unacquainted with salvation by grace. It must, however, be granted, that the more pure our views are of the glory of God, the more perfect is our obedience, and the more acceptable in the sight of our heavenly Father. Yet, far be it that we should indulge the thought of our duties, when performed to the utmost of our ability, being accepted of God for their own sake! The acceptance with which they meet at the hand of God, is not because they are perfect, or we worthy; but in consequence of our union with Christ, and the justification of our persons in him. These duties, being the fruits of holiness, are produced in virtue of our union with him; are considered as evidences of that union; and accepted through him, as our great High Priest in the heavenly sanctuary—Accepted, not to the justification of our persons, but as a testimony of our love and gratitude, and of our concern for the glory of God.

That these are *all* the motives to obedience, with which the Scriptures furnish believers, and which they are bound to keep in their view, I am far from supposing; but they, I conceive, are some of the principal. If, therefore, these have their proper influence upon them, they will *be neither idle, nor unfruitful, in the knowledge of our Lord Jesus Christ.*

It is evident, from the foregoing paragraphs, that sanctification is an important part of that salvation and blessedness, which are promised to the people of God, and provided for them. Let the reader, therefore, be careful to look upon it, and seek after it, under its true character. Be diligent in the pursuit of holiness, not as the condition of your justification; but as the brightest ornament of a rational nature, as the image of the blessed God, and as that by which you bring the highest honour to his name. In this the perfection of your intellectual powers consists, and everlasting glory is its genuine result. The children of God should always remember, that though holiness and good works give them no title to life; for that is the prerogative royal of Divine grace, through the Mediator's work; yet a higher, and still higher degree of holiness is to be sought with all assiduity. It being their proper business, as well as their great blessing, while they walk in Christ the Way, to evidence, by holiness and good works, that they are in him, and so free from all condemnation.

It also appears, that as no obedience is acceptable to God, except it proceed from a principle of love to his name, and be performed with a view to his glory; and as no man is possessed of that heavenly principle, or capable of acting for that exalted end, but the true believer, or the justified person: so it must be very preposterous, and entirely unavailing, to exhort sinners to do this or the other good work, in order to gain an interest in Christ; or as preparatory to justification by him. For an interest in Christ is not acquired by the sinner, but freely bestowed of God; and is a primary fruit of eternal, distinguishing love. Nor are the best works of an unbeliever, any other than splendid faults; neither spiritually good in themselves, nor acceptable to Him that searches the heart. Till we receive the atonement which is by Christ, and that forgiveness which is with Jehovah, all our duties arise from a slavish principle, and are directed to a selfish end. "Without this, all that you do," says Dr. OWEN, 'however it may please your minds, or ease your consciences, is not at all accepted with God.—You run, it may be, earnestly; but you run out of the way; you strive, but not lawfully, and shall never receive the crown. True gospel obedience is the fruit of the faith of forgiveness. Whatever you do without it, is but a building without a foundation; a castle in the air. You may see the order of gospel obedience, Eph. ii. 7—10. The foundation must be laid in grace; riches of grace by Christ, in the free pardon and forgiveness of sin. From hence must the works of obedience proceed, if you would have them to be of God's appointment, or find acceptance with him."*

Hence it is evident, that as it is the gospel of reigning grace, under the agency of the Divine Spirit, which produces true holiness in the heart, and furnishes the Christian with such excellent motives to abound in obedience; this glorious truth is absolutely necessary to reform the world—necessary to be known, experimentally known, that we may please God, or answer any valuable purposes in a holy conversation. For the gospel only can furnish us with such principles and motives to obedience, as will cause us to take delight in it. When we know the truth as it is in Jesus, then, and not till then, *the ways of wis*

---

* On the Hundred and Thirtieth Psalm, p. 266, 267.

dom will be ways of pleasantness. Then faith will work by love to God and our neighbour.

Be it your concern, believer, to keep in view the many inducements to holiness, with which the book of God abounds and urges upon you. Always considering it as your indispensable duty and proper business, to glorify God by an holy, heavenly, useful conversation. Remember, you *are not your own: you are bought with a price:* your whole person is the Lord's. As nothing is a more powerful persuasive to holiness, than a consideration of the love of Christ and the glory of God, that are manifested in the atonement made on the cross; let that be the subject of your frequent meditation. For the cross, and the work finished upon it, exhibit the brightest view of the Divine perfections. Endeavour, then, to obtain clearer views of Jehovah's glory, and of your reconciliation to him by Jesus Christ; and you will have a greater abhorrence of all sin, and be more abased in your own eyes. Contemplate the bitter sufferings which Jesus underwent, not only for your good, but in your stead; and you will be pained at the heart on account of your past transgressions and present corruptions.* The more you become acquainted with that Divine philanthropy which was manifested in the redemption of your soul from the pit of destruction; the more will it constrain you to love, to adore, and to glorify the Lord Redeemer.† For as the love of God, manifested in Christ, proclaimed in the gospel, and experienced by faith, is that which first fixes our affections on him; so the more we view it, the more will our love be heightened. And as love to God is the only principle of true obedience, the more it is heightened, the more will it influence our minds and conduct in all respects. Thus grace, that very grace which provided, reveals, and applies the blessings of salvation, is the master who teaches, is the motive which induces, and the sovereign which sweetly constrains a believer to deny himself, and to walk in the ways of holiness.‡

* Zech. xii. 10.   † 2 Cor. v. 14.   ‡ Tit. ii. 11, 12.

CHAPTER IX.

CONCERNING THE NECESSITY AND USEFULNESS OF HOLINESS, AND OF GOOD WORKS.

Having considered the nature of sanctification, the character and state of those happy souls who enjoy the blessing, the way in which they come to possess it, and the many cogent motives to engage believers in the pursuit of holiness, and in the practice of true virtue, I shall now proceed to show the necessity of holiness, and the various important purposes which are answered by the performance of good works.

Love to God, being by regeneration implanted in the heart of a sinner, he is fitted for spiritual communion with the great object of all religious worship, in his ordinances and with his people in the church below; and for a more perfect communion with Him in the world of glory. In this fellowship with the Father, and with his Son Jesus Christ, with which believers are indulged in the present state; and in that more intimate fellowship with God, enjoyed by the spirits of the just made perfect above, true happiness, both in time and in eternity, consists. But the unsanctified soul is absolutely incapable of such refined pleasures. There must be a spiritual discernment, and a heavenly taste, before things of this kind can be either enjoyed or desired. For while a man continues in his natural state, at enmity with God and in love with sin; he neither has, nor can have any real pleasure in approaching his Maker. *Two cannot walk together except they be agreed.* Hence it is that our Lord says, *Except a man be born again, he* CANNOT *see the kingdom of God.* With whom the apostle agrees, when he asserts, *Without holiness no man shall see the Lord.*

That holiness which the Scripture so expressly requires in order to the enjoyment of God, is possessed by every one that is born from above, and in a justified state. For every subject of regenerating grace loves God. Love to God being the grand principle of holiness, and the source of all acceptable obedience, none can enjoy it, and not be possessed, in some degree, of real holiness. Nay, we may venture to assert, that whoever loves the infinitely Amiable, is possessed of all that holiness, in the principle, that shall at any time flourish and adorn his future conversation, or that shall shine in him to all eternity. Such a one, therefore, must not only have a title to heaven, but also be in a state of preparation for it.

Some professors, who espouse the notion of sinless perfection, and look upon themselves as uncommon friends to the interests of holiness, talk, indeed, of persons being in a regenerate and justified state, while they are yet unsanctified. Consequently, quite incapable of having communion with God, in his ordinances here; entirely unfit for the sublime enjoyments of the heavenly world hereafter; and, therefore, if they leave the present state in such a situation, everlasting misery must be their portion. But as the doctrine of sinless perfection in this life, is a bold opposition to the testimony of God, and contrary to all Christian experience; so this imagination is equally false and uncomfortable. For, either they mean the same things by the terms, *regenerate* and *justified*, which the Scripture does, or they do not. If not, what they say is nothing at all to the purpose; and therefore unworthy of a moment's regard, whatever may be their meaning. But if, by these expressions, they intend the same things which the Holy Spirit does, in the volume of infallibility; then it is evident, from the tenor of Divine revelation, that they labour under a great mistake. For what is intended by the *justification* of a sinner, but that the eternal Judge pronounces him righteous according to law, and freed from every charge? What is implied in the *regeneration* of a sinner, but a communication of spiritual life, and the restoration of the image of God in man? Now, is it possible that a person should be regenerated and justified; that he should stand clear in the eye of the law, and be viewed by Omniscience as possessed of spiritual life, and as bearing his Maker's image, while he is yet unsanctified, and quite unfit for glory? There is no such law in the blessing of justification, nor any such imperfection in the state of a regenerate person, as to leave him at such a distance from the eternal inheritance. We are not, in order of time, first renewed by the Spirit of truth, and justified by an imputed righteousness, in virtue of which we are entitled to glory; while yet we remain entirely destitute of holiness, or a capacity of enjoying eternal bliss, for which we must labour and strive in hope to attain it at some future period. For, being freed from the curse, and entitled to blessedness, we are the members of Christ; in a new state, and live a new life—Possessed both of a right to glory, and of a preparation for it; at the same time, though not by the same means.

As holiness of heart is absolutely necessary to communion with God, and to the enjoyment of him; so holiness of conduct, or an external conformity to the Divine revealed will, is highly useful, and answers various important purposes in the Christian life; the principal of which I would now consider. By obedience to the commands of God, we evidence the sincerity of our holy profession. By this our faith is declared genuine before men; who have no other way to conclude that it is unfeigned, but by our works. Whoever pretends to believe in Jesus, and is not habitually careful to perform good works; his faith is worthless, barren, dead. By a good conversation, in which our light shines before men, we edify our brethren, silence opposers, and preserve the gospel from those reproaches which would otherwise be cast upon it, as if it were a licentious doctrine. An exemplary conduct in Christian professors has often been owned of God and made happily useful, by convincing the ignorant, and by removing their prejudices against the truth; so as to make them impartial inquirers after it, and frequently of winning them over to an approbation of it. By walking in the paths of duty, we express our gratitude to God for his benefits, and also glorify his holy name; which is the great end of all obedience.

The works of faith and labours of love which believers perform, will be remembered by Jesus the Judge, at the last and great day of accounts: those especially that are done to the poor, despised members of Christ, and for his sake. These will be mentioned, at that awful time, as fruits and evidences of their union with Christ, and of their love to him. They will distinguish real Christians from open profligates and mere formalists; from all that were punctual in the performance of a round of duties, that cost them nothing; which raised their character among men, and exposed them to no shame nor suffering; but exceedingly backward to part with their unrighteous Mammon for the support of the cause of God, or to assist the poor and the persecuted members of Christ. These are the principal of those *necessary uses*, for which good works are to be maintained.

It is, notwithstanding, carefully to be observed, that neither our external obedience, nor inherent holiness, constitutes any part of that righteousness by which we are justified. Neither the one nor the other is either the cause, or the condition, of our acceptance with God. For, as before observed, that righteousness by which we are justified, must be absolutely perfect. But our personal obedience is greatly defective, even in the best of men and in their most advanced state, while in the present life. So that if God were to enter into judgment with us, on the ground of our own holiness or duties, none of us could stand in the awful trial. Our holiest dispositions would be found far short of that perfection which the law requires; and our best duties could not answer for themselves, much less atone for our transgressions. *All our righteousnesses are as filthy rags;* and we have need of a High Priest *to bear the iniquity of our holy things.* For who among mortals dare say to the omniscient God, "Search and try this, or the other duty, performed by me; thou shalt not, on the strictest examination, find any defilement cleaving to it, nor any sinful defect attending it!" Who dare add, "I am willing to risk my soul's eternal salvation on its absolute perfection, after such an exact scrutiny made?" The boldest heart must very much tremble at such a thought; nor dare the most upright make the solemn appeal, or venture his immortal all on such a foundation.

Hence the great teacher of the Gentiles, who was a most eminent saint, notwithstanding all his extraordinary gifts, his beneficent labours, exemplary conduct, and painful sufferings, for the cause of truth and the honour of his Divine Master, utterly disclaimed all pretensions to personal worthiness. For, when taking a prospect of the awful tribunal, he earnestly desired to *be found in Christ; not having his own righteousness, which was of the law,* consisting in his own holiness and righteous deeds; *but that which is through the faith of Christ, even the righteousness which is of God by faith.* This obedience, and this only, can support our hope, and comfort our hearts, when we think of standing before Him who *is a consuming fire.* That righteousness which was wrought out before we had a being, is the only ground of a full discharge before our final Judge; and, being so, it is the source of all our comfort and of all our joy, as to that grand affair. If any person, therefore, solicitously inquire, How shall I appear before my Maker? the answer is, in the obedience of Christ, which is perfect in itself, and entirely free for the guilty. But if the inquiry be, How shall I express my thankfulness to God for his benefits and glorify his name? then the answer evidently is, by living in conformity to his revealed will; and by devoting yourself, all that you are, and all that you have, to his honour and service. Thus provision is made, in the covenant of grace, for the believer's peace and joy, by a direct view of the finished work of Christ; and for the exercise of every virtue, the performance of every duty, whether it be religious or moral; and all for the noblest end, even the glory of God.

Hence it is manifest that though our good works are of no consideration at all, in the article of Justification, or in obtaining a title to life; yet, on many other accounts, they are highly necessary: and it is an affair of the last importance, to be rightly acquainted with the proper uses of good works. Otherwise, we shall inevitably run into one of those opposite and fatal extremes, Arminian legality, or Antinomian licentiousness. The former will wound our peace, infringe on the honours of grace, and exalt self. The latter will turn the grace of God into wantonness, harden the conscience, and render us worse than infidels avowed. We should therefore be exceedingly careful rightly to distinguish between the foundation of our acceptance with God, and that superstructure of practical godliness which must be raised upon it.

Let us once more hear the judicious Dr. OWEN. Speaking to this point he says: "Our foundation in dealing with God, is Christ alone; mere grace and pardon in him. Our building is in and by holiness and obedience, as the fruits of that faith by which we have received the atonement. And great mistakes there are in this matter, which bring great entanglements on the souls of men. Some are all their days laying of the foundation, and are never able to build upon it to any comfort to themselves, or usefulness to others. And the reason is, because they will be mixing with the foundation, stones that are fit only for the following building. They will be bringing their obedience, duties, mortification of sin, and the like, unto the foundation. These are precious stones to build with, but unmeet to be first laid to bear upon them the whole weight of the building. The foundation is to be laid, as was said, in mere grace, mercy, pardon in the blood of Christ. This the soul is to accept of, and to rest in, merely as it is *grace;* without the consideration of any thing in itself, but that it is sinful and obnoxious unto ruin. This it finds a difficulty in, and would gladly have something of its own to mix with it: it cannot tell how to fix these foundation-stones, without some cement of its own endeavours and duty. And because these things will not mix, they spend a fruitless labour about it all their days. But if the foundation be of grace, it is not at all of works; for otherwise *grace is no more grace.* If any thing of our own be mixed with grace in this matter, it utterly destroys the nature of grace, which if it be not alone, it is not at all.

"But doth not this tend to licentiousness? Doth not this

render obedience, holiness, duties, mortification of sin, and good works needless? God forbid! Yea, this is the only way to order them aright unto the glory of God. Have we nothing to do but to lay the foundation? Yes, all our days we are to build upon it, when it is surely and firmly laid. And these are the means and ways of our edification. This then is the soul to do, who would come to peace and settlement. Let it let go all former endeavours, if it had been engaged in any of that kind. And let it alone receive, admit of, and adhere to mere grace, mercy, and pardon, with a full sense that in itself it hath nothing for which it should have an interest in them; but that all is of mere grace through Jesus Christ. *Other foundation can no man lay.* Depart not hence until this work be well over. Surcease not an earnest endeavour with your own hearts, to acquiesce in this righteousness of God, and to bring your souls into a comfortable persuasion that God, for Christ's sake, hath freely forgiven you all your sins. Stir not hence until this be effected. If you have been engaged in any other way; that is, to seek for the pardon of sin by some endeavours of your own: it is not unlikely but that you are filled with the fruit of your own doings: that is, that you go on with all kinds of uncertainties, and without any kind of constant peace. Return then again hither. Bring this foundation work to a blessed issue in the blood of Christ; and when that is done, up and be doing."*

It is greatly to be feared, that the distinction so judiciously pointed out in the preceding quotation, is but little known or considered, even by many who are earnestly concerned in a religious profession. And it is undeniably plain, that there are great numbers denominated Christians, who, as they know nothing in reality concerning Christ; so, in their conduct, they are more like incarnate devils than real saints.—Nor are there a few that perform a round of duties very exactly, and have a high opinion of their own religious profession; who, notwithstanding, are far from possessing that holiness, and from performing those

* On the Hundred and Thirtieth Psalm, p. 307, 308.

good works, which are essential to the Christian character. View them in their places of public worship, and in the performance of devotional duties; they assume a serious air, as though they were greatly concerned about their everlasting welfare. See them in their families and in the common concerns of life, there they are full of levity, unsavoury and loose in their conversation. Some of these pretenders to Christianity will also attend that seminary of vice and profaneness, the playhouse, and other amusements of this licentious age, as far as their circumstances will permit. You may see them vain and extravagant in dress and show, while their pious neighbours of the same religious community, with all their industry, are hardly able to acquire decent clothing: yet these children of carnal pleasure, either do not at all regard their distress, or content themselves with saying, *Be ye warmed.* They will be lavish at their own tables, while the poor among the people of God are almost starving by their side: yet such is their love to Christ and his members, that they will think it an instance of great condescension if they vouchsafe to visit them and say, *Be ye filled.*

If these pretenders to piety be naturally of a more grave and serious disposition, view them in their trade and business; there you will find them covetous, griping, and oppressive; making it their chief design to lay up fortunes for their dependents, and to raise their families in the world. These, like their forefathers, *for a pretence make long prayers;* even when, by usury, extortion, and oppression, they *devour widows' houses, and grind the faces of the poor.* They lay up that in their coffers, which of right belongs to the needy who labour under them; the rust of which shall be a swift witness against them another day, and *shall eat their flesh as it were fire.* Is not the church defiled, and is not the gospel dishonoured, by such sanctimonious wretches as these? Such persons, whether more light in their disposition and conduct, or more grave in their temper and behaviour, are alike the children of the devil and the slaves of sin; are on a level, in the sight of God, with the most profane. As to the covetous, those votaries of Mammon, whatever dislike they may have to their associates, they stand ranked in the book of God with extortioners and thieves, with drunkards and adulterers. Nay, they are branded with the most detestable character of *idolaters.*

The sin of covetousness is, I fear, greatly misunderstood, and much overlooked by many professors. Were it not, the remark would not be so often made; " Such a person is a good Christian, but a covetous man." Whereas it might with as much propriety be said ; " Such a woman is a virtuous lady, but an infamous prostitute." For the latter is not more contrary to sound sense, than the former is to the positive declarations of God, recorded in Scripture. When we hear people, in common, talk about covetousness, we are tempted to look upon it as a merely trifling fault. But, when we open the volume of heaven, we find it pronounced idolatry, and considered as a capital crime; while Jehovah denounces damnation against the wretch that is guilty of it.*

In what then does this aggravated sin consist? I answer, *Covetousness,* in the language of inspiration, *is the desire of having more;* the desire of obtaining or of increasing in wealth. Whoever, therefore, is habitually desirous of riches, is, in the estimate of Heaven, a covetous man, whatever his station in life, or profession of religion may be. The language of the covetous heart is that of the horseleech's daughters, *Give, give.* The covetous man is always desirous of *more,* whether he have little or much: and, if a professor, he will always find some pretence to hide the iniquity of his idolatrous heart. But however such a professor may cover his crime under plausible pretences of any kind ; or however safe he may imagine himself, as being a member of some visible church, and free from her censure ; the time is coming when the mask shall be stripped off, and then it shall be fully known where his affections have been, and what God he hath served. Then it shall plainly appear, whether Jehovah, or Mammon, swayed his affections and ruled in his heart. Perhaps there are few sins for the

---

* 1 Cor. vi. 9, 10. Eph. v. 5. Col. iii. 5. Ps. x. 3.

practice of which so many excuses are made and plausible pretences urged, as that of covetousness, or a love of the world: consequently, there are few sins against which professors have greater occasion to watch. It was not, therefore, without the greatest reason, that our Lord gave that solemn caution to all his followers; *Take heed, and beware of* COVETOUSNESS.*

* Luke xii. 15. None will suppose, from what is here asserted, that I mean to encourage idleness or extravagance. No; far be it! Those who, through indolence, pride, or prodigality, waste their substance and fail in the world, can hardly be too severely censured. They not only impoverish themselves, but injure their neighbours; are the pests of society, and public robbers.

The reader, I presume, will not be displeased, if I present him with a quotation on this subject, from my worthy and honoured friend, Mr. HENRY VENN.—" It is remarkable," says he, " that the covetousness against which we are so earnestly warned in God's word, is not of the *scandalous* kind; but such as may govern the heart of a man, who is esteemed very virtuous and excellent by the world. In the tenth Psalm, *the covetous*, whom the Lord is there said to *abhor*, are the very persons of whom the wicked *speak well;* which could never be the case, did their love of money make them either villanous in their practice, or miserably penurious in their temper; for men of this stamp none commend.—The same thing is observable in that solemn caution given by our Redeemer; *Take heed, and beware of covetousness.* By which it is evident, he meant no more than a rooted persuasion that the comfort of life consists in abundance, and desiring, from such a persuasion, to be rich; this was the covetousness our Lord condemns. And, that this admonition might sink the deeper, he represents the workings of that avarice which he condemns, in a case which passes every day before our eyes. It is this: A man grows rich in his business, not through fraud and extortion, but by the blessing of God upon his labour and skill. As is usual, he is highly delighted with his success; he exults in the prospect of being master, in a few years, of an independent fortune. In the mean time, he is determined to be frugal and diligent, till he takes his final leave of business, to enjoy all the sweets of ease and splendour. Luke xii. 19. Now, where are the people governed by the common maxims and principles of human nature, who see any thing the least to blame in this man's sentiment or conduct? Who do not applaud and imitate it themselves? Yet this very man our Lord sets before our eyes, as the picture of one engrossed by a covetous desire of the things of this world. This very man he represents as summoned, in the midst of all his golden hopes, to appear a most guilty criminal at the bar of his despised Maker. Lo! this is the man whom our Lord exposes, as a miserable wretch for all others

We may, therefore, conclude, that though the absolute freeness of Christ, as exhibited in the gospel to the worst of sinners, must be maintained with confidence; yet we are bound to affirm, with equal assurance, that he who pretends to faith in Jesus, and does not habitually live under the benign influence of love to God, and of love to his brother *for the truth's sake;* and that he who does not manifest his heavenly affection by a suitable conduct, has no claim to the Christian character.

to take warning by and resist covetousness. *So, such a fool and such a sinner as this is he that layeth up treasure for himself;* that is, every earthly minded man, who seeks after wealth, as if it was the foundation of happiness; *and is not rich towards God ;* rich in faith, hope and holiness. Luke xii. 21.

"Paul, in perfect harmony with his Lord, forbids the desire of wealth as a criminal effect of avarice. *Let your conversation be without covetousness, and be content with such things as ye have: for He hath said, I will never leave thee, nor forsake thee.* Heb. xiii. 5. And where, instead of this self-denied temper, a desire of increasing in wealth is cherished, there snares, defilement, and ruin are declared to be the certain consequences. For 'they that will (the original signifies the simple desire) be rich, fall into temptation and a snare, and into many foolish and hurtful lusts, which drown men in destruction and perdition. For the love of money is the root of all evil: which while some have coveted after, they have erred from the faith, and pierced themselves through with many sorrows.' 1 Tim. vi. 9, 10.—If it should be said, Do you mean then to affirm, that it is wrong for any man to arise to a state of great wealth? The Scripture, I answer, condemns only the *desire* of riches and the *passion* for them, as defiling and sinful. Therefore, if whilst your whole heart is given to God, he is pleased to prosper whatever you take in hand, and give you an abundant increase; then your wealth is evidently as much the gift of God, as if it came to you by legacy or inheritance. It is God's own act and deed to call you up, who was content to sit down in a low place, to a higher point of view, and to intrust you with more talents, to improve them for his glory. Now the difference between possessing wealth, thus put into your hands, and *desiring to grow rich,* is as great as that between a worthless, ambitious intruder into a place of honour, seeking nothing but his own base interest; and a man sought out for his worth and invested with the same office, for the public good. And those who can see no material, no necessary distinction in the two cases, are already blinded by the love of money."—*Complete Duty of Man,* p. 389—392, second edition.

CHAPTER X.

OF GRACE, AS IT REIGNS IN THE PERSEVERANCE OF THE SAINTS TO ETERNAL GLORY.

It appears, from the preceding chapters, that the state of believers, whether considered as relative, or as real, in their justification, adoption, and sanctification, is highly exalted; and that the privileges attending it are of incomparable excellence, and of infinite worth. In each of these particulars it has also been proved that grace reigns; that the exceeding riches of grace are manifested.

The believer, notwithstanding, who knows himself, will be ready to inquire with great solicitude; "How shall I persevere in this happy state? By what means shall I attain the desired end? What provision has the Lord made, that, after all, I shall not come short of the expected bliss? Grace, I thankfully acknowledge, has done great things for me: to reigning grace I own myself unspeakably obliged. But if grace, as a sovereign, do not still exert her power, I not only possibly may, but certainly shall finally miscarry." Thus will every Christian conclude, when he considers the number and power, the malice and subtilty, of his inveterate spiritual enemies, compared with his own inherent strength to resist them. For the world, the flesh, and the devil are combined against him. These, in their several ways, assault his peace and seek his ruin. These attempt, in various forms, to cause him to wallow in the mire of sensuality, as the filthiest brute; or to puff him up with pride, as Lucifer. By insinuating wiles or open attacks, with the craft of a serpent, or the rage of a lion, they endeavour to compass his ruin: and, alas, how small his ability, considered in himself, to resist and overcome! The corruption of nature, even in the regenerate, renders the believer's desires after that which is good, too often exceedingly languid, and enervates all his moral powers

His pious frames are fickle and uncertain to the last degree; nor can he, with safety, place the least confidence in them.

This humbling truth was exemplified in the case of Peter. *Though all men be offended because of thee, yet will I never be offended—Though I should die with thee, yet will I not deny thee*—was his confident language. But, alas! in a very little while his frame of mind is altered. His courage fails. His pious resolutions hang their enfeebled heads: and, notwithstanding his boasted fidelity, he cannot watch with Christ so much as one hour, though there be the greatest necessity for it. He is brought to the trial, and, like Samson, his locks are shorn; his presumed strength is gone. He trembles at the voice of a silly maid; and, shocking to think! denies his Lord with dreadful oaths and horrid imprecations. Such are the inherent abilities of those who are to fight against the world, the flesh, and the devil. Such, considered in themselves, are the best of saints.

Now, can these unstable and impotent creatures hope to persevere, and to attain eternal life? Can those who know not how to trust their own hearts for a moment;* whose moral strength, in a comparative view, is mere weakness; who are continually surrounded with crafty, powerful, and unwearied adversaries, rationally expect a complete victory and an everlasting crown? Yes; these very persons *can do all things through Christ strengthening them.* God can enable even a *worm to thrash the mountains.* They shall not only come off victorious, but be *more than conquerors* over all their enemies. Nor can this appear strange, or in the least incredible, when it is considered, that omnipotent *Grace reigns*—that the love, the power, the wisdom, the promises, the covenant, and faithfulness of God—that all the divine persons in the eternal Trinity, and every perfection in the Godhead, are concerned in their preservation, and engaged to maintain it.

The *love* of God is engaged for their everlasting se-

* Prov. xxviii. 26. Jer. xvii. 9.

curity. Having chosen them to life and happiness, as a primary fruit of his own eternal favour, his love must abate, or his purpose be rendered void, before they can finally fall. But if *the Lord of hosts hath purposed, who shall disannul it?* If *his hand be stretched out,* for the execution of his gracious designs, *who shall turn it back, before the end be accomplished?* As he *thought, so it shall come to pass;* and as he *purposed, so shall it stand.** Nor shall his love to their persons ever abate. For *he rests,* he takes the highest complacency *in* the exercise of *his love,* and in all its favoured objects. Such is Jehovah's delight in his people, that *he rejoices over them with singing,* and takes a Divine pleasure in doing them good.† His love is unchangeable as himself, and unalterably fixed upon them. Consequently, though the manifestations of it may vary, yet, while infinite wisdom is capable of directing, and almighty power of executing his gracious purposes toward them, they shall never perish. Agreeable to which, we hear the apostle exulting in God's immutable love; affirming, that nothing in the heights above, nor any thing in the depths beneath; nothing present, nor any thing future, should be able to separate him from it.‡

The *power* of God is also engaged on the behalf of all those who are *begotten again to a lively hope.* They *are kept by it,* as in a garrison, *through faith to salvation.*‖ His power surrounds them as a fiery wall, to be their protection and the destruction of their adversaries.§ Omnipotence itself is their shield, and keeps them night and day.¶ As omnipotence is their guard, so omniscience is their guide; the honour of Divine *wisdom* being concerned in their preservation. For if a regenerate soul, one that has been rescued out of Satan's hand, were finally to fall and perish forever; it would argue, if not a want of power in God to maintain the conquest, yet a change of resolution; and so would bring no honour to the wisdom

---

* Isa. xiv. 24. 27.   † Zeph. iii. 17.   Jer. xxii. 42.
‡ Rom. viii. 38, 39.   ‖ 1 Pet. i. 2—4.
§ Zech. ii. 5.   ¶ Isa. xxvii. 3.

of his first design. It is no reputation to the wisdom of an artificer to suffer a work, by which he determined to manifest, in ages to come, his exquisite skill, and upon which his affections were placed, to be dashed in pieces, before his eyes, by an inveterate enemy, when he had power to have prevented it. Now the Scriptures inform us that, in the method of redemption, the wisdom of God is peculiarly concerned, is greatly diversified, and in the most wonderful manner displayed. Jehovah *abounded in all wisdom and prudence,* in forming the stupendous plan, and in choosing suitable means to attain the wonderful end. But if any of the chosen, redeemed, and called, were to be finally miserable, how could this appear?

The *promises* of God, those *exceeding great and precious promises* which are made to his people, afford them strong consolation respecting this matter. For the Father of mercies has declared that he will *confirm them to the end, and preserve them to his kingdom.* That the *righteous shall hold on their way, and grow stronger and stronger;* that they *shall never depart from him, but fear him forever;* that as they are in his hand and in the hand of Christ, they shall never be plucked thence; and, consequently, *shall never perish.* Yes, the blessed God has repeatedly and solemnly declared, that *he will never,* no never *leave them, nor forsake them.* And the reason is, not because they are worthy, or any way better than others; but for the glory of his own eternal name, and because he has chosen them to be his peculiar people. *The Lord will not forsake his people, for his great name's sake; because it hath pleased the Lord to make* them *his people.** These promises, with many others of a similar kind, *are yea and amen;* are made, and unalterably confirmed, *in Christ Jesus.* Divine faithfulness is pledged in them, and infinite power is engaged to perform them. These promises, let Christians exult in the cheering thought! these promises were made by Him that cannot lie; to which he has annexed, amazing to think!

---

* 1 Cor. i. 8. 2 Tim. iv. 18. Job xvii. 9. Jer. xxxii. 39, 40
Deut. xxxiii. 3. John x. 28, 29. Heb. xiii. 5. 1 Sam. xii. 22

his most solemn oath; with this professed design, that every sinner who *flees for refuge to lay hold on the hope set before him, might have strong consolation.* Now, the promise and oath of God, being two immutable things, must ascertain the believer's final happiness.

Jehovah's *covenant* with his people in Christ affords another glorious attestation to the comfortable truth That covenant, which is *ordered in all things,* which is stored with heavenly promises, replete with spiritual blessings, *and* absolutely *sure ;* that covenant of peace which never shall be removed, runs thus : *They shall be my people, and I will be their God. And I will give them one heart and one way, that they may fear me forever, for the good of them and of their children after them. And I will make an everlasting covenant with them, that I will not turn away from them to do them good; but I will put my fear in their hearts, that they shall not depart from me.* The stability of the new covenant is here asserted in the strongest terms. This gracious covenant is entirely different from that which was made with our great progenitor Adam; the condition of which was perfect obedience, and the promise of life was suspended on that condition. It is also very different from that which was made with the people of Israel at Sinai; which, being broken by them, was abrogated by the Lord himself. The language of this is *testamentary.* It consists of absolute promises, requires no condition to be performed by man, and is perpetual. Here that sovereign Being, who cannot lie, declares in the strongest manner, that those who are included in this covenant *shall not depart from him,* and that he will *never cease to do them good.* Security greater than this is not to be conceived, nor can be had. It would indeed be absurd to suppose, that God should make a new and better covenant than that which he made with Adam, or with Israel at Sinai ; a covenant without conditions to be performed by man ; a covenant which displays rich goodness and boundless grace ; and that, after all, the covenantees should be as liable to the dreadful forfeiture of life and happiness, as our first father, when under the covenant of works. Nay, if the new covenant had been conditional; if perseverance and immortal happiness had depended on our performance of any condition, whether greater or less; our state, as believers, would have been much more hazardous than Adam's was, while under the covenant of works; because of the very great disparity between that state of uprightness, in which he was created, and ours of corruption, into which we are fallen. Perfect obedience was easier to him than the least possible condition would be to us.

The *faithfulness* and inviolable *veracity* of God give further assurance of the saint's perseverance. The rocks, though of adamant, shall melt away; the everlasting mountains shall be removed; yea, the whole terraqueous globe itself shall disappear; but the faithfulness of God in executing his covenant, and the veracity of God in performing his promises, are unchangeable and eternal. *The Lord is faithful who shall establish you and keep you from* the destructive power of every *evil:* and he has declared, that he *will not suffer his faithfulness to fail.* Yea, he hath *sworn by his holiness*, by the glory of all his perfections, that he will be faithful to his covenant and promises, respecting Christ and his chosen seed.* So that if there be immutability in the purpose of God, if any stability in his covenant, if any fidelity in his promises, the true believer shall certainly persevere.—Rejoice, then, ye feeble followers of the Lamb. The basis of your confidence and consolation is firm and strong. Stronger than all the troubles of life; stronger than all the fears of death; and stronger than all the terrors of approaching judgment. Why should not you dismiss every slavish apprehension, when the God of power, of truth, and of grace, has made such ample provision for your deliverance from every evil you had any reason to fear; and for the enjoyment of every blessing you ought to desire, whether in this or a future world?

The *merit* of the Redeemer's blood, his *intercession* for his people, and his *union* with them, strongly argue their final preservation, and heighten their assurances of

---

* 2 Thess. iii. 3. Ps. lxxxix. 33—34.

it. *The merit of his blood.* For, is it probable that he who so loved them as to give his life a ransom for them; that he who suffered such tortures of body and horrors of soul in their stead; that he who drank the very dregs of the cup of wrath, on purpose that joy and bliss might be their portion forever—is it probable, I say, that he should ever suffer those who are in the most emphatical sense his *peculiar*, his *purchased people*, and his own property, to be taken from him by craft or power, and that by the most abhorred of beings and his greatest enemy? Such a supposition is very absurd. Such an event would be highly injurious to the Saviour's character. What, will not He who underwent so much for them in the garden and on the cross; who bore the curse and suffered the pains of hell in their stead, even while they were enemies, protect them now they are become, by converting grace, his friends? Why was he willing to be at such an amazing expense in their purchase, if, after all, he permit their avowed enemy to make them his easy prey? That be far from him! The thought be far from us! No; while there is compassion in his heart, or power in his hand; while his name is JESUS, and his work SALVATION; he must *see of the travail of his soul, and be completely satisfied.* It cannot be, that one soul for whom he gave his life and spilled his blood; whose sins he bore and whose curse he sustained, should ever finally perish. For if that were the case, divine justice, after having exacted and received satisfaction at the hand of the Surety, would make a demand on the principal; in other words, would require double payment. Besides, the faithfulness of Christ to his engagements is greatly interested in the everlasting happiness of all his redeemed. For we cannot forget who it is that says, *I came down from heaven, not to do mine own will, but the will of him that sent me. And this is the Father's will which hath sent me, that of all which he hath given me,* I SHOULD LOSE NOTHING, *but should raise it up again at the last day.* Now if Jesus. to whom the elect were given, and by whom they were redeemed, became responsible for them to the Father at the last day, as his own declarations import; were he

not fully to execute the Divine will, in raising up all that
were committed to his care, he would (I speak it with
reverence) fail in the performance of his own engagements. Consequently, either his power, or his faithfulness, would be impeached: a supposition of which is
absurd, and the assertion blasphemy.

The *intercession* of Christ for his people, in the heavenly sanctuary, affords another evidence of the glorious
truth. This intercession is founded on his perfect atonement for all their sins: and it is a firm foundation for that
purpose. So that, notwithstanding all the accusations of
Satan lodged against them, notwithstanding all their
weakness and all their unworthiness, the intercession of
Jesus the Son of God, of Jesus Christ the righteous, must
afford them the highest security. For *their Redeemer is
strong, the Lord of hosts is his name, he shall thoroughly plead their cause.* And as every believer is interested
in this intercession, so Jesus, the Advocate, is never denied in his suit.* His plea is always valid, and always
effectual to the end intended: which is, as he expressly
informs us, *that their faith fail not;* and, that they may
be *preserved from* destructive *evil.*† Our ascended
Redeemer is not, in this part of his mediatorial undertaking, like a mere petitioner, who may or may not succeed;
for, to all the blessings he solicits on their behalf he has
a previous right. He can claim them, in virtue of the
promise made to him and his spiritual seed, having, as
their substitute, fully performed the conditions of the
everlasting covenant. Yes, believer, the compassion of
Him who bled on the cross, and the power of Him who
pleads on the throne, ascertain your final felicity.

That ineffable *union* which subsists between Christ and
his people involves the truth for which I am pleading,
and clearly evinces the important point. For as every
believer is a member of that mystical body of which He
is the head; so, while there is life in the head, the members shall never die. neither by the wiles of craft, nor the
assaults of power. For He who rules over all, with an

---

* John xvii. 20, and xx 42.   † Luke xxii. 32. John xvii. 11, 15.

unremitting regard to the church, declares concerning his people ; *Because I live, ye shall live also.* His life, as Mediator, is the cause and support of theirs ; and they are *the fulness* and glory *of Him who filleth all in all.** As it is written, *Christ is our life—Your life is hid with Christ in God.*† Your life is *hid*, like the most valuable treasure in a secret place. *With Christ;* committed to his guardianship, and lodged under his care, who is able to keep that which is intrusted to his hands. *In God;* the bosom of the Almighty is the sacred repository in which the jewel is safely kept. Cheering thought! For Jesus, the Guardian, will never be bribed to deliver up his charge to the power of an enemy ; nor shall any sacrilegious hand ever be able, by secret fraud or open violence, to rifle the casket where Jehovah lays up his jewels.‡ The life of believers is *bound up in the bundle of life with the Lord their God;*§ and the bond of that union shall never be broken, the mysterious connexion shall never be dissolved. For *he that is joined to the Lord is one Spirit* with him, and, therefore, absolutely inseparable.‖

The *indwelling* of the Holy Spirit in believers furnishes them with another cogent argument in proof of the joyful truth. He is *in them a well of living water, springing up unto everlasting life.* As a guide and a comforter, he is given to *abide with them forever.* His design, in regeneration, is their complete holiness and everlasting happiness. His gracious purpose, in taking up his residence in them, is to fit them for sublimer enjoyments, to secure their perseverance, to guard them through life, and conduct them to glory. By him they are *sealed to the day of redemption :* and he is *the earnest of their inheritance.* Now as an earnest is part of the whole, and is given in assurance of enjoying the whole ; and as the Holy Spirit is called the earnest of our everlasting inheritance; the words must import the utmost certainty of our future bliss, if possessed of this earnest. Otherwise, which would be shocking to affirm, it must be

---

* Eph. i. 22, 23.   2 Cor. viii. 23.   † Col. iii. 3, 4.
‡ Mal. iii. 17.   § 1 Sam. xxv. 29.   ‖ 1 Cor. vi. 17.

esteemed precarious, as not answering the end for which it was given.

The *word* and *ordinances* of God, on which it is both the duty and privilege of believers to attend, happily subserve the great design. By these, as through the whole, the great Agent of the covenant works in a way suited to the nature of a rational being. For though the saints *are kept by the* invincible *power of God;* yet not by means merely physical but *through faith.* Whatever, therefore, is adapted to increase and confirm our faith in the great Redeemer, at the same time tends to our preservation. This the word and ordinances do. In the Divine word, believers have many great and precious promises to encourage them; many exhortations to direct and animate them in the performance of duty; many warnings given, and dangers pointed out, to deter them from evil; many examples of suffering patience and victorious faith, for their imitation, comfort, and support, whenever they come into similar circumstances; and many glorious things affirmed concerning that inheritance which God has provided for them, in order to raise their affections to heavenly things, and to invigorate their hope of eternal blessedness; all which are adapted to promote their edification, and to preserve them in the way of peace. The *ordinances* of God in general, which are compared to green pastures, in which the sheep of Christ delight both to feed and rest,* being adapted to nourish their souls, and to increase the vigour of their spiritual life, must be happily conducive to their preservation. By a suitable attendance on Divine institutions, believers have their faith confirmed, their holiness advanced, and their hope brightened. In them they have the bread of God dispensed, by which they are nourished up to life eternal. On those appointments of Heaven, therefore, it is their duty and their blessing to attend: nor can they, without the highest presumption, expect preservation in the faith, while they neglect the salutary means. Nor are the Divine *chastisements* without their use, in this respect. For the children

---

* Ps. xxiii. 2.

of God are chastened of their Father, *that they might not be condemned with the world.**

On the whole, then, we have the utmost reason to conclude with Paul, that wherever God begins *a good work, he will* certainly *perform it until the day of Jesus Christ.* For He that formed the universe is not such an inconsiderate builder, as to lay the foundation of a sinner's complete happiness in his own eternal purpose, and in the blood of his only Son, and then leave his work unfinished. No; it shall never be said by his infernal enemies, Here *God began to build, but was not able to finish.* He once loved, redeemed, regenerated, and designed to have saved these wretched souls. But his love abated; his purpose altered, or, which is more to our honour and his disappointment, we have rendered his plan of operation abortive: and now we torment, with a vengeance, myriads that were once high in Jehovah's favour, and numbered among his children. But, though this be the consequence of the opposite doctrine, Lucifer himself, with all his pride and enmity, will never entertain such a thought, nor thus blaspheme his Maker.

The following quotation may serve to exhibit, in a compendious view, the substance of the foregoing paragraphs: " Since we stand not, like Adam, upon our own bottom; but are branches of such a vine as never withers; members of such a head as never dies; sharers in such a Spirit as cleanseth, healeth, and purifieth the heart; partakers of such promises as are sealed with the oath of God—since we live, not by our own life, but by the life of Christ; are not led or sealed by our own spirit, but by the Spirit of Christ; do not obtain mercy by our own prayers, but by the intercession of Christ; stand not reconciled to God by our own endeavours, but by the propitiation wrought by Christ; who loved us when we were enemies, and in our blood; who is both willing and able to save to the uttermost, and to preserve his own mercies in us; to whose office it belongs to take order that none who are given unto him be lost—undoubtedly, that life of Christ in us, which is thus underpropped,

* 1 Cor. xi. 32. Ps. lxxxix. 30—34.

though it be not privileged from temptations, no, not from backslidings, yet it is an abiding life. He who raised our soul from death, will either preserve our feet from falling, or if we do fall, will heal our backslidings, and will save us freely."*

Some, perhaps, may be ready to object: "If the preservation of believers depend upon God, in the manner asserted, they have no occasion to be at all careful how they live. No great harm can befall them, for they are certain of being finally safe." In answer to which I shall only observe; that the strength of this objection was long since tried, by Satan, upon our Lord himself. But as it appeared of no force to him, though the tempter proposed it as the necessary consequence of those promises made by the Father to Christ, as man and mediator, respecting his preservation; so it appears to have as little in the present case. The major proposition in the devil's argument was; if thou art the Son of God, his angels will certainly preserve thee: thou canst not be injured. And his conclusion was, therefore, without any danger, thou mayst cast thyself down from this eminence. So, in the present case, the argument contained in the objection, is, If you be a child of God and in union with Christ, your perseverance must be certain. For, being the charge of Omnipotence, it is impossible you should finally fall. Therefore, you may safely bid adieu to all circumspection. You need not fear sin, or its consequences; nor is there any occasion to be solicitous about walking with God in the ways of holiness. But as our Lord, who had not the least doubt of the special care of his Father over him, rejected Satan's proposal with the utmost abhorrence; knowing it was a temptation to evil, and that the argument used to enforce it was an abuse of the Scripture: so the believer, though fully persuaded that grace reigns in every part of salvation: and though it strongly appears in that special care of God, which is incessantly exercised over him in his perseverance to eternal life; yet he is well convinced, that he must not continue in sin that *grace may abound*. On every such suggestion, therefore

* Bp. Reynolds' Works, p. 173, 174.

he will from his heart say, *God forbid!* Besides, there are many important purposes answered, by walking in the ways of obedience, respecting the Christian himself, his neighbour, and his God; which, having been considered already, I shall not here particularly mention.

Nor can it, with any propriety, be objected against the doctrine for which I am pleading; " that the saints are exhorted to pray for the continual aids of grace; for Divine support, in times of trial; and for protection against their enemies," as if it argued their state uncertain, with reference to the final event. For Christ, who was absolutely sure of happiness, nor could possibly fail of enjoying the reward that was promised to him, as Mediator; or come short of possessing that glory which he had with the Father before the world was; yet prayed for it with as much fervour as any saint can possibly do for the most desirable blessing.* A noble example this, of the assurance of faith, respecting our eternal state; and of an unreserved reliance on the Divine promises, being perfectly consistent with earnest and constant prayer for the fulfilment of them ! Besides, whoever dares to act on the principle of this objection has no reason to consider himself as a Christian; but rather as dead in sin, and in the broad way to final ruin.

But notwithstanding the Lord has promised that his people shall never perish; yet as he has nowhere engaged that they shall not fall into sin, and as moral evil is provoking to the eyes of his holiness; they are bound to use the utmost caution, lest by disobedience they move him to use the scourge. For the frowns of a father will be hard to bear; as their spiritual peace and joyful communion with him will be much interrupted, by such disobedience and chastisement for it. The children of God, when careless in their walk and guilty of backsliding, have severely smarted under his correcting hand. The sorrowful confessions and bitter complaints of David, after his scandalous intrigue with Uriah's wife, are a standing incontestible proof of this observation. Their persuasion of interest in the everlasting covenant has been terribly

* John xvii. 1. 5. Compare 2 Sam. vii. 27—29. Dan. xi. 2, 3.

shaken, if not lost for a season, so as to wound their hearts with keenest anguish; till, after many prayers and great watchfulness, they have been again indulged with the smiles of Jehovah's countenance, and with the joys of his salvation.* The remembrance of this, and a consideration how God the Father and his incarnate Son are dishonoured, the Holy Spirit grieved, the glorious gospel reproached, weak believers offended, and the hands of the wicked strengthened, by the careless conduct of Christian professors, afford a sufficient reason for those multiplied cautions, which are given to the disciples of Christ in the book of God, that they indulge not any criminal passion in the least degree; without supposing that their final happiness depends on the steadiness of their walk, or on the goodness of their conversation. For our perseverance in faith and holiness depends on the excellency of our state; as being in covenant with God, his adopted children and the members of Christ; not upon our obedience and endeavours.

Hence you may learn, believer, that as the enemies of your soul are inveterate, subtle, and powerful, and your spiritual frames inconstant, it is highly necessary you should live under a continual remembrance of those awakening considerations. What more advisable, what so necessary for you, as to walk circumspectly; to watch and pray, lest you enter into temptation? A sense of your own weakness and insufficiency should ever abide on your mind and appear in your conduct. As the corruption of nature is an enemy that is always near you, and always in you, while on earth; and as it is very strongly disposed to second every temptation from without; you should *keep your heart with all diligence.* Watch, diligently watch, over all its imaginations, motions, and tendencies. Consider whence they arise, and to what they incline, before you execute any of the purposes formed in it. For such is the superlative deceitfulness of the human heart, *that he who trusteth in it is a fool;*† ignorant of his danger, and unmindful of his best

* Ps. li. 8, 12. and lxxxix. 30—32.
† Prov. xxviii. 26. Jer. xvii. 9. Prov. iv. 23.

interests. This consideration should cause every child of God to bend the suppliant knee, with the utmost frequency, humility, and fervour: to live, as it were, at the throne of grace; nor depart thence till far from the reach of danger. Certain it is, that the more we see of the strength of our adversaries, and of the danger we are in from them; the more shall we exercise ourselves in fervent prayer. Can you, O Christian, be cool and indifferent, be dull and careless, when the world, the flesh, and the devil, are your implacable and unwearied opposers? Dare you indulge yourself in carnal delights, or in a slothful profession, while the enemies of your peace and salvation are ever active and busy in seeking to compass your fall, your disgrace, and, if possible, your eternal ruin? *Awake, thou that sleepest!* Mistake not the field of battle for a bed of rest. *Be sober; be vigilant.*

Are there, notwithstanding the believer's weakness and the power of his enemies, such strong assurances given of his perseverance, complete victory, and final happiness? then, though with fear and trembling he should often reflect on his own insufficiency, he may rely on a faithful God, as his unerring guide and invincible guard, with confidence and joy. The remembrance of that will be a constant motive to humility and watchfulness. The exercise of this will maintain peace and consolation of soul; will be an inexhaustible source of praise, in spite of all the attempts of inveterate malice in his most enraged foes. For the Almighty says, *Fear not: I am thy shield*, forever to defend thee; *and thy exceeding great reward*, to render thee completely happy. While *the eternal God is his refuge, and everlasting arms* his support, there is no occasion to fear. *If God be for us, who can be against us?* When the gates of hell and the powers of earth united, assail the believer, menacing destruction to both body and soul, then the *name*, the promises the oath, and the attributes *of Jehovah* are *a strong tower*, an impregnable fortress: and, conscious of his own inability to resist the enemy, he *runneth into it, and is safe* from every attack, however crafty or violent. The righteous man, the real Christian, *dwelleth on high*, out of the reach of every evil. *His place of defence is the munitions of rocks;* immovable as their solid foundations; inaccessible as their lofty ridges. Nor shall the favoured inhabitants of this everlasting fortress ever be obliged to surrender for want of provisions. A fulness of living bread, and streams of living water, are united with invincible strength. For, it is added, *Bread shall be given him,* and *his waters shall be sure.* He shall want neither nourishment nor protection; outward defence, nor inward comfort. Happy, then, thrice happy they that are under the reign of grace! Every attribute of Deity is engaged to promote their felicity. All the eternal counsels terminate in their favour; and Providence, in the whole course of events respecting them, has a special regard to their advantage. Thus Divine grace appears and reigns in the perseverance of true believers. For grace provides the means necessary to it; grace applies them; and omnipotent grace crowns them with success, to its own eternal honour and praise.

CHAPTER XI.

CONCERNING THE PERSON OF CHRIST, BY WHOM GRACE REIGNS.

The person of Christ, considered in connexion with his work, is a copious and exalted subject; infinitely deserving our most attentive regards. For his person is dignified with every excellency, divine and human; and his work includes every requisite for the complete salvation of our guilty souls.

The constitution of our Mediator's wonderful person was an effect of infinite wisdom, and a manifestation of boundless grace. The hypostatical union of his Divine and human nature, is a fact of the last importance to our hope of eternal happiness. For, by the personal union of these two natures, he is rendered capable of performing the work of a Mediator between God and man. If he had not possessed a nature inferior to that which is Divine, he could neither have performed the obedience required, nor have suffered the penalty threatened by the holy law; both which were absolutely necessary to the salvation of sinners.

Nor was it sufficient merely to assume a created nature; for it was to be that which is common to men. The law being given to man, the obedience required by it, as the condition of life, was to be performed by man, a real, though sinless man. Because the wisdom and equity of the Supreme Legislator could not have appeared in giving a law to our species, if it had never, so much as in one instance, been honoured with perfect obedience by any in our nature. As man was become a transgressor of the law, under its curse, and bound to suffer eternal misery; it was necessary that he who should undertake his deliverance, by vicarious sufferings, should be himself a man. It would not have appeared agreeable, that a different nature from that which sinned should have suffered for sin. Had it pleased the infinite Sovereign to have saved the angels that fell, with reverence we may suppose, that it would have appeared suitable to Divine wisdom, that their deliverer should have assumed the angelic nature. But as man, having lost his happiness, was the creature to be redeemed; and as humanity, having lost its excellence, was the nature to be restored; it was necessary that redemption, and this restoration, should be effected in the human nature. For *as by the disobedience of one* man, *many were made sinners*, brought under condemnation, and liable to eternal death; *even so, by the obedience of one* man, Jesus Christ, must *many be made righteous*, be delivered from condemnation, and accepted to everlasting life.

It was necessary also that the human nature of Christ, in which he was to accomplish our deliverance, should be derived from the common root and fountain of it in our first parents. For it does not appear suitable to answer the various purposes designed by the assumption of our nature, that it should be created immediately out of no thing; nor yet that his body should be formed out of the dust, like that of the first man. Because, on that supposition, there would not have been any such alliance between him and us, as to lay a foundation for our hope of salvation by his undertaking. It was necessary that he who should sustain the character and perform the work of a Redeemer, should be our *Goel, or near kinsman;* one to whom the right of redemption belonged.* So it was declared in the first promise; *The seed of the woman*, and no other, *shall bruise the serpent's head.* He was not only to assume the nature of man, but to partake of it, by being made of *a woman.* Thus he became our kinsman, and our brother. According to that saying, *both he that sanctifieth, and they who are sanctified, are all of one* nature: *for which cause He is not ashamed to call them brethren.*† Amazing condescension this! That the son of the Highest should become the child of a virgin; that the God of nature should become the seed of her who, with a bold, presumptuous hand, plucked the fatal fruit which entailed death on all our species; that He whom angels adore should appear in our nature when sunk in ruin, that he might obey, and bleed, and die for our deliverance! What words can express, what heart can conceive the depth of that condescension, and the riches of that grace, which appear in such a procedure!

It was absolutely necessary, notwithstanding, that the nature in which the work of redemption was to be performed should not be so derived from its original fountain as to be tainted with sin; or partake, in any degree, of that moral defilement, in which every child of Adam is conceived and born. It behooved us to have such an High Priest, as was *holy, harmless, undefiled, and separate from sinners;* for as a priest, he was to atone for our sins and ransom our souls. If the human nature of Christ had partook, in any measure, of that pollution which, since the fall, is hereditary to us; it would have been destitute of the holy image of God, as we are prior to regeneration: and, consequently, he would have been ren-

---

* Lev. xxv. 48, 49. Ruth ii. 20, iii. 9. *Margin.* † Heb. ii. 11.

dered incapable of making the least atonement for us. He who is himself sinful, cannot satisfy Divine justice on the behalf of another; because, by one offence, he forfeits his own soul. Here, then, the adorable wisdom of God appears in its richest glory. For though it was necessary our Surety should be man, and the seed of the woman; yet he was conceived in such a manner as to be entirely without sin. Yes, Jesus, though born of a woman, was absolutely free from the guilt of the first transgression, and from every degree of that depravity which is common to all the offspring of Adam. The perfect purity of our Mediator's humanity, being an article of the last importance to our salvation, is frequently and strongly asserted in the sacred writings. The complete rectitude of his heart, and the unspotted sanctity of his life, are there displayed in lively colours.

A little to explain and illustrate this momentous truth, it may be of use to consider, how it is that we, who are the natural descendants of Adam, became guilty through the first transgression, and are made partakers of a depraved nature. As to *guilt* by the first offence, it may be observed, that the whole human nature subsisted in our original parents when it was committed; and that Adam was our public representative. Hence it is that his offence became the sin of us all; is justly imputed and charged upon us. *In him*, as our common representative, *we all sinned*. Such being our natural state, as the descendants of an apostate head, we justly bear that humbling and awful character; CHILDREN OF WRATH, BY NATURE. But Adam was not a federal head of Christ. *The Lord from heaven* was neither included in him, nor represented by him. He was not included *in him*. For the blessed Jesus was conceived in a way entirely supernatural, and born of a virgin. He was not born in virtue of those prolific words, by which the great Creator blessed the connubial state before the fall, *Increase and multiply;* but in virtue of a *gracious promise*, made after the fall, when Adam ceased to be any longer a public person. He was not represented *by him*, for our grand progenitor was the representative of none but his natural offspring

The holy Jesus, therefore, not being naturally descended from him, could not be represented by him. It appears indeed, highly incongruous for us to imagine, that he who was *of the earth, earthy*, should be the representative of him who is *the Lord from heaven;* of him who is, in all respects, his Great Superior. It could not be, that One who is the Son of God, as well as the seed of a woman, should acknowledge Adam for his federal head. Our Lord therefore had no concern in his guilt, as a descendant from him, which is the case of all his natural posterity. The promised seed not being included in that covenant under which the first human pair stood, could not be chargeable with any part of that guilt which attended the violation of it. Original guilt becomes ours in virtue of Adam's relation to us, as our public representative; and hence it is imputed to us by a righteous God. For if we had not been some way involved in the first transgression, before it was imputed to us, it could not justly have been charged upon us. Because it is not the *imputation* of Adam's offence that makes it ours; but, *being legally ours*, in consequence of our natural and federal relation to him, it is justly imputed to us.

Nor could the Lord Redeemer be liable to the necessary consequence of Adam's offence; that is, a *depravation* of nature. This immediately followed, as the natural effect of his first transgression, which transgression being committed by him as our representative, is legally ours; and hence we share with him in its natural and awful effects. In other words, we derive a corrupt nature from him, because we were guilty with him. Nor was the imputation of his offence to us, the cause of this woful effect; but his offence being legally ours, prior to that imputation. But as Christ was not concerned with him in original guilt, having no relation to him as a federal head; the natural consequence of that guilt could not take place in him, as it does in us, being represented by Adam and descended from him according to the common course of nature. Thus was the human nature of Jesus Christ entirely free from all contamination: and thus that *holy thing*, which was formed in the womb of the virgin, by the power of the Most High, was constituted the second Adam, in opposition to the first. This production of the human nature of our glorious Immanuel, being in a way supernatural and divine, is called the *creation of a new thing in the earth.** Thus Christ became a partaker of the nature which had sinned, without the least sinfulness of that nature.

It was absolutely necessary also, that our Mediator and Surety should be *God* as well as man. For as he could neither have obeyed, nor suffered, if he had not possessed a created nature; so, had he been a mere man, however immaculate, he could not have redeemed one soul. Nay, though he had possessed the highest possible created excellencies, they would not have been sufficient; because he would still have been a dependent being. For as it is essential to Deity, to be underived and self-existent; so it is essential to a creature, to be derived and dependent. The loftiest seraph that sings in glory is as really dependent on God, every moment of his existence, as the meanest worm that crawls. In this respect, an angel and an insect are on a level. Every intelligent creature, therefore, whether human or angelic, having received existence from the Almighty, and being continually dependent on him, as the all-producing, all-supporting first cause; must be obliged to perpetual obedience, by virtue of that relation in which he stands to God, as his Maker and Preserver. It is highly absurd to suppose it possible for any creature to supererogate, or to do more in a way of obedience to Him from whom his all was received, than he is under the strongest obligations to perform, in consequence of his absolute and universal dependence. But whatever is previously due from any one, on his own account, cannot be transferred to another, without rendering the first devoid of that obedience which it is absolutely necessary for him to have. Universal obedience, in every possible instance, is so necessary in a rational creature, as such, being dependent on God and created for his glory, that the omission of it, in any degree, would not only be criminal, but expose to everlasting ruin.

* Jer. xxxi. 22.

The righteousness, therefore, of a mere creature, however highly exalted, could not have been accepted by the Great Supreme, as any compensation for our obedience. Because whoever undertakes to perform a vicarious righteousness, must be one who is not obliged to obedience on his own account. Consequently, our Surety must be a Divine Person; for every mere creature is under indispensable obligations to perfect and perpetual obedience. Now, as our situation required, so the gospel reveals, a Mediator and Substitute thus exalted and glorious. For Jesus is described as a Divine Person, as one who could, without any arrogance, or the least disloyalty, claim independence; and, when thus considered, he appears fit for the task. But of such an One we could have had no idea, without that distinction of Persons in the Godhead which the Scriptures reveal. Agreeably to this distinction, we behold the rights of Deity asserted and vindicated, with infinite majesty and authority, in the person of the *Father;* while we view every Divine perfection displayed and honoured, in the most illustrious manner, by the amazing condescension of the eternal *Son:* By the humiliation of Him who, in his lowest state of subjection, could claim an equality with God. Such being the dignity of our wonderful Sponsor, it was by his own voluntary condescension that he became incarnate, and *took upon him the form of a servant.* By the same free act of his will he was *made under the law*, to perform that obedience in our stead, to which, as a Divine Person, he was no way obliged

The necessity there was that our Surety should be a Divine Person, might be further proved, by considering the infinite evil there is in sin. That sin is an infinite evil, appears from hence. Every crime is more or less heinous, in proportion as we are under obligations to the contrary. For the criminality of any disposition, or action, consists in *a contrariety to what we ought to possess, or perform.* If, therefore, we hate, disobey, or dishonour any person, the sin is always proportional to the obligations we are under to love, to honour, and to obey him. Now the obligations we are under to love, to honour, and to obey any person, are in proportion to his loveliness, his dignity, and his authority. Of this, none can doubt. If then infinite beauty, dignity, and authority belong to the immensely glorious God; we must be under equal obligations to love, to honour, and to obey him; and a contrary conduct must be infinitely criminal. Sin, therefore, is a violation of infinite obligation to duty; consequently an unlimited evil, and deserving of infinite punishment. Such being the nature of our offences, and of the aggravations attending them, we stand in absolute need of a surety, the worth of whose obedience and sufferings should be equal to the unworthiness of our persons, and to the demerit of our disobedience. If to the evil there is in every sin, we take into consideration the vast number of sinners that were to be redeemed; the countless millions of enormous crimes that were to be expiated; and the infinite weight of Divine wrath that was to be sustained; all which were to be completed in a limited and short time, in order to reconcile man to God, and to effect his eternal salvation; we shall have still stronger evidence in proof of the point.

Were a defence of the proper Deity of Christ my intention, the Scriptures would furnish me with ample matter and abundant evidence in favour of the capital truth. For the names that he bears, the perfections ascribed to him, the works he has done, and the honours he has received, loudly proclaim his ETERNAL DIVINITY. But I wave the attempt, and proceed to observe,

That it was necessary our Surety should be *God* and *man*, in unity of person. This necessity arises from the nature of his work; which is that of a Mediator between God, the offended Sovereign, and man, the offending subject. If he had not been a partaker of the Divine nature, he could not have been qualified to treat with God; if not of the human, he would not have been fitted to treat with man. Deity alone was too high to treat with man; humanity alone was too low to treat with God. The eternal Son therefore assumed our nature, that he might become a middle person; and so be rendered capable of *laying his hands upon both,** and of bringing them into a state of

---

* Job ix. 33.

perfect friendship. He could not have been a mediator, in regard to his office, if he had not been a middle-person, in respect of his natures. Such is the constitution of his wonderful person, and hence he is called IMMANUEL, *God with us*, or in our nature.

The perfect performance of all his offices, as priest, prophet, and king, requires this union of the Divine to the human nature. As a *Priest*. For it was necessary he should have *something to offer*, that he should offer himself. But pure Deity could not be offered. It was requisite therefore that he should be man, and taken from among men, as every other high-priest was. And, had he not been God, as he could not have had an absolute power over his own life, to lay it down and take it up at his pleasure; so the offering of the human nature, if not in union with the Divine, would not have made a proper atonement for our transgressions, would by no means have expiated that enormous load of human guilt, for which he was to suffer. Nor could his death have been an equivalent, in the eye of eternal justice, to that everlasting punishment which the righteous law threatens against sin; which must have been the sinner's portion, as it is his just desert, if such an admirable Sponsor had not appeared on his behalf. But when we consider that he who suffered, the just for the unjust, was a Divine Person incarnate, we cannot but look upon him as perfectly able to bear the punishment and to perform the work. For as the infinite evil of sin arises from the majesty, and the excellence of him against whom it is committed; so the merit of our Surety's obedience and sufferings must be equal to the dignity of his person. How great, how transcendently glorious are the perfections of the eternal Jehovah! so great, so superlatively excellent is the atonement of the dying Jesus!

As a *Prophet*. For had he not been the omniscient God, he could not, without a revelation, have known the Divine will respecting his people. Nor could he have had a perfect acquaintance with that infinite variety of cases, in which, through every age and nation, they continually need his teaching. And, if he had not been man, he could not so familiarly, in his own person, have revealed the Divine will.

As a *King*. For if he had not been God, he could not have ruled in the heart, or have been the Lord of conscience; nor would he have been able to defend and provide for the church, in this imperfect and militant state. Neither could he, in his own right, have dispensed eternal ife to his followers, or everlasting death to his enemies at the last day. And if he had not been man, he could not have been a head, either political or natural, of the same kind with the body to which he is united, and over which he is placed as King in Zion. Consequently, he could not have sympathized with the members of his mystical body, as he evidently does. But as his wonderful person is dignified with every perfection, Divine and human; as he possesses all the glories of Deity, and all the graces of immaculate humanity; these render him a Mediator completely amiable and supremely glorious—an adequate object of the sinner's confidence, and of the believer's joy

Hence it appears, that Christ is a glorious, a Divine Mediator; a Mediator that has power with God and with man. He must be able, therefore, *to save to the uttermost*, to all perfection and forever, *all that come to God by him*. The obedience of such a Surety must magnify the law, and render it highly venerable; must have an excellence and a merit, incomparably and inconceivably great. It must be of more value than the obedience of all the saints in the world, or of all the angels in glory. The sufferings underwent by this heavenly Substitute, the sacrifice offered up by this wonderful High Priest, must be all-sufficient to expiate the most accumulated guilt; omnipotent to save the most horrid transgressor. For his obedience is that in worth, which his person is in dignity. This, infinite in glory; that, boundless in merit.

As the greatness of an offence is proportional to the dignity of the person whose honour is invaded by it; so the value of the satisfaction made by the sufferings of any substitute, must be equal to the excellence of the person satisfying. Sin, being committed against infinite Majesty, deserved infinte punishment; the sacrifice of Christ is of infinite worth, being offered by a person of infinite dignity. It was the sacrifice, not of a mere man, not of the highest angel, but of Jesus the incarnate God; of Him who is the brightness of the Father's glory, and Head over all creation. As the infinite glory of his Divine Person cannot be separated from his humanity; so infinite merit is necessarily connected with his obedience and sufferings. In all that he did, and in all that he underwent, he was the Son of God; as well on the cross, as before his incarnation; as well when he cried, *My God, my God, why hast thou forsaken me?* as when he raised the dead, and reversed the laws of nature. He was Jehovah's Fellow when he felt the sword of justice awake upon him; he thought it no robbery to assert an equality with God, even when he was fastened to the bloody tree, and expired under a curse.* Was the sin for which he suffered infinitely evil? the Person who satisfied is infinitely excellent. Did an infinite Object suffer in his honour by our offences? the injury is repaired by a Subject of infinite excellence making an atonement for them. Our sin is infinite in respect of the object; our sacrifice is infinite, in regard to the subject. Jehovah considered our Surety as *the Man his fellow*, when he smote him; and we should consider him under the same exalted character when we believe on him, and plead his atonement before God. "Here is firm footing, here is solid rock." In the Divine dignity of the Redeemer's person, and in the consummate perfection of his work; there is an everlasting basis for faith, the assurance of faith, the full assurance of faith. A basis, firm as the pillars of nature; immovable, as the eternal throne.

Whereas if, with Socinians, we suppose that Jesus had no existence before his conception in the womb of the virgin, and so look upon him as a mere man; or if, with Arians, we imagine him to be a kind of superangelic spirit, united to a human body; yea, though we should compliment him, as some of them have done, with ascribing all Divine perfections to him, except eternity and

---

* Zech. xiii. 7. Phil. ii. 6. 8. Gal. iii. 13.

self-existence, which is absurdly impious; yet we rob him of proper Deity, we make him a dependent being, we reduce him to the rank of mere creatures, and deprive ourselves of that foundation of confidence in him which his true character affords. For we never can persuade ourselves, that the sufferings of a mere creature, and those for so short a time, could be accepted by the most high and holy God, as a righteous compensation to his law and justice, for the sins of innumerable millions of hell-deserving transgressors. Hence it is, that those who deny the proper Deity of Christ, commonly deny that he made satisfaction for sin to Divine justice. Thus far they are consistent, and (what they affect to be called) *rational*. But they may do well to consider, whether they themselves be able to satisfy eternal justice; and how they can expect admission into the kingdom of glory, by the sin-avenging God, without any satisfaction made for their crimes. For, certain it is, that He who governs the universe is inflexibly just, as well as divinely merciful. THE JUST GOD AND THE SAVIOUR is his revealed character. As thus revealed, we must know him, and trust in him, if we would escape the wrath to come.

Here let the reader admire and adore the love of the Eternal Father, and the condescension of the Divine Son. *The love of the eternal Father.* For the glorious person described is the Son of God, and the Father's gift to sinful men. In comparison with whom, all the angels and all worlds, bestowed upon us for an inheritance, would be trifling and next to nothing. Because all created things are equally easy to Divine power, being only the effects of the simple will of God. The formation of an angel, or of an insect; of a thousand systems, or of a thousand grains, is the same thing to Omnipotence. For which reason, there could be no comparative greatness in any such gifts. If, therefore, the eternal Father would manifest his love to an uncommon degree; if he would so gratify his mercy, in blessing his offending creatures, as to have an appearance of doing violence to himself; it must be by *giving his only begotten Son*, who is one in nature and equal in glory with him—by giving him to be their substitute, their propitiation, and their Saviour. In this view, how great the propriety, how striking the beauty of those apostolic sayings! *He that spared not his own Son, but delivered him up for us all, how shall he not with him also freely give us all things? God commendeth his love toward us, in that while we were yet sinners Christ died for us.* Here Divine love appears to the utmost advantage: here it shines in all its glory. For its rich donation is infinitely excellent, and the blessedness resulting from it is consummate and eternal. *The condescension of the Divine Son.* That He *who was in the form of God, and thought it no robbery to be equal with God;* that He whom angels obey; that He whom seraphs adore, and before whom they veil their faces; as conscious of their own comparative meanness, or as dazzled with the blaze of his infinite glories—that HE should be made flesh, take upon him the form of a servant, perform obedience, and give up himself to the most infamous death, is amazing! But that he should surrender himself to die for sinners, for enemies, and for such as were in actual rebellion against him, is unspeakably more amazing! These are demonstrative proofs, that the Lord Redeemer is as much superior to his creatures in the riches of his grace, as he is in the depths of his wisdom, or in the works of his power. Let all the heavens adore him! and let the children of men be filled with wonder, and burn with gratitude! For this glorious Redeemer is accessible by sinners, who was designed for sinners; and on them his power and grace are magnified.

Such is that representation which the gospel gives of Divine, redeeming love. But were we to deny the proper Deity of Jesus Christ, and to reject the reality of his atonement, we should, in reference both to the Father and the Son, obscure its glory, weaken its force, and almost destroy its very being. On Socinian principles, many of the most emphatical terms and phrases of inspiration, relative to our salvation by the Son of God, must be understood in a sense directly contrary to their natural import; or, in other words, the language of Scripture must be reversed. For instance: our Lord says, *God so loved*

THE WORLD, *that he gave his only begotten Son.* But Socinianism teaches us to understand the Divine declaration thus: " God so loved the *son of Mary*, that he gave him the government of the world." Paul says, *Ye know the grace of our* LORD JESUS CHRIST, *that though he was rich, yet for your sakes he became poor.* But, according to this hypothesis, the meaning and the fact are, " Ye know the grace of *God* to the man Jesus Christ; who, though he was *by nature poor*, as any that are born of a woman; though, in the whole of his life, he was equally dependent on the Father's power and pleasure as any other person can possibly be, and though neither the labours of his ministry, nor the pains of his martyrdom, were equal to those of many among his disciples; yet, for his *own sake*, and as the reward of his obedience, *he became*, through divine bounty, *incomparably rich.*"

In another epistle the same apostle says: *Christ Jesus, being in the form of God, thought it not robbery to be equal with God; but made himself of no reputation, and took upon him the form of a servant, and was made in the likeness of men: and being found in fashion as a man, he humbled himself and became obedient unto death, even the death of the cross.* Now this, according to the principles of SOCINUS, may be paraphrased thus: " Christ Jesus, being a merely human creature, existed in the form of a man. Conscious of this, he thought it the most impious robbery on the honours of Deity, for him to be equal with God; whether it were by bearing his names, by claiming his attributes, by presuming to perform his works, or by receiving his worship. Yes, being made in the form of a servant, (because as a mere creature, it was impossible he should exist in any other form) and feeling his own emptiness, he was contented to appear in the likeness of men. And seeing he was a mere man, there is no reason to wonder that he was found in fashion as a man; or that, as a righteous person, and a teacher of truth, he was greatly humbled, as many other good men have been, by poverty and reproach. Nor yet, feeling himself entirely at the Divine disposal, is there any reason to be surprised that, as a martyr, he became obedient to death, even the death of the cross : Because he knew that such was the will of his Creator and Sovereign. But as he had no bodily disease to affect his imagination with melancholy gloom ; no guilt on his conscience, to excite despondency ; no unhallowed attachment to family connexions, to religious friends, or to any sensible object: no doubt of special interest in the Father's love ; nor any fear, with regard to his own final felicity ; the wonder is, that, in his last sufferings, and before any human hand was upon him, he should be so full of consternation, so penetrated with anguish, as to sweat blood, and to exclaim, *My soul is exceeding sorrowful, even unto death—My God, My God, why hast thou forsaken me!* At this we may well be astonished; because many of his disciples, even when in the hands of their barbarous executioners, and though conscious of personal guilt, have sustained the extremest sufferings without one complaint, and sometimes with indications of exuberant joy.

" Besides, Jesus dying only as a martyr, being perfectly innocent of the crimes laid to his charge, and suffering nothing at all from the hand of eternal justice for the sins of others ; the love he expressed to men like himself was far from being so disinterested, so fervent, or so great, as multitudes have imagined. For he was absolutely certain of rising again from the dead within the space of three days ; and, as the reward of his obedience to death, of being exalted to the throne of universal empire. Yes, he knew that God would *highly exalt him, and give him a name above every name: that at the name of Jesus every knee should bow, of things in heaven, and things in earth, and things under the earth ; and that every tongue should confess that Jesus Christ is Lord, to the glory of God the Father.* Now, as he was a mere man; as his death was only that of a witness to Divine truth ; as he lost his life only for three days; and as he had the most certain expectation of such an unbounded reward; it cannot with reason be supposed that his love to men considered as neighbours, or his compassion to men, considered as perishing in ignorance and in superstition, was much superior to that philanthropy which prophets, apostles, and martyrs have discovered. Because it is manifest that, had self-love been the only principle of his conduct, he could not have promoted his own advantage so effectually in any other way. Who, that loves God and man; who, that pursues his own supreme honour and happiness, would refuse to undergo similar sufferings, provided he were absolutely certain of an equal reward? Nay, did not CODRUS, did not the DECII, voluntarily devote themselves to death for the good of their respective countries; though, being enveloped in Pagan darkness, the only reward they had to expect was a little posthumous renown?"

So abhorrent are the grand principles of Socinianism to the language and sentiments of Divine revelation! On those principles, the phraseology of inspired writers is extremely strange, and very obscure: so obscure, that instead of saying, *Great is the mystery of* GODLINESS; we may justly exclaim, Unaccountably singular, and profoundly mysterious, is THE LANGUAGE *of prophets and of apostles,* respecting the person and work of Jesus Christ! For though the *things* intended are plain, and easily apprehended by common capacities; yet the *terms* by which those things are expressed are so extremely abstruse, that the most ardent study, and the greatest acumen, are absolutely necessary to develope their meaning. Christians have been used to consider Scripture mysteries, as relating to the MODUS *of certain important facts;* which facts, being plainly revealed, are believed on the authority of Divine testimony: but this new theology teaches us to look for those mysteries in the unparalleled MODUS *of biblical expression.* I said, *unparalleled.* For, surely, if the Socinian system be true, no set of writers, who had not lost their senses, and who intended to be understood, ever expressed common ideas in such mysterious language, as that which is used by the inspired penmen relative to Jesus Christ, and to the great work of redemption by him.*

Fully persuaded, therefore, that the Scriptures mean as

* See Dr. ABBADIE on the Deity of Jesus Christ essential to the Christian Religion, *passim.*

they speak, let the sinner who is conscious of nothing but misery and wretchedness about him, flee to the all-sufficient Mediator; trust in him as mighty to save; and veracity itself has engaged that he shall not be disappointed in his expectations. As a Divine person, he must be able to act agreeably to every character he bears; perfectly qualified to execute every office he has undertaken; and completely fitted to fill up each relation in which he stands to his people. Let us repose the most unreserved confidence in his atonement and intercession, as our Priest; look to him for instruction, as our prophet; be subject to him, and expect protection from him, as our King. Let us manifest the most fervent love to him, as our Redeemer; yield him the most cordial obedience, as our Lord; and pay him the sublimest worship, as our God. I will add, let all those who deny his proper Deity, and reject his vicarious death; who refuse to honour him as a Divine person, and to accept his righteousness as Mediator; be aware lest, when it is too late, they feel their want of his atonement, and be compelled to acknowledge, that He IS OVER ALL, GOD BLESSED FOREVER.

Let my reader contemplate with wonder and with joy, the infinite honour that is conferred on the human nature, in the person of our great Mediator. For it is in everlasting union with the Son of God; is now seated on a throne of light; is the most glorious of all creatures, and the eternal ornament of the whole creation. Yes, believer, He on whom you rely, in whose hands you have intrusted your soul, still wears your nature while he pleads your cause. That very body that hung on the cross, and was laid in the grave; that very soul which suffered the keenest anguish, and was *exceeding sorrowful, even unto death;* are now, and ever shall be, in close connexion with the eternal Word. Mysterious, ineffable union! big with wonder and replete with comfort! How encouraging it is to consider, that as Jesus is clothed with that very humanity, in which he suffered afflictions and trials of every kind and of every degree; he cannot forget his tempted, despised, afflicted people in this militant state. In himself he sees their image; in his hands he beholds their names. He feels for them, he suffers with them:[*] he never will, he never can overlook their persons, or be unmindful of their best interests.

CHAPTER XII.

CONCERNING THE WORK OF CHRIST, THROUGH WHICH GRACE REIGNS.

HAVING taken a view of the person of Christ, and of his qualifications for the work of a Mediator, arising from his personal excellencies considered as Immanuel; we must now advert to that perfect *work*, through which grace reigns, and in virtue of which her favours are dispensed.

Grace reigns, says the oracle of heaven, THROUGH RIGHTEOUSNESS. Righteousness, in this place, I understand as including the whole of that obedience which the Redeemer, under the character of a surety, performed to the preceptive part of the law; and all those bitter sufferings which he underwent, in conformity to its penal sanction. Through this obedience grace reigns, in a way strictly conformable to the rights of Divine justice. By this most perfect work of Christ, the tenderest mercy is manifested to miserable sinners, and meets with the truth of Jehovah's righteous threatenings against sin. Here the righteousness of God, as the lawgiver, appears in taking vengeance on sin; so as to be productive of substantial and lasting peace to the sinner. Happy expedient! Wonderful grace! But let us a little more particularly consider the nature and excellencies of this evangelical righteousness.

As to its *nature:* it is a complete conformity to the Divine law. Whatever the precepts of Jehovah's law demanded, the adorable Jesus performed in its fullest extent. His nature being perfectly holy, the principle of

---

[*] Heb. ii. 18, and iv. 15. Isa. xlix. 15, 16.

his actions was absolutely pure; the end for which he did them entirely right; and the matter of them, and rule of their performance, without any defect. Whatever the law, considered as broken, threatened by way of punishment against the offender; to that he submitted in all its dreadful severity. For *he was made sin; he was made a curse.* He suffered—amazing love! unparalleled condescension!—he suffered the greatest shame, the most excruciating pain, that the malice of men, or the subtilty of devils, could invent or inflict; and which was infinitely more, the wrath of God. The duration of his passion was indeed comparatively short; but for this the infinite dignity of his person was a full compensation. When we consider that it was the Son of God and Lord of glory, who bled and died under every circumstance of infamy and pain; all the dreadful monuments of Divine justice inflicted on the sons of rebellion in past ages, and transmitted to posterity in the most authentic records; all the misery that awaits the licentious world, and is denounced in the Scripture; cannot raise our ideas of Jehovah's vindictive justice to so high a pitch, as a remembrance of the bitter, though transitory sufferings of the Divine Jesus.

The *excellencies* of this righteousness appear from the characters it bears in holy writ. For to signify its unspotted purity, it is called *fine linen clean and white*. To denote its completeness, it is called a *robe*. To hold forth its exquisite beauty, richness, and glory, it is called *clothing of wrought gold, and raiment of needle-work*. To point out its unequalled excellency, it is called the *best robe*. It is better than the robe of innocence with which our first parents were clothed before the fall; yea, better than the righteousness of angels in glory. For theirs is but the obedience of mere creatures; of dependent beings. But this—which is the highest epithet that language can give—this is *the* RIGHTEOUSNESS OF GOD. Its nature and properties are such, that the Lord himself seems to glory in it, frequently calling it *His righteousness.**

---

* Rev. xix. 8. Isa. lxi. 10. Ps. xlv. 13, 14. Luke xv. 22. 2 Cor. v. 21. Rom. x. 3. Jer. xxiii. 6. Isa. xlvi. 13: li. 5—8; lvi. 1.

It is an *everlasting* righteousness.* It is a robe, the beauty of which will never be tarnished; a garment that will never decay; and clothing that will never wear out. When millions of ages have run their ample round, it will continue the same that it was the first day it came into use; and when millions more are elapsed, there will be no alteration. The continuance of its efficacy, beauty, and glory, will be lasting as the light of the New Jerusalem; unfading as the eternal inheritance.

It is a righteousness *already performed*. It is not something now to be wrought in us, by the operation of the Holy Spirit. No; it was completed when the Divine Redeemer cried, *It is finished, and gave up the ghost*. But here many persons fall into a fatal mistake. Ready they are to imagine, that sinners are accepted of God in virtue of righteousness wrought in them, and performed by them, through the assistance of the Holy Spirit; which assistance, they suppose, was purchased for them by the death of Christ. But while such an imagination prevails, they never can experience what it is to be in a justified state. Besides, when the blessed Jesus died, he did not do something to assist our weak, but willing endeavours to save ourselves; he did not lay in a provision of grace, or purchase the Spirit for us, by which the defects of enfeebled nature might be supplied, and we rendered capable of performing the condition of our justification. But, at that awful and ever-memorable period, when he bowed his head and expired, he, by himself alone, perfectly finished that righteousness which is the proper condition, and the grand requisite of our justification. That the Spirit of grace and truth, as given to any, is a precious fruit of the death, resurrection, and glorification of Christ, is freely acknowledged; but that Jesus died to purchase the Spirit, to work in us any part of that righteousness, on account of which we are accepted of God, must be denied. For the principal work of the Spirit, in the method of grace, our Lord himself bearing witness, is to testify of him, and reveal his glory to the sinner's con-

* Dan. ix. 24.

science. *He shall testify of me—He shall glorify me; for he shall receive of mine, and shall show it unto you.** Nor does the Spirit of truth act as a sanctifier, till, in order of nature, we are perfectly justified: and when justified, he effects our sanctification by that very truth which reveals the obedience of Christ as a finished work. To think otherwise, is according to the Popish scheme, which confounds justification with sanctification; but is very far from being the doctrine of the apostles. It is also contrary to the sentiments of our first reformers, and of all their genuine successors, both at home and abroad.

Notwithstanding what has been said concerning the matchless excellence of the Redeemer's righteousness, the reader whose mind is enlightened to behold the defects attending his own best performances, and whose conscience is affected with a sense of deserved wrath, may, perhaps, be ready to say; " As to the glorious nature and superlative excellence of this obedience, there is no dispute. But, is it free for a mere sinner? Is it not rather designed for those who are some way qualified for it, by a set of holy principles, and a series of pious actions; those who are distinguished from the altogether worthless and vile? Is there any possibility for a miserable sinner, a condemned criminal; one whose transgressions are great and whose corruptions are strong, to partake of it, and be made happy by it? And if there be, which is the way?" To these momentous inquiries the oracles of God furnish a substantial answer. For they inform us that there is another excellency attending it, which has a special regard to the manner of its communication; and therefore ought by no means to be overlooked. Yes, blessed be God! the unerring word warrants me to assert that this righteousness is absolutely free. It was wrought for the sinner; it was designed for the sinner; and is freely bestowed on the vilest of sinners. It is not matter of bargain, or the subject of sale; it is not proposed on certain *conditions;* as, the performing some arduous course of duties, or the attaining some notable qualifica-

---

* John xv. 26; xvi. 14. 1 Cor. ii. 12.

tions; but it is a free gift. Grace, as a sovereign, is exalted to confer it; and grace, we know, deals only with the unworthy. As a gift it is imparted; as a gift, therefore, it must be received; and as for an absolutely free gift, the professor of it should be thankful. From these considerations we may with confidence affirm, that the mere sinner, the condemned creature; he who feels himself in a perishing condition, and is conscious that he deserves no favour; has the strongest encouragement given him to rely on it, as quite sufficient for his justification, and absolutely free for his use. Yes, disconsolate sinner, you have no reason to hesitate, whether you have a right to conceive it, and to call it your own. Believing the testimony which God has given of his Son, you receive it, and enjoy the comfort arising from it. Heaven proclaims your welcome to Christ, and eternal faithfulness insures acceptance to all that believe in him.

By a figure of speech that is frequent in Scripture, this righteousness is represented as *speaking*. Doubtless, then, so noble a righteousness must have a charming language; and a little attention will discover its import. The language of this righteousness is represented by Paul, as directly contrary to that description which Moses gives of *the righteousness of the law;* and thus it addresses the anxious inquirer. *Say not in thy heart who shall ascend into heaven? That is, to bring Christ down from above;* as though he had not appeared in our nature, to perform a righteousness for the justification of sinners. Nor does it bid thee inquire, *Who shall descend into the deep? That is, to bring up Christ again from the dead;* as if he had not perfectly paid the debt for which, as a surety, he became responsible; and received in his resurrection, from the hand of his Father, an acquittance in full for himself and his people. *But what saith it*, what then is its language? *The word* of grace which reveals this righteousness *is nigh thee*, sinful and wretched as thou art. *Even* so near, as to be *in thy mouth* to proclaim its excellence, *and in thy heart*, to enjoy its comfort; *that is the word*, the doctrine *of faith which we preach.* It further says, *That if thou shalt confess with thy mouth the Lord Jesus,* as dying an accursed death for the redemption of sinners, *and shalt believe in thy heart that God hath raised him from the dead,* as a Divine testimony that the atonement made was accepted by eternal justice; *thou shalt be saved* from final misery, and exalted to the joys of heaven.*

The language of this Divine righteousness is here described, both negatively and positively. *Negatively*, we are not commanded to do some arduous work, in order to obtain acceptance; nor are we required to do any thing at all for that purpose. Because it is evident that *believing in Christ*, which is here mentioned, is, in the business of justification, opposed to works and doings of every kind.† The faith here designed, is, therefore, to be considered as the *receiving* of Christ and his righteousness; or, as a *dependence* on him alone for salvation. Believing the gracious report, we receive the atonement; we enjoy comfort; and have the earnest of eternal glory.

But as the awakened sinner is ever disposed to imagine that he must do some great thing, in order to obtain the pardon of sin and peace for his conscience; therefore the language of this righteousness is also described *positively.* Thus considered, it plainly declares that the only obedience by which there is favour with God, and a title to happiness, is already performed: and that the anxious inquirer is not left in a state of uncertainty how it may be enjoyed; for it is brought near in the word of grace, with a free welcome to rely on it and use it as his own, to the everlasting honour of its Divine Author.

By comparing what the apostle says about the *righteousness of faith,* with what Moses declares concerning the *righteousness of the law,* we learn, That whoever thinks of doing any good work, as the condition of life, is ignorant of that obedience which the gospel reveals; is under the law, as a covenant; is a debtor to perform the whole; and, as a breaker of it, is obnoxious to its awful curse. This is his case, even when, with the Pharisee in the parable, he thanks God for assisting him to per-

---

* Rom. x. 5—9.   † Rom. iv. 5. 16. Gal. iii. 12. 13.

form the supposed condition, whether great or small. For the righteousness of the law, and the righteousness of faith, are here directly opposed. This is evident from the scope of the place in general; and especially from the adversative *but*, with which what is said about the righteousness of faith is introduced.

This vicarious obedience is no less useful to the sinner, than perfect in itself. By this work of our heavenly Substitute, that holy law which we have broken is highly honoured; and that awful justice which we have offended is completely satisfied. By this righteousness the believer is acquitted from every charge, is perfectly justified, and shall be eternally saved. In this consummate work, Jehovah declares himself well pleased, and in it all the glories of the Godhead shine. Yes, the obedience of our adorable Sponsor is perfect as Divine rectitude could require; and excellent as eternal wisdom itself could devise. Admirable righteousness! Who that is taught of God, would not, with Paul, desire to *be found in it?* and who, that is conscious of an interest in it, can cease to admire and adore the grace that provided, and the Saviour that wrought it?

Is the obedience of the Lord Redeemer so glorious in its nature, so excellent in its properties, so free in the manner of its communication to the ungodly, and so extensively useful to all that possess it? What encouragement, then, has the miserable sinner to look to it? How safely may he confide in it, as all-sufficient to justify his ungodly soul! For, be the demands of the Divine law and infinite justice ever so great, or numerous, or dreadful; the work of Christ completely answers them all. There is greater efficacy in the grace of God, and in the work of his incarnate Son, to justify and save from deserved perdition, than there can be demerit in the offences of a sinner, to incur condemnation and ruin.

Nor can it seem strange that the work of Christ should be thus efficacious. For God the Son performed it, in the capacity of a substitute. God the Father declares his delight in it, and treats as his children all those that are vested with it. And it is the principal business of God the Holy Spirit, as a guide and a comforter, to testify of it. So that every other righteousness, in comparison with it, is quite insignificant: if set in competition with it, is viler than dross, and worse than nothing. In this righteousness Christians of all ages have gloried, both living and dying, as the only ground of their hope. In this most perfect obedience believers are now exalted and the saints in heaven triumph. For the work of Christ finished on a cross is the burden of their songs. But who can point out all its beauties? Who can show forth half its praise? After all that has been written or said about it, by prophets or apostles, here on earth; after all that has been sung or can be conceived, by saints or angels in the world of glory; considered under its Divine character, THE RIGHTEOUSNESS OF JEHOVAH, it exceeds all possible praise. The inhabitants of the heavenly world must be conscious that their loftiest strains, though expressed with seraphic ardour, fall vastly short of displaying all its excellence. So that,

"When Gabriel sounds these glorious things,
He tunes and summons all his strings."

CHAPTER XIII.

CONCERNING THE CONSUMMATION OF THE GLORIOUS REIG OF GRACE.

As Divine grace is glorious in itself, and infinitely superior to all that is denominated free favour among men; as the way in which it reigns is absolutely without a parallel, and such as will render it forever dear to all the disciples of Christ; so the end of its benign government is equally glorious: for it is eternal life. Reviving, ravishing thought! This, in subordination to his own glory, is the great design of God in every gracious dispensation towards his people. The emphatical phrase is hsed in Scripture to signify, *An everlasting state of complete holiness and consummate happiness, in the presence and fruition of God, in all his persons and perfections.* To this blissful state, grace, as a sovereign, infallibly brings her subjects, through the person and work of Immanuel.

To assist our feeble and contracted minds in forming some faint ideas of celestial blessedness, and to inform us by whom it shall be enjoyed; it is compared by sacred writers to the most delightful and glorious things that come under our notice in the present world. For instance: To denote its superabounding delights, it is called *paradise*, in allusion to the garden of Eden: for at God's *right hand are pleasures forevermore.* To signify its grandeur, magnificence, and glory, it is called a *crown* and a *kingdom.* As a crown, it is unfading and incorruptible. To intimate that none shall enjoy it, except in virtue of the Redeemer's obedience, it is denominated a *crown of righteousness.* It is also called a *crown of life* and a *crown of glory.* As a kingdom, it was prepared for believers *before the foundation of the world,* and is the *kingdom of their Father;* who bestows it upon them here, in right to possess; hereafter, in perfect enjoyment. To ascertain its perpetuity, it is called an *everlasting* kingdom: and those that enjoy it are called *kings,* are said to *sit upon thrones,* and to *reign in life.* To inform us who shall possess it, and on what ground, it is called an *inheritance.* Plainly denoting, that none but the children of God shall enjoy it: for a servant, considered as such, cannot inherit. We must, therefore, be the sons of the Highest, by adoption and regeneration, before we can justly hope to enjoy the heavenly patrimony. For however diligent the sons of God may be in keeping his commands, and in performing his will; they shall not possess it under the notion of a reward of duty, or as wages for work; but under the idea of a testamentary gift. Yes; it is a gift by way of legacy, and is bequeathed to them in the everlasting testament of our Lord Jesus Christ. According to those words; *I appoint, by testa-*

ment, unto you a kingdom.* The kingdom is most glorious, the inheritance most free to the children of God, and absolutely unalienable.

Nor are the heirs of this boundless bliss without some joyful foretastes of it in this life. Faith being, as the apostle defines it, *the substance of things hoped for, and the evidence of things not seen;* they anticipate, in some degree, the joys of the upper world. In the present state, they receive the earnest of their future inheritance, and rejoice in hope of the full fruition. Nay, at some bright intervals, they *rejoice with joy unspeakable, and full of glory.* For *he that believeth hath everlasting life,* in the promise, and in the earnest of it. Having *fled for refuge to lay hold on the hope set before them;* those *two immutable things*, the promise and the oath of God, in either of which *it is impossible for him to lie,* afford them *strong consolation* respecting their final preservation and eternal happiness. Living by faith on the dying, the ascended Redeemer, as their surety and sacrifice, their righteousness and advocate ; and viewing the stability of the promise, the covenant, the oath of Jehovah ; they have the greatest assurance that, *when Christ who is their life shall appear,* they also *shall appear with him in glory.*

The future happiness of believers may be considered, either as it is enjoyed by the *separate spirit,* before the resurrection and the last judgment; or by the *soul and body united,* after that awful period is come, and those grand events have taken place. That the separate spirits of the saints are possessed of thought and consciousness, and that they enjoy ineffable bliss in communion with Jesus their exalted Head ; are truths manifestly contained in the unerring word. Soon as that mysterious union, which subsists between soul and body in the present state, is dissolved by death ; the soul, being made perfectly free from the being of sin, immediately enters into glory. Death, to the saints, far from being a penal evil, is num-

---

* Luke xxii. 29. Thus the celebrated Witsius renders and interprets the passage, Œcon. l. iii. c. x. § 28. To the same effect, Beza and Castalio translate the words

bered among their privileges, and makes one article in their comprehensive inventory of Divine blessings.* Death is the gate by which they enter those heavenly mansions prepared for them; in the possession of which they enjoy delights that could not be experienced in this mortal state. The knowledge of that sublime blessedness, and of an interest in it, made Paul *desire to depart and to be with Christ, which is far better;* infinitely preferable to all that can be enjoyed in this world.

The same incomparable man and infallible teacher says; *Whilst we are at home in the body, we are absent from the Lord:* at the same time declaring, that it was far more eligible to him and his pious contemporaries, to be *absent from the body and present with the Lord.* Now, if the apostle's words have any sense, and if their meaning be at all intelligible, we cannot suppose him to have imagined, that his immortal soul, when separated from the body, would lie in a sleepy, unconscious, inactive state, till the sound of the archangel's trumpet should awaken it; which notion is by some warmly espoused. For in such a state of absolute insensibility he could not, with any propriety, be said to *be with Christ,* or to enjoy the presence of God. Before the dissolution of his body, he rejoiced in the light of Jehovah's countenance and had much communion with his God; was indulged with bright manifestations of Divine favour, and exulted in the certain prospect of a blissful immortality; all which, according to the sleeping scheme, he instantly lost by death. Under the deprivation of which he must continue for a long series of years; even till the voice of the Omnipotent, and the alarming crash of a falling world, shall rally his dissipated, and awaken his drowsy powers into act; and so bring him into a second enjoyment of himself, and of his God. How uncomfortable such an idea to the real Christian!

That the departing spirits of the children of God enter immediately into happiness, might be proved from a great variety of Divine testimonies. Among which there are

* 1 Cor. iii. 22.

few more apposite, than that which contains the remarkable and gracious answer of Jesus to the converted thief, when they were both on the verge of the unseen world. *Verily I say unto thee, to-day shalt thou be with me in paradise.* These words include a particular answer to the request of the expiring penitent, who prayed that Christ would *remember him.* As if our Lord had said; "I will not only remember thee, as absent; for, verily, thou shalt be with me in the everlasting mansions, to behold my glory." As the dying petitioner desired his request might be granted, when the bleeding Jesus should enter into his kingdom; the suffering Saviour certified him, not only of the place where he was to reign, which he calls *paradise,* but also of the *time* when he was to enter on the possession of his kingdom, signified by *to-day.* Nor is it unworthy of notice, that when this promise was made, the day was half elapsed; for *it was about the sixth hour,* yet Christ promised him the joys of paradise before that very day concluded; knowing that, in the interim, they should both make their exit. As the gracious promise to this thief was very extraordinary, and as the person to whom it was made was in such circumstances, and bore such an infamous character; Jesus confirmed it with the asseveration, *verily.* As if he had said, "I, the Amen, who am truth itself, solemnly declare that what I have promised shall certainly be fulfilled this day."

The different punctuation and sense of the text, that are given by those who adopt the sleeping scheme, appear farfetched, strained, and jejune. They contend, that the words ought thus to be pointed; *I say unto thee to-day, thou shalt be with me in paradise.* As if our Lord had not the least intention to fix the time, when the converted malefactor should behold his glory; but only declared, by the expression *to-day,* the certainty of what he promised. To which forced, unnatural, and insipid interpretation of the passage, it may be justly objected, that as the thief could not be ignorant of the time when the gracious promise was made; so he had no occasion to have that particular distinguished and confirmed in so solemn a manner. Nor is it the expression *to-day*, but the word *verily*, which indicates the truth of what was affirmed, and the certainty of enjoying the promised blessing. For as *to-day*, in our Lord's answer, denotes a precisely limited time; so it evidently corresponds to the adverb *when*, in the thief's petition.

This hypothesis appears not only uncomfortable to the real Christian, and antiscriptural to the impartial examiner of the sacred records, but also unphilosophical. For as the soul is a thinking being, if, when the animal frame is dissolved, it were to be entirely deprived of thought and consciousness; it must, for aught appears to the contrary, lose its existence. But if so, instead of a resurrection at the last day, there must be a new creation; which is contrary to the analogy of faith, and to the hope of saints in every age. A mind without thought and consciousness, and matter without solidity and extension, being equally absurd ideas.

The separate spirits of saints, therefore, being lodged in eternal mansions, and abiding at the source of all felicity, enjoy inconceivable pleasures. They are completely released from all troubles of every kind; from all sins and sufferings; from all temptations and sorrows. Moral evil, with all its attendants, is eternally banished from those bright abodes: for the people that dwell there are all perfectly righteous; nor shall any of the inhabitants of that land say, *I am sick.* Their garments are always white; their harps are always tuned. Being with Christ, according to his promise, they behold his glory, and are delighted with his beauty. The infinite excellencies of Jesus, the incarnate JEHOVAH, are illustriously displayed in that exalted state. Those Divine and mediatorial perfections, of which, while here below, we can form but very low conceptions; beam forth on the holy and happy spirits in a blaze of glory. With adoring gratitude and pleasing astonishment they reflect; This is HE that once raised a feeble cry in the stable at Bethlehem! This is HE that spent his life in one continued series of beneficent actions, when surrounded with meanness and poverty, with reproaches and sorrows! This is HE—but, O how changed!—who made his exit on Calvary, under every mark of infamy, under the severest sensations of pain, both in body and soul; and all this to accomplish our salvation!—To view HIM eye to eye, who was once a man of sorrows and sufferings to the highest degree; to behold HIM who is their husband and head, after all the abasement and misery to which he submitted on their account, thus exalted and glorified, must fill their souls with ecstatic bliss.

Nor are they mere spectators of his glorious exaltation. They not only behold their beloved, and have intercourse with him, as loyal subjects with an exalted sovereign; but he entertains and rejoices over them as his friends and brethren, as his bride and portion. This we may learn from the friendly freedom he used with his disciples while here on earth. For though, as their sovereign Lord, he required supreme respect, and accepted profound adoration; yet he did not keep them at an awful distance, but conversed with them in the most familiar manner. Doubtless, then, he does not behave with less freedom, or keep them at a greater distance, because of his exalted state; but rather takes them into a state of exaltation with himself. For though he is exalted above all blessing and praise, yet not as a private person, nor merely for his own sake; but as the head of his numerous family, and as the Saviour of all his people. The advancement of him, the head, could not be intended to remove the members to a greater distance: for there is the same relation, and the same union, subsisting between him and them. Consequently, they must be honoured and exalted with him. Beholding his infinite glory, their adoring regards are heightened; but this is far from diminishing their nearness to him, or their delight in him. It only serves to increase their astonishment and joy, as they find him still condescending to admit them into such a familiarity with him, and so liberally communicating his glory to them.

When in this lower world, they discerned the signatures of Deity in the works of creation and of providence. They beheld yet brighter displays of Jehovah's glory in the operations of grace, and the amazing effects of his love; in the gift of a Saviour, and in his death on the cross. But now, having their intellectual powers abundantly strengthened, they have manifestations of his infinite excellence, compared with which, all their previous discoveries of Divine perfection, by the material creation, and all the happiness they enjoyed in the church militant, were poor and mean, were low and languid beyond expression. For they are surrounded with the opulence of God, and eternally enriched with his munificence.

If Paul, ravished with the more obscure appearances of Divine wisdom, could not forbear exclaiming; *O the depth of the riches, both of the wisdom and knowledge of God!* what holy transports of wonder must it afford *the spirits of the just made perfect*, to have the counsels of Heaven laid open to their view? The contemplation of Divine power, under the conduct of infinite wisdom, and leagued with boundless goodness, must heighten their pleasure. How delightful to behold, in the light of glory, that power which raised the vast frame of nature, and from the beginning sustained all things—That power, which turned the mighty wheels of providence in every age of the world, through all the revolutions of time—That uncontrollable power, which restrained legions of malignant spirits and accursed fiends, in ten thousand different instances, from perpetrating their malicious designs and from filling the world with mischief; which wrought upon the obdurate hearts of rebellious creatures, caused them to acknowledge Divine sovereignty, and made them willing to accept salvation in the appointed way—That power, which, having formed their souls anew, preserved them in the midst of innumerable dangers that continually lay in their way to the regions of happiness; nor ever intermitted its guardian agency, till it brought them safe to glory!

If the power of God, as beheld by the saints in light, be so delightful a subject of contemplation, what exuberant joy must the views of his love afford! For as love is the noblest passion of the human breast, so it is the brightest beam of Divinity that ever irradiated the wide creation. Love is a pleasing theme, and the meaning of that divine sentence, GOD IS LOVE, is there unfolded to the very life. The happy spirits are no longer obliged to learn Jehovah's love from his names and works; for they now behold it as essential to his Being. The day they had long expected, that happy day which is appropriated to the full discovery of Divine love, having dawned upon them, they take their *fill of loves*. Now the immortal spirit is invigorated in all its powers, enlarged in all its faculties, on purpose to render it capable of taking in more copious views, and of receiving abundantly larger emanations of Divine love, than it could possibly before enjoy. They have now traced up the streams to the eternal fountain; the beams, to the very sun of love. The bosom of their Father, where the thoughts of love were lodged from everlasting, and where its noble designs were formed, is laid open to their view. Now they clearly see why the Son of God became incarnate, undertook the redemption of man, and, in order to accomplish the arduous work, obeyed, and suffered, and died the most painful and infamous death— Died, a sacrifice, an atonement for sin; a spectacle to the world, to angels, and to men. The wondering soul penetrates the vast design, and sees, with warmest gratitude, why itself was not made an everlasting monument of Divine justice; why its native enmity against God was completely subdued, and why its enormous crimes were pardoned. All which is resolved into the free, distinguishing love of God. The adoring soul beholds, with ecstasies of delight, how well the admirable effects correspond to their grand, original cause. Certainly, nothing short of heaven itself, which gives the experience, can give an adequate idea of such exalted bliss.

Nor will their views of Divine justice; no, not in its awful effects considered as vindictive, and manifested in the damnation of innumerable myriads of apostate angels and sinful men, in the least allay their joys, or damp their pleasures. For, however infidels may now object against an eternal punishment being inflicted for transient crimes; and arraign the Book of God itself, which asserts that so it shall be; to them it appears, in the clearest light, that sin is an infinite evil, and therefore, justly deserving of perpetual misery. Their holy wills, being perfectly conformed to the pleasure of God, fully acquiesce in the sentence pronounced upon offenders, and rejoice in the execution of it on all the daring sons of rebellion, whether angels or men. They now more fully discover, how holiness in the Lawgiver, the demands of his law, and the rights of his justice, were all displayed and perfectly satisfied, in the redemption of their souls by the blood of the cross. The remembrance and views of which are a scene of wonders, and an inexhaustible source of joy.

Divine holiness they contemplate with supreme delight. God is *glorious in holiness*. This perfection of the Godhead has frequently been celebrated in lofty strains of devotion, by saints on earth.* Now, if those who dwell in houses of clay; whose views, at the best, are so feeble and partial, have been so affected by meditating on it; what thoughts must they have who behold it in all its glory? with adoring hearts and ravished eyes, with inflamed devotion and notes divinely sweet, they join the heavenly choir in that seraphic hymn: *Holy! holy! holy! is the Lord of hosts! Heaven and earth are full of his glory!* How inconceivable the pleasure! how divine the joy! and may I not venture to add, the views of this glorious holiness must have such a transforming efficacy on the happy spirits, as to produce in them a perpetually advancing conformity to God in holiness and in glory?

If the face of Moses shone with peculiar brightness, after he had been admitted to familiar converse with Jehovah on the mount; how much greater must that effulgence be, which God communicates to those who constantly behold him without any interposing veil! The transcendent amiableness of Jehovah greatly consisting in his immaculate holiness, (for holiness is nothing but intellectual beauty,) and he presenting himself to beatified saints as the Infinite Beauty; they must perpetually rest in him as the proper object of their love, and as the centre of their delight. Nor can they cease to admire the equity of hat command, which requires the most perfect love to

---

* Exod. xv. 11.   1 Sam. ii. 8.   Ps. xxx. 4; xcvii. 12.

God, on account of his own infinite loveliness and all-surpassing excellence.

Being favoured with a more perfect knowledge of God, and more intimate communion with him, their love to him is proportionally heightened. That grace which reigned in their whole salvation, being discerned by them in a stronger light, inflames them with the most ardent love to its adorable Author, and to Jesus, by whom it reigned. All the amiable and infinite perfections of Deity, shining upon them in the light of glory, their holy bosoms cannot but glow with the utmost fervour. They cannot but make returns of love, and in such a manner, as are suited to their happy and exalted state. Their supreme love to God causes them to contemplate his Divine perfections and astonishing operations with evernew delight; by which they are more and more assimilated to his Divine image. Hence that sublime delight, which, in the sacred page, is called *the joy of their Lord.*

Absolutely free from that pride and selfishness which tarnish our best services while here, and quite remote from all those imperfections which attended them in a militant state, songs of sincerest gratitude and hymns of holy wonder, the profoundest acknowledgments of multiplied obligations to reigning grace, and the loftiest strains of thanksgiving to God and the Lamb, are their uninterrupted and sweet employ: Ever free to declare, that the only cause of their enjoying the beatific vision, and being seated on thrones of glory, is that grace which, as a mighty, magnificent, and bountiful sovereign, reigned through the person and work of Immanuel. Hence it is that grace, as it appears, and shines, and triumphs, in rescuing them out of the hands of Satan—in preserving them through all dangers—in supporting them under the severest trials—in bringing them safe to glory, and in crowning them with unutterable bliss—is the grand and unvaried burden of their songs. To the GOD OF ALL GRACE, the triune God, they address all possible praise with divine delight.

Peculiarly great and glorious is that sublime blessedness which is possessed by the separate spirits of saints in heaven; it, nevertheless, comes far short of that happiness which shall be enjoyed in their *whole persons*, and which belongs to the consummation of that celestial state. For the oracles of God frequently intimate that the bliss of the saints will not be absolutely complete, till the general judgment is past, and the end of the world is come.* We may, therefore, take notice of some things, by which their blessedness will then be enhanced.

Their bodies being raised in glory, and reunited to their immortal spirits, will not only be a demonstration of Divine power, and a display of Divine goodness, very wonderful in their eyes, but also an addition to their blessedness. For, so long as any of the children of God continue in this perplexing, miserable world, and so long as the bodies of saints departed are confined in the grave, the happy spirits in glory cannot be ignorant, that the power which sin obtained over man is not yet entirely abolished; and, consequently, that something must be wanting to the consummation of their joy. But by the resurrection, death itself, which is the last enemy, shall be destroyed, never more to have the least power, but over the enemies of God, and of his people.

That the dead shall be raised, is a fundamental article of the Christian creed. That the same bodies shall be raised, which fell by death, the justice of God and the comfort of believers apparently require, is clear from the Scriptures, and is implied in the word *resurrection*. But though, as to their substance, they shall be the same; so far at least as to support the identity of them; yet as to their qualities, the alteration will be so great, that we cannot form suitable ideas concerning them. That surprising change, which shall pass upon them, is absolutely necessary to fit them for the exalted state into which they shall be introduced, when reanimated by their immortal spirits. Hence those words: *Flesh and blood cannot inherit the kingdom of God.* The present constitution of our bodies renders them incapable of bearing the splendour of the heavenly world; and, consequently, of

---

* Col. iii. 4. 2 Tim. i. 12; iv. 8. 1 Pet. v. 4.

partaking in the joys of that state. The glory of it would be insupportably bright; too dazzling for them to sustain. Like herbs and flowers of the most delicate kind, exposed to the scorching glare of the meridian sun, they would faint under it. But when that which was *sown in corruption* shall be *raised in incorruption;* when that which was *sown in dishonour and weakness*, shall be *raised in glory and power;* when this *corruptible shall put on incorruption*, and this *mortal shall put on immortality*—in a word, when that which was *sown a natural body* shall be *raised a spiritual body;* it will then be capable of partaking in the employment and bliss of heaven. When the bodies of believers shall be raised by almighty power, and fashioned by infinite wisdom, like to the glorious body of Christ,* they will be fit companions for their souls to all eternity. *Then shall the righteous shine forth as the sun*, both in body and soul, *in the kingdom of their Father*.† Then shall the body, which partook in the sorrows and sufferings of this present world; which suffered various hardships and acts of violence, from the enemies of Christ; and which assisted the intellectual powers in performing religious duties, be a partaker of the joys of that triumphant state. Yes, the earthly tabernacle, being the purchase of redeeming blood, and the temple of the Holy Ghost, even when surrounded with imperfections, shall then be bright as the sun, vigorous with celestial youth, and undecaying as the power that shall support it. We may, therefore, conclude, that the bodies of the saints being raised from the dust of death, will contribute much to augment their bliss. But who can form adequate ideas of the nature and excellence of a *spiritual body?* Who can declare the power and grace that shall be exercised and manifested toward the children of men, in raising their sleeping dust, and in forming their bodies afresh for an eternal world, after so dignified an exemplar as the glorious body of Christ? Here we must leave them, till we behold the glorified body of our exalted Redeemer, or experience the happy transformation. For

---

* Phil. iii. 21   † Matt. xiii. 43.

OF THE GLORIOUS REIGN OF GRACE. 281

the beloved disciple himself declares, *It doth not yet appear what we shall be: but we know that when he shall appear we shall be like him, for we shall see him as he is.** To which I may add, in allusion to the words of the psalmist, we shall certainly be *satisfied* with the amazing alteration, *when we awake* from the sleep of death, in the *likeness* of our adorable Saviour.†

Another thing which will add to the blessedness of saints at that day, is their public acquittal by Jesus the judge, when standing before his tribunal. *Behold he cometh with clouds and every eye shall see him!* Infinitely grand and awfully amiable he now appears. Innumerable angels attend his approach, and pour around his chariot. The brightness of ten thousand suns is lost in the blaze of his glory, and in the lustre of his countenance. Behold! A great white throne is erected;‡ clear as light, and fiery as flame. The Judge, inflexibly just and immensely glorious, ascends the tribunal; and before his presence *the heavens and the earth flee away.* Those innumerable millions of rational creatures that people the universe are now assembled. The books are opened. Myriads of adoring seraphs, and countless multitudes of anxious spectators, await the grand result. The wicked, with trembling hands and throbbing hearts, with horror in their aspect and damnation in view, would be glad to lose their being; but the righteous are bold and intrepid: for the Judge is their friend, and their Saviour. The righteousness in which they appear, was performed by Him. The plea which they make, he cannot reject. For it is the blood which he shed to atone for their sins, and the promise he made to comfort their souls, under the expectation of this important event. They there stand, not to have any fresh indictment brought against them; nor to have any thing laid to their charge, by Satan, or the law, or justice; but to be honourably acquitted in the presence of angels, and of the whole assembled world. The sentence of justification, long before pronounced in the court of heaven, and in the court of conscience, at the time of

* 1 John iii. 2. † Ps. xvii. 15. ‡ Rev. xx. 11.

their conversion, is now recognised in the most solemn and public manner. The works of faith and labours of love performed by them, in the time of their pilgrimage here below, toward their needy fellow-christians, are now produced by the omniscient Judge, as fruits and evidences of their union with him, of their faith in him, and of their love to him.* The nature and quality of their works;

---

* Matt. xxv. 34—40. It is very observable how different the conduct of saints will be, at this awful and glorious time, from that of nominal professors, as represented by our Lord in Matt. vii. 22. Here we find the Judge taking notice of his people's works, when they make no mention of them. Not only so, but when he is pleased to mention their labours of love, with high approbation, they seem to have forgotten them. A plain proof they did not expect salvation by them, nor ever thought of any such thing. No; Christ was their righteousness, and that was sufficient. The works they performed were designed to glorify him, and to express their gratitude to God for his benefits. But, so conscious were they of the imperfections cleaving to their performances, that they were ashamed to mention them. Whereas, when our Lord represents the reason of hope in self-righteous persons, he tells us that they will say, with great importunity; *Lord! Lord! have we not prophesied in thy name? and in thy name have cast out devils? and in thy name done many wonderful works?* But he will answer, *I never knew you: Depart from me, ye that work iniquity.* They plead their own works, religious duties, and great usefulness, as a sufficient reason why they should be admitted into the kingdom of glory. Not that they pretend to have done these things by their own strength, or natural abilities. No; they acknowledge that all was done in *the name of Christ*, by his authority, and his assistance. For which reason, we may suppose, they would be the more confident of acceptance with him. Hence, *we have done this*, and *we have done the other*, is their cry and their plea. They thought of coming to heaven by their own works. They did them for that end, and were loath to be disappointed. But what is the issue? Why, truly, these mighty workers and very useful persons are branded as the workers of iniquity; not acknowledged as the people of God. They are thrust down into hell, with all their fine recommendations and imaginary goodness; and notwithstanding all their pleas and promising hopes founded upon them. While the *poor in spirit*, those who are sensible of their own unworthiness; who live by righteousness imputed, making that the only ground of their hope; and who, from love to the truth, and to Christ, as revealed by it, perform good works with a view to the glory of God, not in the least expecting admission into the eternal kingdom for the sake of their pious performances—these, who say not a word about any thing which they have done, are accepted

the principle from which they proceed, and the end for which they were done, together with the character of those that were benefited by them, will afford sufficient evidence to whom the performers of them belong. These expressions of love and fruits of holiness being remembered by Christ, though forgotten by the saints, he will avow them for his own; he will number them among his jewels; he will confess them before his Father and all the holy angels. Then shall their characters, which, in the time of their sojourning here below, were aspersed with every foul reproach, be fully vindicated to their everlasting honour, and to the eternal confusion of all their adversaries. For, with a smile of Divine complacency, the Judge will say, *Come, ye blessed of my Father, inherit the kingdom prepared for you from the foundation of the world.* Reviving words! Having long desired to be near the Lord, they are invited to come, and to be with him forever. Now the painful fears which they once had are eternally removed; for they are pronounced *blessed of the Father*, by a voice which the whole assembled

by the Judge of all, into everlasting honour and joy.—Let the legalist be cautioned by this, not to trust in his own duties, though of the most splendid kind; and let all who love the truth be encouraged to abound in every instance of duty to God; especially in that of communicating to the indigent members of Christ. For the Judge will say to them on his right hand; *Inasmuch as ye have done it unto one of the least of these my brethren, ye have done it unto me.* Matt. xxv. 40. What condescension is here! Christ is not ashamed to own the meanest of his people under the character of *brethren.*

There is reason to fear that many professors, whose situation in life is a little more elevated than that of their neighbours, are almost above looking at the *poor* brethren of Christ; and would be extremely offended, if one of those indigent disciples were to address any of them, under the character of a *brother.* But who art thou, reptile of the earth! that thou shouldst be ashamed of them whom Jesus, the Lord of glory and Judge of the world, will acknowledge as HIS *brethren?* What! shall a little shining dust, or worldly honour, so elate thy ignoble mind and swell thy contracted heart, that the poor members of Jesus Christ shall have no place in thy affections! Beware, lest after all thy profession, thou shouldst go down to hell with a lie in thy right hand; and all thy expectations of eternal happiness prove no better than "the baseless fabric of a vision!"

world shall hear. They were all poor in spirit, and the generality of them poor in temporals ; how agreeably, then, must they be surprised, to hear that they are called to possess a kingdom ; called to inherit it, as princes of the blood royal, who are born to thrones and crowns! Lost, they will be, in pleasing astonishment, to find that, before they had a being, or the foundations of the world were laid, the eternal God had prepared this kingdom for them ; and every reflection upon the way in which they came to possess it must heighten their amazement and joy. Then shall they be admitted, in their whole persons, into the fulness of bliss ; into a nearer and more perfect fruition of God than they ever before enjoyed.

Their blessedness thus heightened shall be eternal. It is eternity stamped on their enjoyments that gives them their infinite worth. For could they, who are so high in bliss, be apprehensive of an end of their happiness, however remote ; " that ghastly thought would drink up all their joy." But their inheritance is unalienable, their crown unfading, and their kingdom everlasting. Jehovah himself is *their light*, and the Most High *their glory*. Yes, the infinite God is their portion, and their exceeding *great reward*.* Their felicity, therefore, is permanent as the Divine perfections they adore and enjoy ; and made certain to their own comprehensive minds beyond the possibility of a doubt. This makes their state supremely glorious. This constitutes it heaven indeed. Nay, what if the limits of their capacities should be forever enlarging, and forever receiving greater measures of glory ? For the Deity is an infinite source of blessedness ; and finite vessels may be forever expanding, and forever filling, in that ocean of All-sufficiency. What an amazing state of evergrowing pleasure! and what an astonishing scale of bliss! Jehovah shall open inexhaustible stores of blessings, as yet unknown to angels, and feast their souls with joys that are ever new. Nothing equal to this can be conceived by mortals ; nothing superior can be enjoyed by mere creatures. Yet this—hear it, O ye nations! and

* Isa. lx. 19   Gen. xv. 1.

listen, ye isles from afar! while the millions of beatified saints dwell on the stupendous truth!—this is the END of the victorious reign of grace. Grace reigned in the eternal counsels, when contriving the way to this glorious end. Grace reigned in providing the means, and in bestowing the blessings, that were necessary to its accomplishment. Grace reigned to the complete execution of the noble, the astonishing design, from first to last. Surely, then, reigning grace should have the unrivalled honour of all the blessings enjoyed by believers on earth, or by saints in light. Yes, and it shall have the glory, in all the churches of Christ below, and in all the triumphant hosts above. For when the last stone of the spiritual temple shall be laid, it will be *with shoutings*, GRACE, GRACE UNTO IT!

In these respects the blessedness of saints, in their entire persons, after the resurrection and the general judgment, will exceed that of their separate spirits: and in how many other particulars the proceedings of that day will add to their happiness, I neither affirm nor presume to inquire. It is quite sufficient for us to know, while in the present state, that we are heirs of this blessedness, and that it is inconceivably great. We should rest contented with what is revealed concerning it, without indulging a curious imagination, in searching after those particulars of which the Spirit of wisdom has given us no intimations, or those that are very obscure; for such inquiries are sure to be attended with vanity, rather than edification.

Nor will the angelic hosts be unaffected spectators, when that grandest of all Divine works, REDEMPTION, shall be completed. For as they had often been charged with offices of great importance to the church of God, and to its particular members, while in this lower world; so hey had seen with astonishment the incarnation of their Sovereign, his feeble appearance in the manger, his life of poverty, of reproaches, and of sufferings. They saw his agony in the garden, and heard his cries and complaints. They saw him extended on the cross, and beheld him laid in the grave. They were witnesses of his victorious resurrection, and they attended his triumphant ascension into the realms of glory. They beheld, and often reflected on these things, with amazement. They diligently looked into these works of Divine contrivance, these mysteries of infinite love,* wondering what would be the grand result. They had long desired the evolution of the mysterious plan, and now they have it.

> "Now they are struck with deep amaze,
> Each with his wing conceals his face;
> Now clap their sounding plumes, and cry
> *The glories of the* DEITY."

If those first-born sons of light and love could not forbear *shouting for joy* when they beheld the material world rise into existence, and saw its finished form,† how much greater reason will they have to rejoice, when they behold all the redeemed world brought safe to glory and confirmed in bliss? Those morning stars, those children of ardour and sons of God must exult with joy, when they view the spotless perfection and ravishing beauty of the whole church, considered as the bride, the wife of the Lamb.‡ Nor can any thing short of transport seize their breasts when they reflect, that all this immaculate innocence and matchless beauty arose from reigning grace, through the person and work of their incarnate Sovereign; her own original being base and miserable.

And now, reader, what are your thoughts of this blessedness? Very probably you are one of those that hope to go to heaven when they die. If so, what is your hope? Is it a mere wish, or a well-grounded expectation? Remember, that the word of God requires you, as a Christian professor, to *be ready to give an answer to every man that asketh you a reason of the hope that is in you.* Have you ever seriously inquired, why *you* hope to be happy, when so many millions will be eternally miserable; when it is certain from the Scripture, that there are comparatively very few that find the way to life? You have, perhaps, never thought much about these interesting sub-

---

* 1 Pet. i. 12. Eph. iii. 10. † Job xxxviii. 7.
‡ Eph. v. 27. Rev. xxi. 9.

jects. But why, then, do you call yourself a Christian? Why hope to go to heaven? For if this be your condition, you are *in the gall of bitterness, and in the bond of iniquity.* You are—may God enlighten your mind to see it! may reigning grace deliver you from it!—you are at present, a child of wrath, and an heir of destruction.

But why hope for heaven, when you have no delight in God; no pleasure in his ways; no love to his people; in a word, possessed of no holiness: and, without holiness, intellectual happiness is impossible. Heaven, were you there, would be no heaven to you; nor, as an unregenerate sinner, can you desire it for the sake of its enjoyments. For they are contrary to the prevailing inclination of your will. You do not love heaven, but are afraid of hell. The inhabitants of the celestial world would be no companions for you. Their business would be a toil, and their language unknown; their sweetest hosannas would afford you no pleasure, and the symphony of their golden harps would be discord in your ears. Nay, the fruition of God, their highest joy, would be your greatest uneasiness, were you to be admitted into those mansions of purity in an unregenerate state. For happiness consists in the enjoyment of an object that is completely suitable and satisfying to our desires. A holy God, therefore, cannot be our happiness, without partaking of his holiness. Remember, sinner, that if you leave the world in an unsanctified state, as you cannot be fit for heaven, so you must not enter those abodes of blissful purity, or taste their sublime pleasures; but your state will be eternally fixed, where there is *weeping, wailing and gnashing of teeth.*

Are you a serious person, and a strict professor? Be it so; yet it behooves you to consider what is the foundation of your hope. For *there is a way that seemeth right unto a man, but the end thereof are the ways of death.** A man may be zealous for God, and, in many respects, exemplary in his conversation; yet, after all, perish forever.† What then is the reason of your hope?

* Prov. xvi 25. † Rom. ix. 31, 32; x. 2, 3.

Is it that grace which reigns through the person and work of Christ? Can you say with the primitive Christians, *We believe that through the grace of our Lord Jesus Christ, we shall be saved?* Are you come to a point about that most interesting and solemn affair, the salvation of your immortal soul? Is your hope of glory lively and bright, or languid and obscure? Is it such as is attended with rejoicing, as purifies the heart and conduct?* Has it Christ and his finished work, together with the promise of him that cannot lie, for its everlasting support?—O, professor! seek for certainty and satisfaction: they are to be had in the knowledge of Christ, and in the belief of his truth. If you love your soul, rest not in uncertainty about an affair of infinite consequence. You are building for eternity; be cautious, therefore, with what materials you build, and upon what foundation. A mistake in the ground of your trust will ruin your soul. Read your bible, meditate, and pray that the Spirit of truth may direct you in the momentous concern.

Are you a child of God and an heir of the kingdom? endeavour, by a conscientious attendance on all the public means of grace, and by maintaining communion with your heavenly Father in every private duty, to make a swift progress in vital religion, and in real holiness; remembering, that holiness is the health, the beauty, and the glory of your immortal mind. Seek after it, therefore, as a Divine privilege, and as a heavenly blessing. Watch and pray against the insurrections of indwelling sin, the solicitations of worldly pleasure, and the assaults of Satan's temptations. Watch, especially, against spiritual pride and carnal security. As to the former, rejoice not in your knowledge, or gifts, or inherent excellencies; no, nor yet in your Christian experiences. Be thankful for them, but put them not in the place of Christ, or the word of his grace; so as to make them the ground of your present confidence, or the source of your future comfort. For so to do, is not to rely on the promise of God, and to live by faith in Jesus Christ; but to admire your own accomplish-

---

* Rom. v. 2.   1 Pet. i. 3. 5.   1 John iii. 3.

ments, by which you differ from other men, and to live upon your own frames. The consequence of which most commonly is, either pharisaical pride, imagining ourselves to be better than others; or desponding fears, as if, when our frames are flat and our spirits languid, there were no salvation for us. The peace and comfort of such professors must be uncertain to the last degree. But as a guilty, perishing sinner, as having no recommendation, nor any encouragement, to believe in Jesus, or to look for salvation by him, but what is contained in the word of grace, depend upon him, live by him. The more you behold the glory of God in the face of Jesus Christ, the more will you see of your own vileness. The more you grow in real holiness, the more sensible you will be of the power of your own corruptions, and of the imperfections attending all your duties. You will be more and more convinced that if the gospel did not warrant your dependence on Christ, under the character of a sinner, you could have no hope, even after ever so long and zealous a profession of religion. You should live under a continual remembrance, that you are still an unworthy, a guilty, a damnable creature; but accepted in Christ, and freed from every curse. That will keep you truly humble, and provoke to self-abhorrence: this will make you really happy and excite to praise and duty.

Watch against carnal security and spiritual sloth. Forget not that you have many enemies. *Be sober*, therefore, *be vigilant*. Time is short and absolutely uncertain. Husband well your precious moments. Lay them out for God. Be careful that the fruits of gratitude to your infinite Benefactor may adorn your whole behaviour. Make the holiness and usefulness of the life of Jesus your fair example: copy after that brightest of patterns. Remember, that the eyes of God, of angels, of accursed spirits, and of men, are all upon you. Both friends and enemies inspect your conduct and mark your steps. How necessary then is watchfulness and circumspection! lest, falling into sin, your spiritual joys be impaired, your friends and allies be grieved, and your adversaries triumph. Having received the earnest of your future inheritance;

having had some joyful foretastes of that immense bliss, of which you, O Christian, are an heir; make it your constant business, as it is your indispensable duty, to live above the world, whether your temporal circumstances be affluent or penurious, prosperous or adverse. Let your conversation be in heaven, as becomes a citizen of the new Jerusalem. It is your duty and blessing to live in the prospect of the world to come, and as on the confines of it. Converse much with the Eternal Mind, in prayer, and praise, and holy meditation: so shall you contract a blessed intimacy with that sublime Being whose favour is better than life, whose frown is worse than destruction. By such an intercourse with God, you will taste more exquisite delights than all the pleasures of sin can boast; than all the riches of the world can bestow. Yes, believer, by such converse with God, you shall find your mercies sanctified, and your afflictions alleviated; your holy dispositions invigorated, and your corrupt affections weakened. Be it your constant endeavour that, whenever your fair, your glorious, your heavenly Bridegroom shall come, he may find you ready; having your loins girt, your lamp burning, and waiting for his glorious advent. So shall your soul be peaceful, your life useful, and your death triumphant.

While we soar on the wings of faith and holy meditation, in order to explore the wonders of reigning grace; while we endeavour to sound its depths and to measure its heights, we are elevated, as it were, to the suburbs of heaven. We taste of joys divinely sweet, and savour the entertainments of angels. But, alas! how soon the pinions of divine contemplation flag! How soon are we interrupted by the workings of indwelling sin, or by the impertinencies of a noisy, busy, transient world! Yet, for our comfort, we have to remember, that when a few more of our fleeting days are elapsed, we shall enter on a state unchangeable, to enjoy those infinite delights which are ncluded in the beatific vision; in the fruition of the eternal JEHOVAH.

To conclude: from this imperfect and brief survey of *The Reign of Grace;* from this feeble attempt to illustrate its power and majesty, we may learn, that the free favour of God manifested in our salvation, is a theme so copious and so sublime, that all which can be said by the most evangelical and eloquent preachers; all that can be written by the most accurate and descriptive pens; all that can be conceived by the most excursive and sanctified imagination among the sons of men, must come infinitely short of a full display. Yes, after all that is imagined or can be sung, by angels or men, by seraphs or saints, in the church below, or in the choirs above; the charming subject will remain unexhausted to eternity. For the riches of Christ are unsearchable, and the grace of God is unbounded. Who, then?—

> " Who shall fulfil the boundless song?
> What vain pretender dares?
> The theme surmounts an angel's tongue.
> And Gabriel's harp despairs."—WATTS.

www.ingramcontent.com/pod-product-compliance
Lightning Source LLC
Chambersburg PA
CBHW070232230426
43664CB00014B/2272